K·I·S·S

DK

The Only Guides You'll Ever Need!

THIS SERIES IS YOUR TRUSTED GUIDE through all of life's stages and situations. Want to learn how to surf the Internet or care for your new dog? Or maybe you'd like to become a wine connoisseur or an expert gardener? The solution is simple: just pick up a K.I.S.S. Guide and turn to the first page.

Expert authors will walk you through the subject from start to finish, using simple blocks of knowledge to build your skills one step at a time. Build upon these learning blocks and by the end of the book, you'll be an expert yourself! Or, if you are familiar with the topic but want to learn more, it's easy to dive in and pick up where you left off.

The K.I.S.S. Guides deliver what they promise: simple access to all the information you'll need on one subject. Other titles you might want to check out include: Playing Guitar, Sex, Pregnancy, Yoga, Online Investing, Sailing, and many more to come.

K·I·S·S

GUIDE TO

Baby and Child Care

JOANNA MOORHEAD

Foreword by **Andrea Barbalich**
Deputy Editor, *Child* magazine

A Dorling Kindersley Book

**LONDON, NEW YORK,
MUNICH, MELBOURNE, DELHI**

DK Publishing, Inc.
Series Editor Jennifer Williams
U.S. Consultants Aviva Schein, M.D., Pam Thomas
Editor-in-Chief Chuck Wills
Publisher Chuck Lang

Dorling Kindersley Limited
Project Editor Jane Sarluis
Project Art Editor Kelly Meyer

Managing Editor Maxine Lewis
Managing Art Editor Heather McCarry

Production Heather Hughes
Category Publisher Mary Thompson

Produced for Dorling Kindersley by

studio cactus ©

13 SOUTHGATE STREET WINCHESTER HAMPSHIRE SO23 9DZ

Project Editors Kate Hayward, Jane Baldock
Project Art Editors Laura Watson, Sharon Moore

First published in 2002 by Dorling Kindersley Limited
80 Strand, London, WC2R 0RL

A Penguin Company

2 4 6 8 10 9 7 5 3 1

Published in the United States by DK Publishing, Inc.
375 Hudson Street, New York, NY 10014

Library of Congress Cataloging-in-Publication data

Moorhead, Joanna.
KISS guide to babycare / Joanna Moorhead.-- 1st American ed.
   p. cm. -- (Keep it Simple Series)
   "Dorling Kindersley Publishing book."
   Includes index.
   ISBN 0-7894-8438-2 (alk. paper)
1. Infants (Newborn)--Care. 2. Infants (Newborn)--Health and hygiene.
3. Infants--Care. 4. Child rearing. 5. Child care. I. Title: Guide to babycare.
II. Title: Kiss guide to babycare. III Title. IV. Series.
RJ253 .M664 2002
649'.122--dc21

2001058105

Color reproduction by Colourscan, Singapore
Printed and bound by MOHN Media and Mohndruck GmbH, Germany

See our complete catalog at

www.dk.com

Contents at a Glance

PART ONE

Your Newborn — the Early Weeks

We're Parents at Last
Feeding Your Baby
Practical Care
Sleeping and Waking

PART TWO

Your Young Baby — 0-6 Months

Will Life Ever Be the Same?
Is My Baby Getting Enough to Eat?
All About Routines
Who Said Babies Sleep All the Time?
Your Baby's Health
Don't Forget to Enjoy Life
Finding the Right Child Care

PART THREE

Your Older Baby — 6-12 Months

Speak to Me!
Safe and Well-Behaved
My Baby's Growing Up Fast
He's On the Move
Childhood Illnesses

PART FOUR

Your Toddler — 1-2½ Years

It Just Gets Better and Better . . .
Potty Training
Choosing Preschool Care

PART FIVE

Your Growing Child — 2½ + Years

Developing in Leaps and Bounds
Your Child's Expanding World

CONTENTS

PART ONE   Your Newborn — the Early Weeks

PART TWO   Your Young Baby — 0-6 Months

Foreword

WHENEVER NEW PARENTS *ask me what I view as the key to successful child-rearing, I give the same answer: Respect. They often look at me, puzzled, and ask, "Well, what about love, patience, or even a good night's sleep?" I smile and say that of course all those things are important (especially the good night's sleep!) but, somehow, I have found respect to trump every other issue. Respect, I've discovered through my work as an editor of a parenthood magazine and as the mother of a wonderful little boy, allows you to find your way to all the other things you need.*

First, you need respect for yourself — a firm belief that you can and will be a good parent, a basic trust in your own instincts, and, not to be forgotten, a commitment to taking care of yourself along with your baby. Then, you also need respect for your partner — that he or she can do just as fine a job of parenting as you can. The fact that you will inevitably do things differently is something not only to tolerate but to celebrate.

And last, and perhaps most important, you need respect for your child. Of course you love him, and of course you will take good care of him, but remember also that he is his own person. He is exactly like every other baby in his need to be fed, changed, and cuddled, but at the same time he is unique. He entered the world with a personality all his own, including traits that you may not have expected. One of the most incredible joys of parenthood is discovering who your child is and guiding him toward becoming all he can be. Along the way, amid countless moments of wonder and fulfillment, you may sometimes feel frustrated at a newborn you can't seem to soothe, a baby who won't stay asleep for as long as you'd like him to, or a toddler who wants to do things his own way. Try to view the world through his eyes. Everything is new to him, and he is trying his best to figure it all out. He depends on you to be confident and secure enough in your parenting to help him through the difficult moments. Set a good example for him — show him how to handle frustration. Stay calm, be patient, laugh with him. Children go through many phases; none of them last very long. And with each one, they're learning, growing, developing — finding their way in the world. They will never cease to surprise you. That's what makes parenthood such a marvelous adventure.

It is on this last point that the Kiss Guide to Baby and Child Care plays such a helpful role. In its tone and its approach, it communicates joy at the incredible journey you've embarked on with your child. It makes clear that there is no right way to do anything; rather, there are many different ways, and only you will know the way that's right for your family. The book has a sense of humor, which is so important in parenthood. And the clear photos and easy-to-understand text work together to demystify countless issues, from feeding and bathing a newborn through all the stages of child development. After reading the book, you'll feel more confident. With confidence comes comfort, and with comfort comes respect.

Enjoy yourself. Enjoy your child. Remember that your baby is lucky to have you — and that together you will find your way. Welcome to parenthood!

ANDREA BARBALICH

Introduction

PARENTING IS THE ADVENTURE *of a lifetime – but don't expect a smooth ride. Few of us who are ahead of you on the journey would want to turn the clock back and have our lives any other way. But most of us would admit that while parenting has brought the greatest joys, the most amazing experiences, and the most wonderful moments, it's also given us our biggest headaches and our greatest worries.*

Whatever else it may be, being a parent isn't easy. And one of the things that you have to face are the people who think they know all the answers – they're the people who tell you the way you "ought" to be bringing up your kids and make you feel like you're getting it all wrong. But most of us who are already treading the path of parenthood know only too well that there's rarely a "right" or a "wrong" way to bring up a child.

That's not to say parenting is all about woolly values, and that there aren't morals and principles you should be instilling in your children. No, what it means is that there are a hundred different "right" ways to bring up a child. And the way that's right for you might not be right for anyone else you know.

The K.I.S.S. Guide to Baby and Child Care will act as your guide to the practical aspects of parenting, but most of all, I hope it will give you the confidence to trust your own judgments and instincts – this is one of the most important principles of parenting. Get to know your inner voice and listen to it when you're faced with a dilemma, or even just a daily situation that you have to find your way through. Believe in yourself as a parent because although we all make mistakes, you're going to be the best mom or dad your child will ever have. That's an awesome responsibility, but it's also a reassuring one.

Along the way you'll learn a lot, but you'll never know everything about parenting – partly because every child is different. However many children you've raised, the new baby in your arms has lots of new things to share with you as well. As I write, I'm the mother of three girls and my fourth baby is due in a few months' time. No doubt I'll face new challenges with my new arrival, as every parent does.

But the most important lesson I would say that 10 years of parenting has given me is this: savor every moment of the early years. Your children are every bit as precious when they're older. But the early years are a special part of the journey of parenting: they're a time of rich memories, quickly changing phases, a lot of laughter, and a whole lot of fun. Hard work is part of the package, but don't let it distract you from the main event. You're taking part in an amazing adventure, and this is the fastest-running part of the action.

Enjoy it!

Joanna Moorhead

JOANNA MOORHEAD
LONDON

Dedication

To my daughters Rosie, Elinor, and Miranda who have taught me everything I know about parenting and doubtless have a lot more lessons to share over the years ahead.

What's Inside?

THE INFORMATION in the K.I.S.S Guide to Baby and Child Care *will lead you through the early days of caring for your newborn, the developments of the toddler years, and your child's first steps towards independence at preschool.*

PART ONE

As a new parent, you will have plenty to learn, but much of it is common sense. In Part One, we'll talk about the early weeks of getting to know your newborn; practical care, such as feeding and bathing your baby; and how to have fun together at home.

PART TWO

In Part Two, we discuss how you can adjust to the demands of your new life in your baby's first 6 months. We'll talk about your baby's developing eating habits; the pros and cons of routines; health issues and child care options; and a baby's social life.

PART THREE

Part Three examines how your baby's character is developing between the ages of 6 to 12 months as he or she builds on communication, mobility, and social skills. We look at safety issues and discuss childhood illnesses and how to encourage good behavior.

PART FOUR

Life with a toddler between the ages of 1 to 2½ years is hard work, but it's also fascinating. In Part Four, we look at your child's increasing independence and see how children develop their talking and walking skills. We explain all about potty training and offer advice on how to choose a preschool.

PART FIVE

In Part Five, we discuss how your child's eating and sleeping habits are becoming more defined at 2½ years and over. We look at how play is one of the most important ways that a child learns at this age and we'll talk about how to settle your child at preschool and school.

The Extras

THROUGHOUT THE BOOK, *you'll notice a number of boxes and symbols. They emphasize the information provided, giving you valuable insights into baby and child care, and guiding you through the sometimes difficult job of parenthood. You'll find:*

Very Important Point

Some information can be crucial to know. If a topic deserves special attention, I'll alert you.

Complete No-No

This warning alerts you to practices or products that you should avoid.

Getting Technical

If there's anything technical that you need to know, I'll point it out so that you can read more carefully.

Inside Scoop

I'll share advice that I've picked up during my years as a parent, and that I think you'll find invaluable.

You'll also find some little boxes that include information I think is important, useful, or just good fun.

Trivia...

These include anecdotes or facts that give you an amusing and interesting insight into the world of baby and child care.

DEFINITION

*I'll **define** words and terms for you in plain English. There's also a glossary of baby and child care terms at the back of the book for easy reference.*

INTERNET

www.dk.com

The internet is a useful place to find advice on baby and child care, on issues ranging from health, sleep, and discipline. I've included some of my favorite web sites.

PART ONE

SPEND TIME GETTING TO KNOW YOUR NEWBORN

Chapter 1

We're Parents at Last

WHEN YOU FIRST FIND OUT that you're having a baby, the months of waiting seem to stretch ahead endlessly. Even as the bump gets bigger, it's hard to imagine that a real baby is in there and, more to the point, is soon going to be out here. In the final weeks of pregnancy, it's difficult to believe that you're about to become parents at last. And then, suddenly, it happens. You can't believe how quickly all those months went by, and you can't really take in the fact that it's happened – and that this tiny, gorgeous baby is actually here, and is actually yours.

In this chapter . . .

✓ This person we knew all along

✓ Is anything wrong?

✓ Debriefing the birth

✓ Getting to know your baby

✓ What your baby can do

This person we knew all along

"SO IT WAS YOU ALL ALONG."
That's what I wanted to say when I greeted each of my daughters after they were born: because when you look into your newborn's face, you're struck by this extraordinary thought – that you both know everything about this new person, and also nothing at all. It's a time of complex emotions: as a mother, this isn't the beginning of your relationship, because you've never been as physically close to another person as you've been to this one over the last 9 months – your own body constantly hugging his tiny, growing form. But for both parents, this is the start of something new – this is the moment that you fully appreciate the whole person you had been preparing to meet.

■ **The moment when** *you hold your baby in your arms for the first time is an intense and emotional experience.*

Love at first sight?

Almost all new parents are intensely fascinated by their new baby, but not all of us fall instantly in love. This isn't a problem, any more than it's not a problem if you didn't fall in love at first sight with your partner – some relationships start one way, some the other, and what emerges isn't dependent on its first moments. For many parents, as for many lovers, love grows slowly and steadily: first you meet, then you get to know one another, and little by little you fall in love.

There are two ways to cope with people visiting you and your newborn. Either invite everyone for one, exhausting day, or limit yourselves to one visitor every second day for the first 2 weeks or so. Try not to schedule too many arrangements – take things day by day.

Remind yourselves that in the early days, your life is going to revolve around feeding your baby, changing his diaper, watching anxiously over him while he sleeps, and being awakened from your own slumbers by him at unwelcome hours when he wakes.

All this is quite exhausting, and it's easy to overlook the fact that the most important part of having a baby is actually enjoying him. Some parents seem to shift effortlessly into enjoying their offspring but, for many of us, it's something we have to learn to do. You can't make it happen, but you can give yourself the best possible environment to allow it to happen.

Trivia...
Although a newborn cannot recognize his mother by sight, he will soon learn to distinguish her by smell. At 7 days, a baby can distinguish his mother's voice from that of another woman; by 14 days, he can recognize his father's voice.

Bonding with your newborn

Stress is a real enjoyment-killer in any situation, and particularly when it comes to your new baby. If you're getting stressed-out by worrying about whether he's getting enough to eat, by whether he's going to weigh enough at tomorrow's weight-check, by what your mother-in-law thinks of your new parenting skills: take action. Stop the clock, take your baby in your arms, and get straight into bed with him.

Undress him: marvel over his tiny body, hold his precious little hands and feet. Play with him: no baby is ever too young to be played with. Smell his gorgeous newborn smell, kiss his beautiful soft tummy, and stroke his downy little head. Talk to him: tell him how you felt about him when he was a bump, about how you feel about him now he's here. Tell him what you hope for him in his life, and about what fun you're going to have in the years ahead. This is parenting: it isn't just about giving him enough milk, putting his diapers on the right way, or applying the cream on his bottom. Of course practicalities matter when you're a parent, but time and love matter most.

Don't overdo the guests: the new person in your life needs you more than anyone else. It's more important that he gets to know his parents, above anyone else.

■ **Get to know** *your newborn, and give him lots of physical contact and love. Let him get to know your smell and your voice.*

Is anything wrong?

ALL NEW PARENTS *are anxious to know that their newborn is fit and healthy. Straight after he's born, your baby will be checked over by a midwife, an obstetrician, or a pediatrician – whoever is with you at the birth. This won't necessarily mean that you can't hold the baby right away. And it is comforting to know that an expert pair of eyes will be checking that, on first impressions, all seems well and that your baby is in good health.*

What happens after a difficult delivery

If the delivery was difficult, or an instrumental or forceps delivery, your baby might be taken immediately to a resuscitation table in the same room. The doctor present will check him over and make sure, in particular, that he's able to breathe easily.

DEFINITION

A **premature** *baby is one that is born before the 37th week of pregnancy, usually weighing less than 5½ lbs (2.5 kg).*

Usually, it only takes a minute or so for this check to be carried out, although it may seem a long time for you and your partner. If there's any cause for concern, or if your baby is very tiny, **premature**, or in any other way vulnerable, he will probably be moved to the special baby unit for specialist care. Usually, unless his life is in the balance, he'll be handed to his parents for a quick cuddle, or at least shown to you both. As soon as you're well enough, you'll be taken to see him in the unit.

All newborn babies are assessed at 1 and 5 minutes after birth and given what's known as the Apgar score.

Your baby will be given an assessment that takes into account his heart rate, breathing, skin color, response to stimulation, and activity level. A baby scoring 7 or more points is making good progress; a baby scoring under 4 points will need resuscitation; and a baby scoring in between the two will be very closely watched and monitored.

The pediatric check

Within 24 hours after the birth, and before the mother and baby leave hospital (if that's where the birth took place), your baby will be checked by a pediatrician. This is a more thorough examination than he had in the delivery room and will involve weighing him, and measuring his length and head circumference.

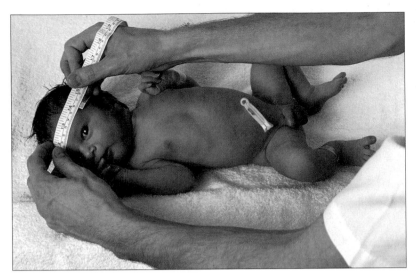

■ **A pediatrician** *will carry out a very thorough check of your baby within the first few days of his life. He or she will take measurements and keep a record of them so that your baby's growth can be monitored over the coming months.*

Your baby's head and the *fontanelles* are examined, and his breathing will be listened to with a stethoscope. The abdomen and genitals are checked, and a boy's testes will be examined to ensure that they have both descended. All the joints are examined, but the pediatrician will be particularly interested in the hip joints because dislocation is not uncommon – if a problem is found and treated early, this can be corrected. Your baby's pulse and reflexes are checked, and you will be asked if you have any concerns or queries.

A few days after the birth, a tiny drop of your baby's blood will be taken from his heel for a Newborn Screen. This is to check for abnormalities such as phenylketonuria, hypothyroidism, and sickle cell disease – tests carried out vary from state to state.

Why is my baby that color?

More than half of all normal babies, and up to 80 percent of all premature infants, develop jaundice. The main symptom is a yellowish tinge to the skin; if you notice this, report it to your caregiver, who should also be on the lookout for it.

The yellowing of the skin is caused by an excess of the chemical bilirubin, which is produced by the breakdown of red blood cells. Your new baby has a lot of red blood cells and his immature liver may be unable to cope with the amounts of bilirubin it has to deal with, resulting in jaundice. Don't be overly alarmed if your baby is affected. The condition is common, and mild jaundice often clears up on its own.

Treating jaundice

If your baby has more severe jaundice, he may need phototherapy. This is a straightforward treatment in which your baby is placed naked, but lying on a diaper, in a special incubator with fluorescent-type lights that help break down the excess bilirubin.

While your baby is undergoing phototherapy, his eyes will be covered with a protective mask so that the light doesn't damage them.

Phototherapy, which can be carried out at home in some countries, is one of the most common medical treatments small babies need. Even so, this doesn't make it any easier to deal with if it happens to your baby. Many parents find watching their tiny newborn lying alone and naked in a plastic box a heart-wrenching experience, and you may find you feel particularly weepy and vulnerable at this time.

Special care units

Around 1-in-10 newborn babies spend time in a special care unit. Premature babies are the most likely candidates for this intensive care, but they're not the only patients on the special care ward. For example, babies whose mothers have diabetes may need to be looked after there, as may babies who have had a difficult delivery.

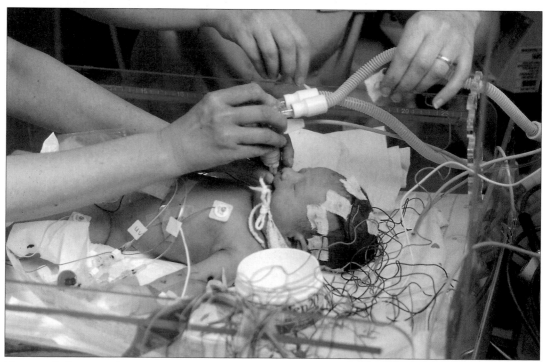

■ **Some babies need intensive,** *specialist care after they are born. A baby needing this type of care will probably be placed in an open incubator so that medical staff have better access to him.*

If your baby needs special care, he'll probably be taken to a care unit straight from the delivery room and you'll be able to see him some time later when you've recovered a little from the birth. Seeing him for the first time in an incubator will be an emotional experience: to make it easier for the nurses to monitor his progress, he'll probably be lying naked or wearing just a diaper. He'll be wired up to various machines, all of which flash and bleep, and you're likely to find it all confusing and upsetting. But just remind yourself that, with a newborn, medical staff always like to err on the side of caution. It may be that your child will be with you on the neonatal ward within a few hours.

Bear in mind that a short period of time in a special care unit isn't a rare event, and nor does it mean that your baby is in danger or has a problem that can't be dealt with.

A longer stay in the special care unit

If your baby has an ongoing problem, such as prematurity, the special care unit may be about to become your home, as well as his, for the forseeable future. This is likely to be a strange time for you: my first baby was born when I was 29 weeks pregnant and the first 2 months of her life were spent in a special care baby unit. I spent almost all day, every day on the unit. Looking back, it felt almost like living in a dream.

What keeps you going is the friendships you develop with other parents and medical staff, and the steady progress you are able to see in your baby. In many ways, however, the real parenting of your child won't begin until you finally get him home – and at that point, you almost need to treat him like a brand-new baby. Get into bed with him and start your babymoon, because he'll certainly need a bit of catching-up on the cuddles and physical contact front.

COMMUNICATING WITH MEDICAL STAFF

If your baby has a medical problem, communicating well with the professionals in charge is vital. You may be in shock, so it is a good idea to ask your partner or a friend to be with you – he or she may be more clear-headed than you are about asking the right questions. Don't worry if you forget to ask something: often the nursing staff will be more able to answer your questions about your baby's day-to-day care than the consultant. Most neonatal intensive care units do not allow parents to be present during the consultant's rounds, but immediately following is a good time to ask questions and to find out if there are any concerns.

Debriefing the birth

MOST WOMEN SPEND some of their pregnancy, especially in the final weeks and days, thinking ahead to the delivery. As an expectant mother, you will inevitably have had hopes and expectations. Even if you felt you'd just "go with the flow" and deal with whatever happened when it happened, you may have found you were unprepared for what did actually happen. Equally, if you had definite ideas about what you wanted, and things didn't go as planned, you may feel shocked about it.

INTERNET

www.thelaboroflove. com

This site contains over 500 birth stories – and you can send your own in too. Mothers share their experiences on a message board.

You'll need to talk

In any of these situations, and even if your delivery went swimmingly, many mothers feel an almost compulsive need to talk about it in the hours and days afterwards. If everything did go well, you may find yourself describing it with an energy and vigor that surprises you. Even if you're not the sort of person who usually likes to talk, this is probably something you'll want to share.

Where events took an unexpected turn, you may not feel so enthusiastic about opening your heart to others, but you do need to talk things through. Research shows that a "difficult" birth experience can mar your early weeks with a new baby. Talking it through with someone who understands and can explain certain aspects of what happened can certainly be useful.

Never keep it to yourself if you're feeling depressed in the early days and weeks after giving birth. It always helps to talk to someone, even if you don't think it's going to.

Who can you talk to?

It may seem difficult to know exactly who to turn to in this situation. Before you leave hospital, if this is where the birth took place, it will probably help to talk to your midwife and/or obstetrician. If you have left, or were not in, hospital, and you are still bothered by what you experienced, you might like to get a copy of your labor notes. However, not all hospitals give patients copies of their notes, and some may require that the patient review their notes in the presence of a physician because the medical terms can be difficult for a layperson to understand.

Talk to your partner and discuss your experiences with friends, particularly those who've had babies themselves. Bear in mind, however, that other mothers may not have got over what happened to them when they gave birth. They may be unable to help you because of experiences of their own that they've not properly worked through.

Talking to medical staff

A community midwife or your own doctor is another possible source of help. Don't feel guilty if you're finding it difficult to come to terms with what happened, despite having a healthy baby and "nothing to complain about". Mental health matters too, and the memories of a difficult delivery are often hard to move on from.

If you are having difficulties coming to terms with the experience of giving birth, your doctor may be able to recommend a counselor.

Be realistic about what happened. If your feelings are stopping you from enjoying your baby as much as you'd like to, be honest about this so that you can deal with your emotions.

If you have worries about what's likely to happen next time you give birth, don't dismiss these as irrelevant: they are relevant, and you do need to deal with them even if you're not planning to get pregnant again for a while.

THE UMBILICAL CORD

The stump of umbilical cord will eventually shrivel and fall off. Usually, this happens within 10 days or so of the birth, but it may take 2 weeks or more. After the cord falls off, there will be a little discharge and bleeding for a few weeks. Clean the area regularly using cotton balls or a q-tip soaked in water or alcohol. Infection at the site of the cord is rare but it does happen, and if the skin seems puffy, red, and shiny bring it to the attention of your doctor.

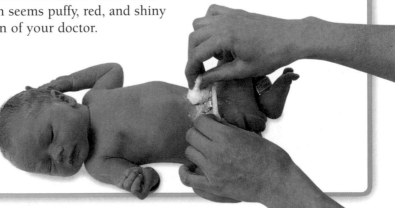

■ **Get into the habit** *of cleaning around your baby's umbilical stump during the diaper-changing routine. Keep an eye out for any signs of inflammation.*

Getting to know your baby

NO NEWBORN WOULD GET FAR in a beautiful baby contest, even if you are inclined to think that your baby is the most divine little creature in the history of the world. But right from the start, your baby's appearance may surprise you: at birth you may have been expecting a pink, plump, pretty baby. In fact, your new addition may be a rather dull, almost gray color initially, changing fairly rapidly to red as he starts to oxygenate his blood (although fingers and toes may remain a bit gray for a few days). He'll be covered in vernix, the creamy substance which protected his skin inside the uterus, and he may have a misshapen head caused by the rigors of the birth. He may even have down-like body hair.

What a newborn looks like

Over the first 24 hours or so, your baby will begin to look more like a baby. Even so, there are definite peculiarities that exist for the first few days and even weeks, such as very dry and flaky skin – a little oil in his bath can help deal with this. A female baby may have swollen breasts and some may even pass a little milk – this used to be known as "witch's milk." The milk in a baby girl's breasts is due to some of her mother's hormones passing into her bloodstream: these hormones are also responsible for occasionally causing a tiny bleed from a newborn girl's vagina. A baby boy, on the other hand, may have a swollen scrotum, caused by retained fluid – this will gradually subside. Rashes and spots are common.

A young baby can change very quickly in appearance. If you notice any difference that seems worrying to you, don't delay in calling for a medical opinion.

If you've got any concerns, talk to medical staff: it's far better to be safe than sorry. Newborn babies are more robust than many people imagine, but their health can change in a very short period of time.

■ **While your baby** *is in hospital, he will have a name tag attached to him so that there is no chance of staff mistaking his identity.*

Pass the diaper bag

It's sometimes said that all a newborn baby does is feed, cry, and fill his diaper, but your new son or daughter is a lot more than a noise-and-food machine. Nonetheless, diapers are a fact of life for at least the next 2 years! Try not to treat diapers with too much negativity: after all, emptying his bladder and bowels is a sign of a healthy child. Six to eight wet diapers and a poo every day or two (and maybe more often), are all signs that your baby is feeding and digesting well. In the early hours, the poo your baby passes is called meconium and is a greeny black, sticky substance – not unlike tar. This quickly changes to bright yellow, dark yellow with seeds, dark green, or lettuce green. At a few weeks old, he may open his bowels less often – even as little as once a week or less.

THIRD DAY BLUES

In the days following the birth, many women find that they have a day when they feel very emotional and weepy. It often seems to coincide with the day their milk "comes in" – usually the third day after the birth.

Between 10 and 15 percent of all new mothers experience some sort of blues in the days and weeks after the birth.

No one knows exactly why it happens, but it's almost certainly to do with a combination of physical and psychological factors. Hormonally, your body is undergoing rapid changes; physically, you're probably still uncomfortable and maybe in pain as a result of the delivery. Your baby is possibly becoming more demanding around this time. Try to put things into perspective: this is a difficult phase, but it will pass (usually quickly). Tell any visitors you can't have a good cry with to stay away, and turn to your partner, friends, or relatives for support.

■ **If you're feeling** *overwhelmed, try to take some time for yourself, sit quietly, and relax.*

What your baby can do

A BABY ARRIVES EQUIPPED with various reflexes, some of which are designed to help him with life now, others of which are primitive leftovers from our ancient ancestors. The useful reflexes include the sucking reflex, which is your baby's most powerful instinct, and the rooting reflex, which means he will turn his head towards the direction of touch and open his mouth expecting to find an available and milk-giving nipple. The gagging reflex stops unsuitable objects from going down his throat.

Basic reflexes

Primitive reflexes include the Moro reflex, in which any sudden change in your baby's balance will make him throw out his arms and legs (a basic attempt to bring him to his parent's attention in case of danger). In a much-documented response, a newborn will also appear to make stepping movements if placed upright with his feet on a firm surface – obviously, he's not strong enough to walk properly yet!

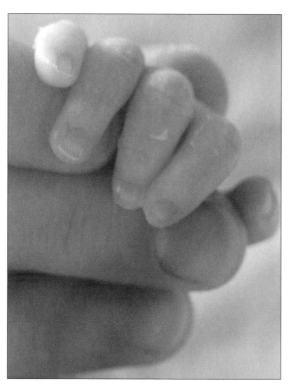

Senses and other abilities

Newborn babies used to be thought to be virtually blind and unable to feel pain or to taste much. It's now known that a baby's eyes are well-focused at a distance of about 12 inches (30 cm), which is the perfect distance for him to see his mother's or father's face clearly as he nestles in their arms.

Babies are also now known to have a strongly developed sense of smell and taste, and their hearing, which was already well developed in the womb, is sensitive to a huge range of sounds within a few weeks of birth.

■ **Your newborn baby** *is able to grasp your hand with his tiny fingers – you may be surprised by his strength.*

Learning fast

More and more is being found out about how much a baby can learn at this early stage of life. In the past, small babies were often consigned for long hours to a crib or baby carriage away from the ordinary goings-on of the household. Today's babies are usually in the thick of things from the start, and they seem to thrive on this. The more there is for them to look at, the more they take an interest, and the more quickly they're likely to learn.

Babies who are born into families that already have one or more children get a ringside seat on life from day one: bear this in mind if yours is a first baby. Don't miss an opportunity to introduce your baby to something new to look at or to the sight of older children playing: babies do love company.

INTERNET

www.parenthoodweb.com
www.drgreene.com

This web site offers lots of information about how to care for your baby.

A simple summary

✓ When your baby is born, you'll almost certainly be fascinated by him, but don't necessarily expect to fall in love and bond with him instantly.

✓ You won't be any less of a parent if it takes a while before you bond with your newborn.

✓ If your baby has a problem, he may need to be nursed in a special care unit where you'll be able to spend lots of time too.

✓ Before leaving the hospital, your baby will have a pediatric check to ensure he is healthy.

✓ In the early days, do all you can to concentrate on your baby.

✓ Friends and relatives will certainly want to visit, but don't forget that your relationship with your baby is more important than anyone else's.

✓ Many women feel down after they've given birth, and it's vital to share your feelings with your loved ones and caregivers.

✓ Newborns don't look like older babies, but their senses and reflexes are surprisingly well developed.

Chapter 2

Feeding Your Baby

THEY SLEEP, THEY CRY, THEY FEED. That's the conventional wisdom about the day-to-day life of a newborn baby. This is a fiction, in the sense that tiny babies do a whole lot more than just the basics of survival. However, it does underline the fact that feeding is one of the fundamental issues in a newborn's life. In the first few months, your baby's growth rate will be faster than at any other time in her life, so it clearly matters, enormously, what she's being fed. And what's more, feeding is about delivering a lot more than food – it's about delivering love and reassurance, too.

In this chapter . . .

✓ Shall I breastfeed?

✓ Early breastfeeding

✓ Sorting out any problems

✓ It's a lot more than food . . .

✓ Bottle-feeding

YOUR BABY WILL ENJOY THE COMFORT AND WARMTH OF YOUR PRESENCE WHILE SHE'S FEEDING

Shall I breastfeed?

ON THE FACE OF IT, THERE'S NO CONTEST. Breast milk is clearly, definitely, and overwhelmingly the best food for your baby. It has proven health benefits for her and a lot of advantages for you, too. Why would you even consider not giving your child this excellent start in life?

Considering breastfeeding

Like everything else in life, the reality isn't as simple as the theory. Almost every new mother living in a Western country in the early 21st century is told about the benefits of breast milk, but not every new mother embarks on breastfeeding. There are also considerable variations in breastfeeding rates based on socioeconomic status and race. In the US, only around 60 percent of new mothers breastfeed; 20 percent are still breastfeeding when their babies have reached 6 months of age.

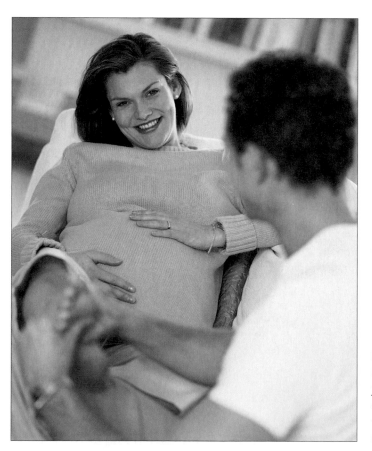

Perhaps that's because they've already tried breastfeeding a previous baby and it didn't work out, or perhaps no one they know has ever breastfed and they don't want to seem "different" from those around them. Perhaps their partner thinks it will push him out, or maybe they feel uncomfortable with the idea of breastfeeding in public. For many mothers, it just seems simpler to give their baby a bottle from the start.

■ **While you're pregnant,** *talk to your partner about how you will feed your baby. Choose a time when you are both feeling relaxed, and discuss any concerns that either of you may have.*

But is breast really still best?

A stream of studies on breast milk have highlighted worries about aspects of breastfeeding and made some women wonder whether breast really is best. One study, for example, carried out by the World Wide Fund for Nature, said that breastfed babies could be exposed to up to 40 times the recommended levels of potentially harmful chemicals. Another piece of research published in the British Medical Journal said that early signs of cardiovascular disease were more likely in people who'd been breastfed beyond the age of 4 to 6 months.

Interpreting the figures

Although these figures look alarming, it's important to realize that these studies say more about whole populations, and the environments they live in, than about individual mothers. The main message behind the World Wide Fund for Nature research, for example, was that pollutants are present in our bodies in greater concentrations than was previously thought, and breast milk is an easy way of checking the amount, that's all. In a polluted world, breast milk is sadly as polluted as anything else, and switching to formula milk would only mean your baby picking up a similar range of contaminants from cow's milk instead.

A breastfed baby is less likely to suffer from gastroenteritis, ear infections, juvenile diabetes, asthma, or allergies. Being breastfed can also result in better eyesight and a lower risk of high blood pressure in later life.

The study on heart disease, meanwhile, is thought to say more about the harmful effects of a Western diet than about breastfeeding – something that humans have practiced for millions of years.

The best reassurances come from the World Health Organization and the American Academy of Pediatrics. It has issued a recommendation that most women should exclusively breastfeed their babies for at least the first 6 months of their lives, to give them the best start in life. That recommendation comes after health experts combed through 3,000 studies on breastfeeding, including the reports which have raised concerns. At the end of the day, they remain convinced that the benefits of breastfeeding are huge and that any dangers are negligible in comparison.

Will breastfeeding suit me?

Some people find it difficult to accept the idea of a woman breastfeeding a baby in public, and think that only a certain "sort" of woman breastfeeds. If this was ever the case, it certainly isn't any more. Breastfeeding has been on the increase in Western countries over the last few years, after a fall in popularity in the 1970s, and the figures are continuing to rise steadily. That means that more and more mothers are deciding to breastfeed, and some of them are certainly women just like you. Also, you may be reassured to know that a lot of women who assume that they won't like breastfeeding find to their surprise that it suits them very well.

If you're dithering over whether to try breastfeeding, it's worth taking a bit of time to ask yourself what's at the heart of the debate for you and what your main concerns are. Involve your partner in your dilemma and your decision. After all, this baby is his as well as yours, and you both want what's best for her.

If you feel it's not fair to breastfeed your baby because you bottle-fed the last, or if you feel that you don't want to breastfeed in case your mother, who bottle-fed you, thinks you're criticizing her decision, stop a moment to think about that. You can't change the past: you can't alter the fact that you bottle-fed your older child, or that your own mother bottle-fed you. But this new baby is just starting out in life, and the evidence is clearer than it's ever been before that breastfeeding is best. Doesn't she deserve the chance to have the finest start in life?

Women who breastfeed have a lower risk of pre-menopausal breast cancer, as well as less risk of fractures from osteoporosis in later life.

Getting used to the idea

In traditional societies, children grow up seeing women breastfeeding their babies, but in the West, breastfeeding can be so discreet that it may be something that you have not consciously come into contact with.

However, even though in some areas it's still not a usual sight, it's becoming more common to see mothers breastfeeding their babies. It's important to remember that breastfeeding doesn't mean exposing yourself, being an exhibitionist, or seeming antisocial. The more women breastfeed in public (not that it's usually obvious what they're doing!), the more it will be seen as an ordinary part of life, and the more other women will be encouraged to do it too, when their turn comes.

> ### Trivia...
> Until 1999, the British House of Commons had its own shooting gallery and barber shop, but no special facilities for breastfeeding. After a record number of women MPs were returned at the 1997 election, a special breastfeeding room was opened – only to be followed by a ruling from the then-Speaker, Betty Boothroyd, that women MPs would not be allowed to breastfeed in committee rooms! Her replacement, Michael Martin, reversed the ban.

Successful breastfeeding begins long before your baby nuzzles into your breast for the first time. It starts when you begin to think positively about breastfeeding. Talk to other women who've breastfed. Ask them about their experiences and learn from them.

I'm afraid of failing...

Unfortunately, a lot of new mothers don't even try to breastfeed because they think it won't work out and they don't want to fail. This is a completely understandable fear, but the fact is that most problems that arise as a result of breastfeeding are solvable. It isn't that women who give up don't want to carry on – surveys show that as many as 9 out of 10 who give up in the first 2 weeks wish they had persevered. The problem is a lack of clear, practical advice at the crucial moment.

Any relaxation techniques that you learn while you're pregnant will come in handy when you start breastfeeding. If you feel positive and are able to relax, feeding will come more naturally.

Determination matters, too. My first baby, Rosie, was born when I was just 29 weeks pregnant and she spent her first 2 months of life in a special care unit. Learning to feed her was a long, hard slog. Often, I'd spend all day in the unit and all she would do was lick my nipple at feeding time (I was expressing milk which was used to tube-feed her). The most important thing I was told came from the hospital feeding adviser, who said simply: "I know you're going to succeed, and I know that you know it too." Believing we'd get there in the end was the most important reason that we did.

■ **Sort out any worries** *you have about how you will feed your baby before she arrives, because when she's finally a part of your life, you won't want any stress to spoil the time you spend together.*

Early breastfeeding

STUDIES HAVE SHOWN *that the earlier a baby has her first breastfeed, the greater the chances of success. Out of the mothers who breastfed their babies immediately after birth, only 14 per cent gave up within the next 2 weeks, compared with the 29 percent who gave up, having begun breastfeeding at between 1 and 4 hours after birth. This doesn't mean that if you don't breastfeed immediately, you're bound to fail. But it does mean that if there's the chance to put your baby to your breast within the first hour or so after the birth, it's worth taking the opportunity. Your obstetrician or midwife will probably encourage it. If not, you should certainly ask.*

A baby's suck is at its strongest in the first few hours after birth. There's evidence that a baby is born "conditioned" for this first feeding, and is more likely to "get it right first time" the younger she is.

The first breastfeed

Because research shows that it's advisable to try to get the baby to nurse as soon as possible after the birth, you'll probably find yourself prompted by your obstetrician or midwife to "have a go at a feeding." Don't be rushed into introducing your newborn to the breast before you're ready, but do bear in mind that if your baby is alert and not crying, this is probably a good moment to see what happens.

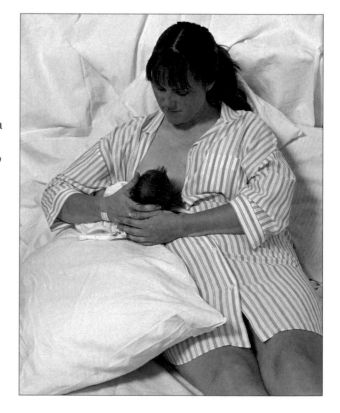

■ **Breastfeeding in** *the early days takes a bit of practice – it helps to start as early as possible after your baby is born.*

An obstetrician, nurse, or midwife will almost certainly stay beside you to help the baby get "latched on" – that is, sucking properly at the breast. You need to make sure that you're comfortable before you begin. It may be difficult if you're still lying on the delivery table, for example, but do ask for more pillows if you need them. Your baby can feed lying down next to you or on top of you, or you can sit up to feed her. It's also perfectly okay to feed her while you're having stitches, in fact, it can be a good distraction.

GETTING THE POSITION RIGHT

The crucial thing about breastfeeding is getting the positioning right. You'll learn more about positioning on the postnatal ward (hopefully) and it will become more natural with practice. But the main thing to remember is that you need to hold your baby right along her body. She should be facing you, with her tummy turned towards your tummy. Here are some tips to help you get it right:

1. If you're sitting up, you should be upright, rather than leaning backwards or forwards

2. Your baby should be lying facing you, with her nose opposite your nipple

3. It can help if you place the flat of your hand beneath your breast, so that your nipple is easily accessible to your baby

4. You need to wait until she "roots" – she must open her mouth really wide, before you move her towards your nipple: this is so that she can latch on. Try "teasing" her with a nipple to encourage her to open her mouth. Make sure her mouth covers the whole nipple

■ **Place a pillow** *on your lap underneath your baby while she's feeding. It will help you support her weight, and it will stop you stooping over her and getting backache.*

Babies aren't always wide awake in the first hour or so after birth – some are very sleepy and barely give the nipple a second glance before settling back down for another slumber. This can be worrying for a new mother who is anxious to make sure that her new baby has her first proper feeding. You can try to wake your baby up by gently tickling her feet or the back of her head. But don't expect it to be a roaring success this first time. After all, you're both novices at this game and very few novices become expert at their first attempt at something new.

Always move your baby to your breast so that she is facing it full on – never move your breast to your baby.

Coping with the ups and downs

You aren't likely to get into a pattern at all in the early days of breastfeeding, so don't have high expectations. This time is, for many women, an emotional rollercoaster. When a feed goes well, it's wonderful – you feel at one with your baby and on top of the world. And then you have a feed when you simply can't get her to latch on, when you think it's all gone completely to pot, and you're terrified your child is going to waste away and never get another drop of milk out of you.

It's completely understandable to feel like this – everyone does. After all, you've got the huge responsibility of keeping this little person going, so of course it matters that breastfeeding is working properly. Don't forget, though, that a newborn baby comes with food reserves already on board, precisely to get her through these early days of learning to breastfeed.

Your baby's tiny stomach is only about the length of your thumb, so she doesn't have to consume gallons of milk to be full up.

Understanding the process

When your baby starts sucking, she will get the foremilk. This will quench her thirst and is light on calories. Her suck will trigger a hormonal response in your body that prompts the higher-calorie, or hindmilk, to flow – this is known as the *let-down reflex*. You may be aware of a feeling like a warm rush into your breasts at this point. New mothers sometimes worry about this reflex, or rather, a lack of it. They fear that if they don't feel it they can't be making enough milk for their baby. This isn't the case: some mothers will notice the reflex, others won't.

> **DEFINITION**
>
> *The **let-down reflex** happens between a few seconds and a few minutes into a feed when hormones trigger the flowing of the milk from the deeper reserves within the breast. Some women feel this "rush," or see their baby's sucking becoming deeper and longer.*

Take each breastfeed as it comes

Try not to get too hung up on feeding if it's not going perfectly; make an effort to just look at your child and touch her tiny fingers and toes. Look into those little eyes that are both wise and unknowing. Remember that milk is important, but love is crucial.

It's easy to make the mistake in the first few days of your baby's life of looking too far ahead. If breastfeeding is difficult, and you and your baby are finding it difficult to get positioning and latching on right, don't despair and worry about whether you'll still be breastfeeding next week or next month. It's far more productive just to concentrate on this feed, rather than fretting about the next one and the one after that. Right now, it's more important than it's ever been to live in the present moment, concentrating on your new baby and her needs and enjoying her as she starts out on this new adventure – life.

The nights are always the worst

Everything seems worse at night, and finding yourself exhausted in a strange hospital bed, and with a crying baby who doesn't quite get the gist of breastfeeding can be seriously depressing. What you need at a moment like this is the experience and support of a knowledgeable nurse or lactation consultant and, with luck, that's what you'll get. The trouble is, not every hospital has enough staff to be of help. If you get the support you need, listen to every word and be guided by it: remember that, for many new mothers, advice sought during a night-time crisis can be the turning point to easier and more straightforward breastfeeding.

You may find breastfeeding easier at home than in hospital. If you need assistance, don't hesitate to contact a lactation consultant. They usually charge an hourly fee, which may or may not be covered by your insurance company.

■ **Breastfeeding** *your baby in the comfort of your own home can give you the positive results you are hoping for.*

Sorting out any problems

*EXPERIENCING PROBLEMS with breastfeeding in the early days
is very common, but it doesn't have to be the end of the world. Unfortunately
for some women, a problem which could be solved with a bit of expert help
does become a major stumbling-block, and the result is a switch to the bottle
long before the mother or baby is really ready.*

This doesn't have to happen to you. The crucial thing you need to do is to get help as
soon as you have an inkling there's a problem. If your nipple is sore, don't wait until the
pain is excruciating before you ask your obstetrician, a lactation expert, or your midwife
what to do; call for help the moment you first notice that there's something wrong.

What to look out for

Sore nipples are the number one symptom that something isn't quite right. In the very
early days of breastfeeding, you may be hypersensitive to the sensation of your baby
feeding, so it may not be a problem – you might just be getting used to the sensation of
the sucking. If you have persistent pain, especially accompanied by redness around the
nipple, ask your doctor or your midwife to watch you feeding and check your positioning.
You've probably got it almost right, but a small adjustment will make all the difference.
As well as getting the position right, sore nipples need to heal. Try to keep your nipples
dry, and expose your nipples to the air in the daytime as much as you're able to.

The pain from a sore
nipple is often worst at
the start of a feed. It
helps to start the feed
with the less sore side.
It may also help if you
can get the milk to
flow before the feed
begins. If you feel the
sensation of your milk
flowing when you're
not actually feeding, put
your baby to the breast
straight away. Once
the milk is flowing,
feeding should not
be so painful.

■ **Talk to your obstetrician,** *your midwife, or a lactation expert about
any problems you're having; most concerns can be sorted out easily.*

FEEDING TWINS

The early weeks and months will be exhausting with twins, but hold onto the thought that this stage won't last forever. Here are some tips to help you through:

a You'll need to feed the babies individually initially until you (and they) are proficient at it. But aim to feed them both at once as soon as you can, because you'll find it a lot more convenient that way

b Even if you're basically feeding on demand, try to wake one for a feeding if her twin is already awake so that they get into the habit of feeding together

c Don't despair! While bottle-feeding may seem like the answer to early breastfeeding problems with twins, breastfeeding may be less time-consuming in the long run and more convenient than using formula milk. After all, you can breastfeed two older babies virtually hands-free using pillows, but bottle-feeding is always a two-handed job for each baby

d Remember that in the early months, all that matters is making sure your babies are fed and happy, and keeping yourself fed, rested, and happy too

e If you're breastfeeding twins, you'll need to drink lots of water and eat plenty of calories to keep your milk supply up

■ **Once you've got** *your twin babies into the habit of feeding at the same time, you'll find that your days will become much easier to cope with.*

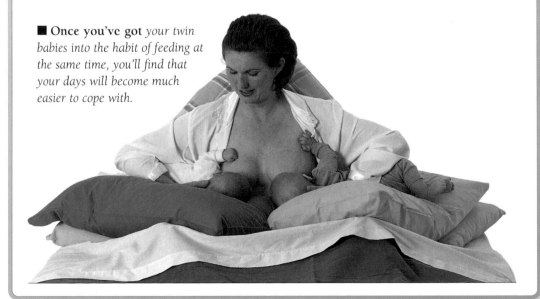

Avoid washing your nipples with soap because it is really drying and also because a scented soap might put your baby off feeding. Your breasts will be quite clean enough if you just wash them with water.

Uncomfortable, lumpy, and full breasts are common in the early days of breastfeeding. That's because it's a supply-and-demand system, and your body is just coming to grips with how much milk your baby needs. At the moment, it's overproducing. Within a few days, this will settle down as your breasts adjust to the amount of food your infant needs.

Don't try to diet or lose weight while you're still in the early days of breastfeeding. Of course you'd like to be back to your old shape as soon as possible, and breastfeeding will help with that. But dieting, or not eating as much as you'd like to, could interfere with your body's ability to produce enough milk for your baby in this all-important early period.

If your breasts are unbearably painful, try putting raw cabbage leaves inside your bra. Keep them in the refrigerator so that they're really cold, and that will be even more soothing.

How to get help fast

Even while you're still in hospital, you can still seek the telephone support of a trained breastfeeding adviser through an organization like the La Leche League. Or ask your obstetrician, your midwife, or a nurse on the ward whether the maternity unit's lactation consultant could come and see you. Most hospitals now have lactation consultants, but in some places they don't routinely visit each new mother unless individuals request it.

Although post-delivery midwife visits are not routine once you're back home, you can expect to take your newborn to her first visit to the pediatrician anywhere from a few days to 2 or 3 weeks after her birth.

INTERNET

www.lalecheleague.org

This is the web site for the La Leche League. It has plenty of information about breastfeeding, and it also has links to other helpful web sites.

Don't let just anyone give you advice on breastfeeding. Decide who your instincts tell you to trust, and listen to them. A lactation consultant, a pro-breastfeeding pediatrician, or a midwife is your best bet.

It's a lot more than food ...

"SURELY YOU'RE NOT FEEDING THAT BABY AGAIN!" People *sometimes unhelpfully said that to me when I was feeding one of my babies, and if anyone says it to you, do your best to ignore them. The truth is, of course, that you're not necessarily "feeding" your baby every time you put her to the breast.*

Sometimes she's having a snack, or even a big supper, but often she's just having a reassuring cuddle, checking that you're still there, getting over a surprise, or comforting herself after something made her sad or jumpy.

A breast is a lot more than just the next meal to your baby: it's a whole emotional support system too.

So don't be afraid of using your breast to soothe, quiet, or reassure your baby. And don't think your baby isn't able to play or learn while she's feeding from the breast. Looking up into your eyes as she sucks is the first thing she'll ever learn to do, and exploring your skin with her little hands as she feeds is one of the first ways she'll reach out beyond her own body. Try to find the time occasionally to go to a quiet place for a feed and take your bra off so you can have a really close skin-to-skin cuddle.

What does breast milk contain?

Mothers make breast milk using the food and drink they've recently ingested. Basically, your milk consists of what you've eaten. A 1-month old baby needs around 24 fl. oz. (750 ml.) of milk a day. To make that, a mother needs between 300 and 600 extra calories daily above her normal requirement – so while the old adage to "eat for two" while you're pregnant is now frowned upon, it's true that you CAN eat a bit more than usual while you're breastfeeding. However, when it comes to celebrating the birth, try and keep alcohol to a minimum. Unlike some substances, alcohol is not broken down by your body before being turned into milk. So if you're feeling drunk, your baby is going to feel the same way too.

■ **Whatever you have** *for your lunch, the milk your baby has later that day will contain the nutrients taken from that meal.*

Bottle-feeding

FORMULA MILK MAY NOT BE *quite as perfect for a baby as breast milk, but it is better than it's ever been. Manufacturers spend a lot of time and effort on mimicking a mother's milk as closely as possible – the days when formula was just something sweet and filling with a few vitamins thrown in are long gone.*

If you have decided you can't carry on with breastfeeding, or perhaps you didn't start in the first place, don't torture yourself with worries over the milk your baby is getting. Ask your pediatrician's or midwife's advice if you're confused over which brand to buy.

Making up your baby's bottles

Always read the instructions on the formula milk package carefully – the ratio of powder to water is important. If you add too much water, the baby won't get enough energy and nutrients. Too little water, however, may lead to dehydration. Put the powder into the scoop provided and level it off with a clean knife – don't compress it. Always use cooled, boiled water, and shake the bottle thoroughly until all the powder is dissolved.

■ **If you are bottle-feeding** *your baby, it means that you can share the wonderful experience of feeding her with your partner, or with grandparents.*

All the equipment you use to feed your baby must be washed and sterilized after use. Wash the bottles with a weak solution of detergent and use a long-handled brush that can reach right inside the bottle. Rinse all the detergent out properly, and then sterilize the bottle by boiling it in water (for at least 10 minutes), using a steam sterilizer, or using water and sterilizing tablets. It's fine to make up a whole day's feedings in one go, because made-up formula milk can be kept in the fridge for up to 48 hours. If you want to warm the milk, stand it in a jug of hot water. It's not necessary for the milk to be heated right through, though, and always check that the milk is not too hot.

A simple summary

✓ Breast milk is the best milk you can give your baby, especially in her early days and weeks.

✓ It's worth at least trying to feed your baby yourself, unless you're completely opposed to the idea or have a medical condition that makes feeding impossible.

✓ Don't decide not to breastfeed because you're "not the type" – talk to other mothers about it.

✓ Breastfeeding doesn't have to limit your life – it's easy to feed on the go, wherever you are, once you've had a bit of practice.

✓ Many breastfeeding mothers have minor problems in the early days and weeks, but these are almost always solvable if you get the right advice quickly.

✓ If you experience any discomfort while you're breastfeeding, or if you notice a lack of weight gain in your baby, speak to a pediatrician or a lactation expert.

✓ Take feedings one at a time and don't rush into any decisions about stopping – it's usually worth persevering.

✓ Don't expect a pattern in the early days because there won't be one. But believe in the future: it won't always be as chaotic as this!

✓ If you need to move on to bottle-feeding, don't feel guilty – formula milk powders are better than they have ever been before.

✓ Make sure that you follow the instructions on the packet when you're making up your baby's milk bottles, and be scrupulous about cleanliness.

✓ Remember that however you choose to feed your baby, you're the best mother in the world for her. Being fed and cared for by someone who loves her is more important than having the best food from someone who's stressed-out and not enjoying life.

Chapter 3

Practical Care

Not many decades ago, the practical care of a new baby was a science in itself. In the 1950s and 1960s, pregnant women and their bemused partners would be invited to lectures at which matrons in starched white uniforms would demonstrate the art of cleaning a baby. However, over the last few years, the tables have turned, and we now spend a lot more time thinking about the emotional and intellectual development of our babies, and less time on how to keep them clean. In general this is a good thing, because a lot of the practical care of a small baby is common sense anyway.

In this chapter . . .

✓ Keeping your baby clean

✓ Heat matters

✓ Dressing your baby

✓ All about diapers

MAKE DIAPER CHANGING FUN FOR YOU AND YOUR BABY

Keeping your baby clean

SOME BABIES LOVE *being bathed and others hate it. There's no rhyme or reason to this. To make things as easy as possible for you, the best thing is to simply go with the flow. If you've got a serious bather, great: give him lots of chances to kick his feet by building a regular bath into his routine. And if you've got a baby that tenses up at the first sign that he is about to be immersed in water, there are other ways to keep him clean until he gets over his fear.*

Giving your baby a quick clean

If your baby doesn't like being bathed, don't worry too much. New babies don't actually need to be bathed very often at all. If it's easier or more convenient for you, or if your baby seems to hate having all his clothes taken off, then **topping and tailing** will do the job very nicely indeed.

DEFINITION

Topping and tailing *is a method of cleaning your baby's head, hands, and bottom without bathing him.*

BATHING A NEWBORN

While your baby is still tiny, you may find it easier to bath him in a tub. Place the tub on a table, so that you can stand up while you're bathing him. Make sure that the water is not too hot, and that the room temperature is warm. It's worth donning an apron, because you're bound to get very wet!

Babies often feel vulnerable when they are being lowered into water, so reassure your baby by talking to him. Once he is in the water, some of his weight will be supported by the water and he may start to play and kick. When he's relaxed, keep one hand under his head, and use your other hand to wash him.

1 **Checking the water temperature**

After you have filled the bathtub with warm water, test its temperature with your elbow to ensure that it's not too hot.

Keep all the things you'll need for topping and tailing together in a bowl in the bathroom – this will cut down the time it takes to a minimum. You'll need: a bowl with lukewarm water; some cotton balls; a towel; a clean diaper; some diaper cream, if you need it; and your baby's next outfit.

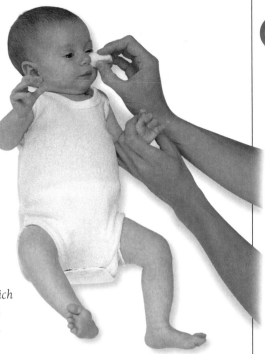

Undress your baby down to his diaper, and then start to clean him with a moist cotton ball. Start with his face. Clean his eyes, his nose, his ears, and his neck – pay particular attention to those creases under his chin, because they can get quite sticky, especially in the summer. Then do his hands, under his arms and around his cord stump, before changing his diaper and cleaning around his bottom.

■ **Babies often produce** *a lot of "sleepers" around their eyes, which they cannot wipe away themselves. Use a fresh piece of moist cotton wool for each eye, and gently swipe from each inner corner outward.*

2 **Placing him in the bath**
Support your baby's head with your forearm, and use your other hand to support his bottom. Gently trickle water over him and wash him.

3 **Drying your baby**
When you have finished bathing your baby, wrap him in a big, warm towel, and gently pat his hair and his body dry.

Heat matters

AS WELL AS KEEPING A BABY CLEAN, *parents also worry about whether their baby is warm enough. However, it's also important not to keep your newborn baby too warm. Although crib death isn't fully understood, research has shown that overheating is a significant factor – and that if babies are kept at an optimum temperature, they're far less likely to become victims of crib death.*

INTERNET

www.sids-network.org

This web site gives advice about Sudden Infant Death Syndrome (SIDS). It's packed with reassuring and useful information on how to keep your baby safe and well.

Why temperature is important

Young babies aren't as good as older children at regulating their own temperatures, which is why it's so important to keep an eye on how warm they are. They simply don't have the mechanism for cooling themselves down quickly, or heating themselves up fast – and getting too hot, or too cold, can be disastrous.

Don't leave your baby wrapped up too warmly when you go into shops or shopping centers, or when you're in the car, or on a bus or train. The Foundation for the Study of Infant Deaths warns that swaddling your baby in heavy clothes can put his or her life at risk.

Regulating temperature

Make a habit of checking your baby's temperature from time to time to make sure that he's not too hot or too cold.

Contrary to popular belief, checking the warmth of his hands and feet is not the best way to do this since in a small baby, it's normal for the extremities to be quite cold, and doesn't mean his core temperature is low. Instead, feel your baby's tummy

■ **If it's warm,** *your baby may not need a blanket over him while he's taking a nap; put him in his bassinet in just his undershirt.*

and the back of his neck. These are a far better indication of whether your infant is the right temperature. If you do decide he's too hot or too cold, act immediately; a baby's temperature will reduce quickly if you simply remove blankets and layers of clothing. If your baby is too cold, the quickest and best way to warm him up is to cuddle him close to you – try holding him between your breasts. You can warm him up more quickly if you pull a fleece or blanket up around his back and bottom.

> ### Trivia...
> In a survey, only 37 percent of parents interviewed knew the correct room temperature for a baby – it should be between 61 and 68 °F (16 and 20 °C.)

Dressing your baby

THERE WAS A TIME when the main clothes in a baby's wardrobe were three white romper suits, a couple of cardigans, and a hat knitted by his proud granny. Things have certainly changed. These days, babies are as much a part of the fashion stakes as their parents. Infants wearing the latest designer kids clothes have even appeared at fashion shows, being carried along catwalks by top models.

When you're buying clothes for your infant, remember that he will only be in his first-size clothes for a few weeks. Save your money and invest in clothes when he's reached 6 months – he'll be able to wear these items longer.

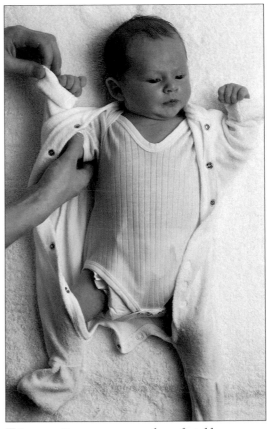

■ **Jumpsuits are warm** and comfortable for your baby to wear, and snap fastenings make dressing and undressing him quick and easy.

Choosing clothes

The world of baby clothes has certainly opened up over the last few years and there's a huge range of different types of garments around. However, there are still a few basics that you wouldn't want to be without and the number one consideration when you're buying for your baby has to be comfort. You don't want to spend hours wondering whether your baby is hungry or in pain only to realize, when you remove his vest, that it was digging into his leg, or that the label was made of scratchy material that bothered him. Look at any item you buy or are given before you put it on; in particular, make sure that you cut off those nasty little plastic tags that tend to get left at the back of the neck on the garment.

ALL YOU REALLY NEED...

The more babies you have, the more you realize how little they really need. The only absolute must-haves are a car seat (unless you go everywhere on foot or public transport), a crib (unless the baby's sleeping in your bed), a from-birth carriage or stroller (or even just a sling for the first couple of weeks), and a changing mat. In fact, as most experienced mothers will tell you, it's amazing how much baby paraphernalia you can do without. But your baby will, of course, need clothing. Here's a basic list of what you'll need:

- At least 6 jumpsuits – get 8 or 10 if you don't want to use the washing machine every day. You could cut the toes out of the suits you have as he gets bigger. If yours is a summer baby, buy a couple of footless suits, and use socks to keep his feet warm – he won't outgrow these suits as quickly
- At least 6 undershirts
- Two or 3 cardigans
- A snowsuit, plus a knitted hat and mittens, in winter
- A cotton hat with a brim for summer

■ **Choose clothes** *that have been made from natural materials, such as cotton and wool. These are warmer than artificial fibers and are less likely to irritate your baby's skin.*

Being practical

There will be lots of diaper changes in the next few weeks and months. Make it easier for both of you by buying outfits that have easy leg access; suits with snaps around the legs and bottom are the best.

Don't forget, too, that "diaper changes" in the early weeks may quite often require whole outfit changes (that's when you get an "up the back" leaky poo – not very pleasant, but a more common occurrence than you might hope). So choose undershirts with "envelope" heads, because they're a lot easier to get over a baby's head (and undershirts are something babies especially hate having put on and off).

If you're on a budget, look for clothes in a good second-hand children's clothes shop: there are often some great bargains in the babywear section, because outfits aren't worn long enough to wear out.

In general, all-in-one suits are the best bet for small babies. Steer clear of dresses as they're far too fussy for such little people, and they mean that you've got to start messing around with tights as well, unless it's a sweltering summer's day.

Getting the right size

When you're buying or advising others on what to buy as presents, remember that clothes labeled as "first size" may not be your baby's first size at all: many are for a baby of UNDER 8 lb. (3.5 kg), and yours may very well be born weighing more than that. Make sure that you keep the receipts so that you can take clothes back (or more realistically, get someone else to take them for you), and do tend towards buying bigger, rather than smaller clothes. After all, your child can always grow into things.

If you find yourself the mother of a tiny premature baby, don't be tempted to buy doll's clothes – they may fit, but they won't be made for comfort. Some neonatal units have a clothes bank for premature babies. Or try phoning around shops asking whether they stock special premature babies' clothes – some do.

All about diapers

WHEN DISPOSABLE DIAPERS were introduced around 40 years ago, they were a convenience revolution. For mothers who had toiled over hot tubs of steaming diapers, and whose every day had been dominated by the cycle of washing and hanging out to dry, they represented a huge step forward in babycare. No longer would a woman with an infant be chained to the laundry tub! The most unpleasant job that went with having a small child had been relegated to history – or at least, that's how it must have seemed.

The great diaper debate

Four decades on, the reusable diaper is making a comeback. It's not that we crave a return to inconvenience, it's just that when we embraced disposable diapers we hadn't considered the effect on the environment. Or at least, for many years we managed to ignore the ecological side effects – but now we can't really ignore them any longer. After all, as you sit gazing down at your cute newborn, you can't really shut your mind to the fact that 7 million trees are being felled daily to provide the pulp for the billions of disposable diapers used annually. And then there are those news scares that pop up every so often about the chemicals used in disposable diapers, and what they might or might not be doing to your precious baby if they're seeping through his skin.

At least 100 viruses contained in human feces have been found to survive for as long as 2 weeks in rubbish bins.

Yet another reason why we can't ignore the problem of disposables is because, literally, we're running out of places to dispose of them. Every day, millions of the smelly things are thrown away – making up more than 4 percent of all household waste.

■ **Although reusable** *diapers may seem more cumbersome and less convenient than disposables, they are more environmentally friendly.*

Traditionally, household waste ends up in landfill sites, but now the World Health Organization is saying that bodily waste should not be included in these because of the risk of infections spreading. What all this means is that the battle against disposables, previously regarded as the province of eco-trendies, has gone mainstream. At the moment, in the United States, 40 percent of diapers changed are non-disposable; in the UK it is 1-in-10 and the figure is on the increase.

Which diapers should I use?

We might be open to the idea of going back to reusable diapers, but very few of us hard-pressed mothers are open to the idea of a return to the life of our grandmothers, dominated by washing dirty diapers. If they're going to persuade us to wash and re-use diapers, manufacturers are going to have to make their diapers a good deal more convenient and user-friendly than the old-style diapers. And the good news is that most of them have.

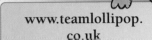

INTERNET

www.teamlollipop. co.uk

This is a comprehensive web site detailing the many reusable diaper options that are available to you.

■ **Disposable diapers** *do have their uses — they are a convenient option when you're visiting friends or relatives, when it's not so easy to cope with carrying or washing reusable diapers.*

53

Considering reusables

Over the 2 to 3 years that your child will be wearing diapers, you could save yourself a lot of money if you opt for reusable ones. Disposable diapers come with a birth-to-potty price tag of $1,500, compared with around $500 for mid-price reusables.

In the early days, when your baby is possibly dirtying several diapers in 24 hours, it's probably best to stick to disposables. Try reusables when your baby's bowels are more settled – at around 1 month.

If you don't like the thought of endless diaper washing, diaper laundering services are available in many areas. Clean diapers are dropped off at your home and dirty ones are taken away in a sealed bin to be laundered and returned. On the downside, this is the most expensive way of using reusable diapers.

Making life easier on yourself

If you do decide to opt for reusable diapers, you're doing a lot more for the environment than a lot of parents, and if it sometimes makes your life easier to use a disposable, go for it. On the other hand, try not to get too wedded to your disposables again. I used

CHOOSING A REUSABLE DIAPER

Although reusable diapers save money in the long term, they are costly in your initial outlay. Contact a manufacturer of reusable diapers and ask them whether they can let you have a trial pack, so that you can test a diaper out before you invest. Talk to other mothers about the sort of reusables that worked for them and bear in mind that different sorts of diaper can be better at different ages.

- **All-in-ones:** This is a complete diaper that's like a disposable. They are easy to use, although they take a long time to dry. A good, comfortable fit is the key
- **Fitted cotton diapers:** This snug-fitting nappy can be used with waterproof pants or wraps. It stays drier than an all-in-one, but wraps must be washed separately
- **Prefold:** These are square diapers that fit neatly into shaped wraps so that they can be held in place. The disadvantage is that they can be a bit fussy to use
- **Terries:** These white squares are folded, fastened with safety pins or plastic clasps, and worn with plastic pants. They are very economical and absorbent, but they can be tricky to use until you get used to them

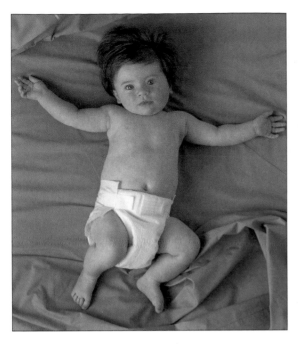

cloth diapers for 9 months and then switched back when we went on a vacation – and never returned to reusables, to my eternal shame! Nor does it hurt to use disposable diapers on a regular basis if it means that you'll stick with reusables for the bulk of the time. I found, for example, that reusables always leaked, no matter what kind of outer pants I used with them. Because our baby shared our bed, three of us waking up to change the sheets at 4 a.m. turned out to be a step too far – so I opted for disposables at night, and reusables during the day.

■ **You may find** *it more convenient, and less messy, if you put your baby in a disposable diaper when he goes to bed.*

A simple summary

✓ There are some aspects of caring for a baby that it helps to have some knowledge about.

✓ You don't have to bath your newborn regularly – topping and tailing can make life much easier.

✓ Small babies can't regulate their own temperature, so make sure that you do it for them.

✓ You don't have to spend a fortune on your baby's clothes.

✓ Choose practical clothes for your baby – there's no point wasting hours dressing him up when he'll probably need a change in a few hours.

✓ Reusable diapers are far kinder to the environment and easier on your pocket than disposables.

✓ If you do go for reusables, give yourself a pat on the back – but disposables can make your life easier from time to time.

Chapter 4

Sleeping and Waking

YOUNG BABIES SLEEP A LOT OF THE TIME, but even when they're tiny they don't necessarily sleep when it's most convenient for their parents. The easiest way to deal with a baby in these early days and weeks is to be flexible. Try to arrange your lives so that you can make use of the baby's sleep time, and when she's awake, try to make yourselves free to feed and play with her. Be aware that she's already laying down patterns of sleep and wakefulness that will serve as a guide to when she'll sleep and when she'll wake later on. You can affect things, if you want to, by being aware of her sleep patterns and by sometimes gently shifting the balance so that she gets the idea of when to have longer sleeps, when it's just a catnap, and when it's time to be properly awake.

In this chapter . . .

✓ Never too young to play

✓ Where will our baby sleep?

✓ Coping with lack of sleep

IT'S WORTH CATCHING UP ON SOME SLEEP WHILE YOUR BABY IS TAKING A NAP

Never too young to play

WHEN I HAD MY FIRST BABY, *I thought for a long time that she was "too young to play." I'd put her in her cot, or lie her on the sofa near me, and she'd look around and watch the sunlight on the sitting room wall or the pattern on the curtains – and I wouldn't realize what a great playtime she was having!*

Watching the world

When my third daughter came along a couple of years ago, she arrived into a house already teeming with toys. Within a day or two of birth, her older sisters were already attaching shaker-bracelets to her wrists and ankles, and waving brightly colored cloth books in her direction. I don't know if all this emphasis on playing from an early age led to a better quality of playtime for her than for my eldest child, but I do know now that babies "play" from the moment they're born. Not that they realize it, of course: your child won't have a concept of play for ages yet. But what she does have, even at her age, is curiosity. Along with feeding, it's the most motivating impetus in her life – one she simply can't help herself from following.

When you lie your baby down on a blanket on the floor or on some other surface, make sure that you put her somewhere with something to look at. It doesn't have to be anything very sophisticated – brightly colored curtains will captivate her, as will a light shade, or the branches of a tree swinging gently in the breeze.

■ **Visual stimulation** *will entertain young babies. A shadow lamp sends patterns of light around the room and is fun for them to observe.*

Endlessly inquisitive

"Finding out" is what life is all about when you're a newborn. The first thing you need to find out about is your mother, the person you've existed inside for so long. That's why, from the moment she is born, a newborn is already able to focus on her mother's face when she's being held in her mother's arms.

Her mother's face is fascinating to a baby and, after her face, so is anyone else's – especially that of the baby's father, whose voice she recognizes from early on.

■ **Spend time looking** *at each other's faces and enjoy getting to know each other. Watch your baby react to the different facial expressions you make.*

From around 4 weeks of age, your baby will be able to distinguish your face from that of other people's.

Talking and singing together

Following your instincts is my motto as far as raising a baby is concerned, and you'll find that talking to your baby will be a natural impulse. Don't hold back: talk to your baby all the time, especially when you're alone together and you don't have to worry about what other people will make of your conversation. Tell your baby everything you want her to know: tell her especially how much you love her, how much you've longed to hold her, how much you've been looking forward to getting to know her. Talk to her about what's happening right now, about what you're doing, where you're going, and what's going to happen next.

Sing to your baby, too. After looking into your face, listening to your voice is a baby's second favorite occupation. You'll find it does usually quiet a crying baby down to hear a familiar voice – especially her mother's – although I can't promise she'll be instantly soothed on every occasion.

Have a "special" song that's just for this baby – a song you've made up, maybe including her name. She'll love hearing it, and it will go on being a song you can sing at night to help her settle down to sleep.

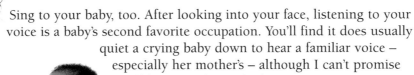

■ **Your voice is** *comfortingly familiar to your baby. Singing to her when she is crying or wakeful will often help to calm her down and relax her.*

■ **Hanging a mobile** *above your baby's cot will provide her with something to play with when she's lying down. The colors and the gentle movement will intrigue her.*

Playthings

Make sure that your baby has things to look at and listen to. Mobiles can be a source of delight to a young baby: if someone you know is looking for an idea of a toy to buy for her, you could suggest a mechanical mobile that attaches to the side of her crib and plays music while it rotates. Your baby won't watch this forever, but she will be quite taken by it in the early weeks of her life.

An unbreakable mirror to attach to the side of her cot near her head could easily be another favorite – as she moves around, she'll entertain herself by watching her own reflection. Sock and wrist rattles are good too. These can be expensive, however, so be inventive and make a rattle by putting grains of rice in a small pot – make sure it doesn't leak.

In the early weeks your baby's vision is still fuzzy, but she'll be drawn to bright colors. You'll notice how she will be particularly attracted to the colorful toys in her collection.

Other good toys that your baby will enjoy at this stage include:
● Any toy that makes a noise or plays a tune
● Soft activity toys
● Wooden spoons from the kitchen (make sure they're not splintered)

Don't forget that, just as everything is play to a young baby, so anything and everything can be a plaything. From wind chimes to a brightly colored plate, from a painting on the wall to the buttons on your jumper – everything at your disposal can entrance your baby for hours on end, and usually the things that you least expect!

Don't forget books and pictures!

Just as she's never too young to play, she's never too young for a book. A tiny baby won't necessarily be able to focus on pictures, or even to hold onto a cloth book, but that shouldn't stop you buying books for her and reading to her. One of the most wonderful delights of early parenthood is remembering the nursery rhymes that were probably so much a part of your own childhood, and enjoying reciting them to your baby. If childhood was a long time ago for you, though, you'll probably need to be reminded of the words. So the first book you'll probably need to buy will be a nursery rhyme anthology, from which you can read and recite to your baby now and in the future.

■ **Show your baby** *pictures or books while you're reading or talking to her; the joint effect of your voice and the colorful images will be fascinating to her.*

Where will our baby sleep?

MY FIRST BABY, ROSIE, *spent the first 2 months of her life in a special care unit, so you'd think we'd have had everything ready when she finally did come home. In fact, we were almost totally unprepared. After all, I'd expected to have another 8 weeks of pregnancy, or at least enough time to prepare her nursery, when she put in her untimely appearance. And from then on, I spent almost every waking hour at the hospital.*

The upshot was that, when the consultant eventually said she was ready to come home, I was suddenly gripped with panic. Goodness knows how such a simple thing had evaded me, but we didn't even possess a crib. I asked the consultant if Rosie could possibly spend a couple of extra days in hospital, while in the meantime I prepared for her arrival at home by buying a few essentials.

The whole thing makes me laugh now because, although Rosie did spend an extra couple of nights in hospital and we did have a crib waiting for her when she came home, she never spent more than an hour or two in it. What I realized within hours of having her home was that, after spending 2 months in a plastic incubator, our baby was not going to be put on her own again for a long time.

Perhaps if I'd had a baby at full term who hadn't had to spend so long in a special care unit, I wouldn't have felt so strongly about **co-sleeping**. But even if things had gone swimmingly for me the first time, I think I'd still have found that my strongest instinct was to keep my baby next to me in bed all the time, and to dispense with a crib fairly swiftly.

Considering co-sleeping

The American Academy of Pediatrics has concerns about co-sleeping, because of the risk of the baby being suffocated. They recommend that a baby should sleep in a crib that meets US Consumer Product Safety Commission guidelines. On the other hand, some American pediatricians *do* advocate co-sleeping.

Never co-sleep with your child if you or your partner has been drinking alcohol, taking drugs, or smoking, or even if you have been in a smoky environment. Experts say that smokers who co-sleep increase their child's chance of a crib death.

Many psychologists believe that sleeping next to his or her parents will add to a baby's sense of security and safety. After all, human beings are the only animals to put their infants in a box away from their warm, cosy bodies to sleep. For other animals, the most natural thing in the world is to curl up with their young.

If you want to co-sleep with your baby, make sure that your bed has a firm mattress, that there are no gaps between the mattress and the wall or headboard, and that there are no soft pillows or heavy blankets in the bed. Babies should never be left to sleep on a waterbed or on a sofa.

■ **At night,** *you may prefer to keep your baby in a bassinet next to your bed, rather than having her in bed with you, or putting her in a crib in a nursery.*

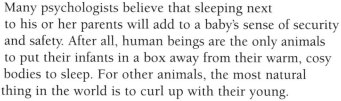

The American Academy of Pediatrics says there is no epidemiologic evidence to support the claim that co-sleeping reduces the chance of sudden infant death syndrome (SIDS).

Having your own space

Co-sleeping certainly isn't for everyone. If it works, it can be a wonderful way of introducing your child to family life. If you're breastfeeding, it maximizes the benefits of doing so because you'll find that, once you get used to it, you're hardly woken at night at all. But not everyone wants to co-sleep, and if it's not for you then that's fine.

Many couples feel that they simply have to reserve a bit of time and space for themselves. For them, sleeping with their tiny child between them is just a step too far – it's a constant reminder of the new person who's quite literally coming between them, and it's too claustrophobic and too demanding. Co-sleeping doesn't mean that you'll have a baby in your bed for ever, and it doesn't mean you'll never have a cuddle with your partner or make love again. But if you feel that you need to create a bit of much-needed space for you, and for you and your partner, then co-sleeping may not work in your case.

Trivia...
A filmmaker, whose 3-month-old son slept with him and his wife in their bed, filmed them through the night. He found that although both parents rolled around in the night, they didn't touch the baby.

The Foundation for the Study of Infant Deaths recommends putting your baby to sleep in a bassinet or crib beside your bed until at least 6 months, since sleeping close to the parents does reduce the likelihood of a crib death.

■ **Babies love** *being brought into their parents' bed when they wake up in the morning, for a cuddle and a play.*

Establishing a sleep pattern with a crib

One of the big advantages of co-sleeping is that you're teaching your baby that there's a difference between night and day, and that what people do at night is lie down in bed and go to sleep. Don't underestimate how powerful that message is: lying down next to your child at night and going to sleep really does teach a baby very quickly what bedtime is about. But that doesn't mean that families who choose not to co-sleep can't teach their baby sleep patterns, too. One of the most important things that you need to do is watch your child and be aware of the signs that she's tired and ready for a sleep. Some babies rub their eyes, while others pull their ears, or they just look tired. As usual, rely on your intuition. If something tells you that your baby is ready for a sleep in her crib, she probably is. Acting on the signs that your baby is tired will help her to understand what her crib is all about.

■ **While you settle** *your baby for the night, speak softly and avoid stimulating her.*

Tailoring behavior

Establish patterns in the kind of playing you do with your baby. In the daytime, when she's alert, play with her and don't worry about noise levels. In the evenings, keep the noise level lower. Don't play with your baby when it's getting near to "bedtime." When she wakes at night, go to her, but don't play or chat needlessly. Keep feedings business-like and talk to a minimum. If you have to change your baby's diaper at night, keep the lights low and don't turn the changing time into a playtime.

Babies of 1 year or more who can't soothe themselves to sleep are more likely to wake during the night.

■ **If your baby habitually** *falls asleep in your arms, it may become difficult for her to fall asleep on her own.*

Most experts suggest that it's a good idea to give your baby at least some opportunities to get herself off to sleep. In other words, don't always let her go to sleep in your arms or during a feeding. You have to be quite dedicated to do this because, when your baby is very young, rocking her or feeding her to sleep is very pleasurable and easy: think ahead, though, and be aware that if your baby is able to settle herself, it will benefit both of you in the long term.

Can you do both?

It is possible for your baby to sleep both in a crib and in your bed, although it won't necessarily always be easy. The best way is to put your baby down to sleep in her crib at the start of the evening, and transfer her to your bed when she wakes for the first time in the night, after you've gone to bed.

This isn't a problem-free tactic: it works for some people (it worked for me), but it can go wrong. What you're doing, in effect, is teaching your baby to wake up and demand a transfer from crib to bed at some point during the night. This behavior will go on, and on, and on. The plus side, from your point of view, is that you won't be disturbed more than once a night (providing you find it easy to sleep with your baby in bed with you, of course). And if you enjoy having your baby cuddling up to you overnight but also like the idea of a bit of "couple time" early on, or just the chance to read with the lights on when you first go to bed, this could be a good way forward.

Coping with lack of sleep

SLEEP IS A VITAL PART OF LIFE FOR ALL OF US, *which is one of the reasons why early parenting is so difficult. Not only are we suddenly faced with a totally new situation, and many of us don't have a lot of clues about how best to manage it, but we're also expected to do it on a fraction of our normal sleep quota. It's not surprising that you start to feel worn out!*

In the early weeks of life with a new baby, you may need to be as creative as possible to get at least some of the sleep you need. Some of the possible solutions to the sleep dilemma may seem drastic. For some couples, sleeping separately for a while is the only way to guarantee a few hours of uninterrupted shut-eye, for one partner at least. Others decide to try co-sleeping with their baby, even though it's not what they'd want in an ideal world.

■ **Take the chance** *to sleep when you can. If you've had a very disturbed sleep the night before, try taking an afternoon siesta while your baby is having a nap.*

According to a recent National Childbirth Trust survey, 1-in-5 new mothers has considered "running home to her parents," and 1-in-10 new parents has considered running away from it all forever.

This isn't a time to be idealistic: it's a time to be practical and to find a solution that makes life a bit easier right now. While it's true that you're laying the foundations for your baby's sleep routine in the future, you are also having to get through some difficult days yourself. So don't worry about bending the rules every so often if it makes your day easier. You certainly shouldn't expect everything to go perfectly every night. And if you are surrounded by friends who are having quiet nights, find some new friends who've faced similar problems to yours. (It won't be difficult.)

Why this stage is so tough

Basically, you've got a lot on your plate right now. Your whole life has changed, irrevocably and totally, and you're still coming up for air. A few short weeks ago, you could decide when you went to bed, how much rest you had, when you got up in the morning, what you did with your day: now, it's all down to someone else.

And if you don't like how that someone else is running your life, you can't appeal to her reason or her good nature or her common sense, because she isn't operating on that kind of level: she can only see the world from her own perspective. All you can do is try to understand her point of view, and believe that things will get easier in the medium to long term. (They definitely will, I promise.)

INTERNET

www.our-space.co.uk/sleep.htm

The web site of CRY-Sis, the organization that advises parents who are experiencing problems with sleepless or excessively crying babies.

How to get through the worst

One of the things that's hardest to accept is the lack of sleep and rest in your life at the moment. Before you can start to come to terms with a lot of the other changes you're dealing with, you need to build more sleep time into your day – at least then you won't feel quite so much like a zombie.

The best trick is to sleep when your baby sleeps: or if you can't sleep, at least rest. Don't see every time your baby goes to sleep as a chance to "get things done." The dish washing, the vacuuming, and even the dinner preparation aren't even on the same scale of importance as looking after yourself at this moment. Think easy meals (they don't have to be unhealthy: salads and fruit are perfect convenience foods). Think take-outs (you deserve a treat or two – and anyway, this is more necessity than luxury). Take up any and every offer of help, and make sure that you take any time you save for yourself.

This isn't the time of life to pride yourself on having a perfect home, or to set yourself impossibly high standards. The most important job in your life is keeping your baby safe and happy, and yourself safe and happy, too.

■ **Don't put pressure** *on yourself. Household chores are not top of your priority list right now, so focus on your baby.*

A simple summary

✓ Play isn't just for older kids. Your baby will enjoy "play" from her earliest days. She likes looking around, seeing interesting things, and watching your face.

✓ Talk to your baby and sing to her as often as you can – your baby will respond to hearing your voice and you'll both enjoy yourselves.

✓ Your baby isn't too young to share a book with you – she'll enjoy the brightly colored pictures on the pages.

✓ Follow your instincts when it comes to understanding your baby's sleep needs and keep her near you as much as possible.

✓ When it comes to deciding where your baby is going to sleep, consider co-sleeping. This isn't right for every family, but it can work for some.

✓ It's a good idea to give your child the chance to get off to sleep on her own. If your baby is always rocked to sleep, she won't learn how to drop off on her own.

✓ If you're not getting a lot of sleep at night, try to catnap during the day when your baby is asleep.

✓ Don't use your baby's sleep time to "get things done" because, in the long term, being properly rested yourself is a priority.

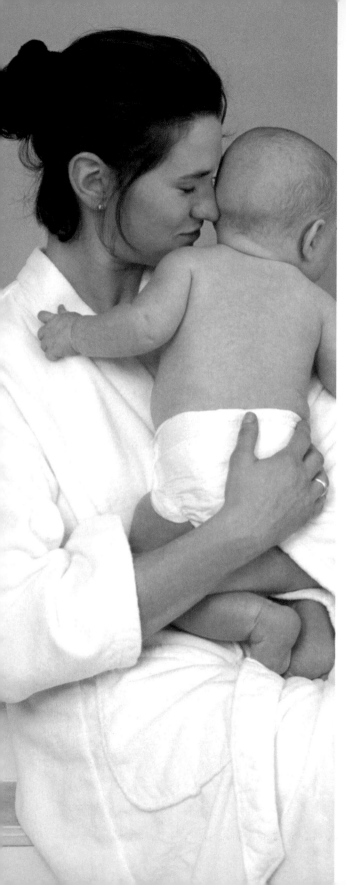

PART TWO

TAKE THE TIME TO RELAX WITH YOUR BABY

Chapter 5

Will Life Ever Be the Same?

LIFE IS NEVER THE SAME AFTER you've had a baby. On the upside, it's a lot more fun: but on the downside, this fun element doesn't always (or even usually) kick in straight away. Many new mothers and fathers find the early weeks and months a bit of a haze – there's just so much about this new life to get used to, and sometimes it can all seem too much. There never seems enough time in the day to do all the things you need to do – let alone have some time left over for yourselves. The thing you've got to remember is to hang in there: it might be tough going at the moment, but it really is going to get better in the not-too-distant future.

In this chapter...

✓ I need some space for me!

✓ Adapting to life with a baby

✓ Avoiding comparisons

I need some space for me!

YOU HAVE SEVERAL *months to prepare yourself and get used to the idea, but somehow the arrival of a baby is always a shock. And nothing is more shocking, particularly when it's your first child, than the realization of how much time looking after a tiny infant can take up. It takes up hours and hours and hours of every day – and, contrary to some expectations, these hours are not merely spent playing with the baby, taking him for walks in his stroller, or having coffee mornings with friends.*

Trivia...

A couple who took their sleeping 5-week-old baby with them to the movies were asked to leave. They were told they couldn't have her at the R-rated film even though she was too young to focus on the screen and fast asleep to boot!

It's all too much!

A lot of looking after a baby is repetitive, boring work. It's worth remembering that it is a lot easier for us than it was for our grandparents when their offspring were young. But even with all the labor-saving machines we've got around our homes, there's still plenty to be done: washing and ironing to get through, diapers to change, doctors' appointments to keep. And that's before you've started on any other household chores, which – whether you were used to doing them or not before your baby arrived – may well be coming your way now if you're at home all day.

■ **When you're used to** *the structure, routine, and social contact of office life, it can be a shock to spend every day at home with no clear pattern to your day.*

One of the reasons why it all gets too much – especially for new mums (or dads, if they're the ones that stay at home) is because you feel you've got so little control over your life after a baby arrives. If this is your first child, your life may become very different. Perhaps you were used to an office life in which you could decide what was going to happen and when. Suddenly, maybe within just a week or two of leaving work, that certainty about what a day will hold vanishes. Instead of feeling in control and on top of things, you feel you're living in disorder, mess, and chaos. There are so many things to sort out and no realistic possibility of doing so.

Making time for yourself

Don't think that being a new parent means taking on some saintly mantle and giving up all hope of an evening out with friends, or a night at the movies, or a swim at the local pool. You do need time for yourself. Not only is it fair that you still have a bit of life for you and you alone, it's actually best for your child and your partner.

It's amazing how much of a lifeline a bit of independence can be in the early months of parenthood. It can help you put your life into perspective and remind you that there are other things going on outside of your immensely absorbing new life. You'll feel better in yourself if you have some interests that are separate from your immediate family, and you'll find you actually enjoy the time you spend with your baby and partner more because you've had some time apart from them.

Don't feel selfish about asking for time on your own when you've got a small baby; look on it as an investment in your sanity, in your own future, and in your relationships with those around you, too.

How to organize time for yourself

Organizing time out for yourself won't necessarily be easy, but if you look hard enough, it will usually be possible. The most important first step is to make your own private time a priority: don't allow it to be pushed to the back burner.

■ **When you're feeling** *worn out by parenthood, a revitalizing bath will lift your spirits and give you time alone.*

Ideally, you need to be able to hand your baby to someone for a few hours so that you can completely get away from being a caregiver for a short while. But if there is no one you are happy leaving your baby with, you can still invest in some "me time." Try this: next time your baby goes down after feeding, run yourself a hot bath, and add your favorite bubbles. Get yourself a delicious cold drink, put on a face pack, play some music if you feel like it, and light some candles in the bathroom. Simply wallow for as long as you can.

Having a massage or enjoying a reflexology session can be very relaxing and will help you switch off. Some practitioners will visit you at home to make it easier for you – a few can even bring a babysitter.

Your support network

It's worth making sure you have a support network you can rely on. This will help you get a bit of time to yourself, because as your child gets older you'll certainly need to rely on others from time to time, whether you're in paid work or not.

If you look after the baby while your partner is working, your partner can enjoy caring for the baby during the evenings or weekends, and this will allow you a bit of freedom.

If you're a mum who's breastfeeding, ask your partner to take your baby for a walk in the sling or stroller once in a while. Your baby is less likely to cry and want milk while she's on the move and if her mum is out of earshot. Meanwhile, you will have some precious peace and quiet.

■ **While your partner** is spending time with the baby, take the chance to do something you enjoy – like reading a good book.

Try to spend more time with people who boost your confidence in your ability to be a parent, and spend less time with those who undermine you – that's those who tell you what to do and how to do it, rather than listening to your views.

Beyond your partner, you may be able to call on family members like your mother or mother-in-law – but if not, you need to start finding other helpers for your network. They could include older neighbors, other mothers, babysitters, and au pairs. As your baby gets older, investigate whether your shopping center has a baby care service where you could leave your baby while you shop.

You don't have to leave your baby for hour after hour with anyone else. In fact, that could be a very bad idea for such a young child. But don't feel that to be the perfect parent you have to be hands-on 24 hours a day – you don't.

INTERNET

www.momsonline.com

A parenting web site that contains useful information about various aspects of pregnancy and babycare.

■ **Most grandparents** *love the chance to get to know their new grandchild, and will cherish time spent one-to-one.*

Adapting to life with a baby

THINGS DO SEEM TO CHANGE *all the time in the first few months of your baby's life, and it can be disconcerting. No sooner do you think that you've got everything figured out and you know when your baby will be asleep and when he's awake, then suddenly he does something you don't expect and the whole routine is up in the air again. It's confusing, but it's actually a measure of how fast your baby is developing and how quickly his life is changing.*

Why things change so much

This may surprise you, but babies do not always take well to being laid in a crib, put down to sleep, or even left to play or kick their legs. What they really, really want is to be held all the time in close proximity to a breastful of warm milk from which they can sup whenever they feel like it. The structure we expect from our babies – that they will feed at roughly similar times of the day, that they will sleep for roughly 3 to 4 hour intervals, that they will sleep for longer at night, and so on – is our invention, not theirs. That's why we're so often confounded by their behavior. Because they didn't write the rule book, we did. And they haven't read it yet!

■ **Your baby will** *often want to be held in the warmth of your arms.*

Coping with an unsettled baby

One particularly difficult problem many parents have to deal with is **colic**. Typically, a bout of colic strikes in the evening, and it can last for 2 hours or more at a time.

It can seem like the thin end of the wedge after a long, hard day, and can make you feel inadequate at a time of day when you're running short on energy and need to have your confidence boosted, not dented.

All my babies have had an unsettled period in the early evening, and I remember how concerned we were when it was happening with our first baby, Rosie. By Miranda, my third, I found the best way to cope was to have a glass of wine, put on a CD, and have a slow dance around the room with her. She didn't always stop crying right away, but she seemed to like the change of pace and I felt a lot more relaxed.

> DEFINITION
>
> **Colic** *is a bout of unexplained screaming, which usually occurs for a spell each evening, day after day. There is very little you can do to soothe your baby's cries. No one really understands what causes colic. Some experts believe that the crying is related to stomach pain. Some say it's the baby's reaction to being over-stimulated during the day; others believe it's because he's accumulated so much wind with his feeding; others that he's exhausted, but can't let go to get to sleep.*

This pattern of unsettled evenings can go on interminably. The only way to deal with a phase of colic is to live with it and to believe it will go away (and it will, usually at around 3 months).

Every day is different

Young children, but especially babies under 6 months of age, don't function as we would expect or always want them to. No two days are alike: their behavior often seems completely random and unfathomable. Occasionally, you will hear stories of a baby who arrived in the world complete with a natural routine that made life a dream for his parents. Don't listen to these stories, because they are almost always fiction and have probably lost every grain of truth in the telling.

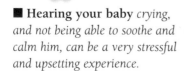

■ **Hearing your baby** *crying, and not being able to soothe and calm him, can be a very stressful and upsetting experience.*

In short, don't expect your baby to behave in an organized fashion in the early weeks, and you won't be disappointed. But that doesn't, of course, mean you can't work around your baby, and introduce an element of order into your lives yourself.

Studies show that 80 percent of normal, healthy babies have at least one period of unexplained crying every 24 hours.

Coping with your new life

It's easy enough to say that you should stop worrying about how your house looks, or whether you've got a meal in the oven, or even how you're looking yourself. Easy to say, but not easy to do. How many of us want to stop caring about our homes, our lives, and ourselves? The truth is that some parents find it relatively easy to cope with the fact that life gets less controlled and more chaotic, and others find it very difficult indeed.

The key to coping is in knowing yourself. Think about the way you lived before your baby was born, and think about the way things are now. Are you the sort of person who can live with piles of ironing everywhere, who doesn't mind surviving on take-out and ready-made meals, and who doesn't mind knowing there's a bit of dust on the top shelves? Or do you know in your heart of hearts that you'll never be happy unless you feel on top of your domestic situation?

There's no "right" or "wrong" sort of parent. It doesn't matter whether you're a control freak or whether you're happy-go-lucky in every way. You just need to find a balance that's right for you and your baby, and try not to set yourself unrealistic expectations to live up to.

■ **The ironing can wait;** *it's not your number one priority right now.*

You're the perfect parent for your baby, so don't torture yourself thinking about whether you'd be so much more successful if you could only be someone else. No one else could be a better parent for your child than you are — although that doesn't mean that you shouldn't always try your best.

Avoiding comparisons

WHATEVER ELSE YOU TAKE ON BOARD from this book, I'm absolutely certain you won't be following the advice I'm about to give you now. Why? Because although every parenting author will suggest you DON'T compare your baby with anyone else's, we all do it – however hard we try not to.

Mothers' groups

In many ways, mothers' groups can be a lifeline: they provide other parents to chat to, share tips with, and make friends with. The downside is that, from the word go, you're secretly comparing your baby with theirs. You discuss things in a neutral way, but inside you're feeling insecure. How come that baby, born 2 days before yours, is already holding her head up? Why does that child sleep through the night, while yours wakes every 3 hours no matter what you do?

■ **Being able to** *discuss your experiences and concerns with other parents can be reassuring.*

THE WAY YOUR OWN MOTHER DID IT

As a new mom, you'll probably not only compare yourself with other mothers, and your baby with other babies, you'll also probably find yourself comparing your performance as a mother to that of your own mother. This is likely to induce a mixed bag of emotions. You may find yourself understanding things from your mother's point of view (perhaps for the first time), or you may start thinking back to your own childhood and find it wanting.

However you feel, the likelihood is that you will find yourself, in the months and years ahead, doing things in the same way as your mother. This is because she is your strongest role model, and you cannot separate your mothering of your baby from your mother's mothering of you. Sometimes this can cause a lot of anguish and soul-searching. If that happens to you, consider seeing a counselor to get your own past in perspective – this may help you be a better mother to your own child.

Have confidence in your baby

As the parenting guru Sheila Kitzinger says in her book *The Year After Childbirth*, the reason we compare our child with others is because we're suffering from low self-esteem. We're not experienced yet in parenting, and it's natural to doubt our own abilities. As time goes on, you'll become more confident in trusting your own instincts. You will worry less about how other people's children are doing and take your cue about how your own are doing from within yourself, not from what you see around you.

Don't get into the habit of saying your own child is "a bit slow" or "not as advanced as yours," because you'll start believing it and your lack of confidence will eventually filter through to your child.

Try not to let the inevitable business of comparing your baby to others lead you to put your own child down. Remember that everyone needs someone to believe in him, and if you can't rely on your mother and father to do this, who can you rely on? You don't need to blind yourself to your child's faults and failings, but don't underestimate the importance of your support and loyalty.

A simple summary

✔ Accept from the start that life is never going to be the same again once you've had a baby.

✔ You need to build some "me time" into your life from the start. Don't feel selfish about this; it's an investment in your sanity, and you'll be a better parent for it.

✔ Put some effort into building up an effective support network so that you've got people you can call on when you need a bit of help with the baby.

✔ Don't expect things to stay the same, even if they suit you as they are – life with a young baby is ever-changing.

✔ Try not to compare your child with others you know.

✔ Concentrate on your own child's personality, abilities, and achievements, rather than worrying that he is not at exactly the same stage as another baby you know – every baby develops at his or her own pace.

Chapter 6

Is My Baby Getting Enough to Eat?

MANY PARENTS WORRY in the early weeks about how much their babies are eating – specifically, they worry because they seem to be eating all the time. Not only does this make moms feel that they're not giving their babies enough food, but they also feel that they are not getting any time to do anything except sit on the sofa while breast- or bottle-feeding their baby. And then as your baby grows, it takes time experimenting with solid foods, finding out what she likes and doesn't like, and slowly weaning your baby off her all-milk diet. It's not the easiest phase to get through, but it's all worth it.

In this chapter . . .

✓ How well is my baby eating?

✓ Introducing solids

✓ Breastfeeding and working

✓ When should I stop breastfeeding?

YOUR BABY WILL BE INTERESTED IN THE NEW TASTES, TEXTURES, AND FLAVORS OF SOLID FOODS

How well is my baby eating?

THIS IS A WORRY THAT *so many parents have, regardless of whether their baby is being breastfed or bottle-fed. If our babies could tell us whether their cries meant that they were cold, hungry, hot, or just generally out of sorts, we'd at least know what the matter was. But whenever your baby cries, the chances are that you'll worry that she's hungry and, over time, that may make you question whether the amount of milk she's getting is really enough to keep her well nourished.*

Almost all pediatricians plot a baby's weight, height, and head circumference on a growth curve, or **percentile chart**.

This may be done every month, or more or less frequently, depending on your baby's age and how well she is gaining weight. Your pediatrician will check that your baby is roughly following the growth line that's expected of her.

> **DEFINITION**
>
> *A **percentile chart** plots your child's growth against her expected growth rate, which is determined according to her weight at birth. It's plotted using information about percentage average growth rates across the population. So if your baby is "on the 50th centile line," it means that her growth is average. If she's "on the third centile line," it means that she's in the lowest 3 percent for growth, and if she's "on the 97th centile," it means that she's in the top 3 percent.*

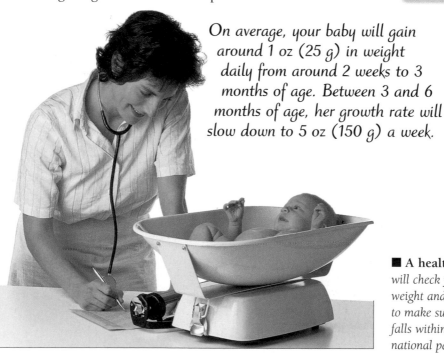

On average, your baby will gain around 1 oz (25 g) in weight daily from around 2 weeks to 3 months of age. Between 3 and 6 months of age, her growth rate will slow down to 5 oz (150 g) a week.

■ **A health provider** *will check your baby's weight and growth rate to make sure that it falls within a general national parameter.*

The signs of a well-fed baby

Actually, contrary to popular belief, you don't need weighing scales to tell whether your baby is thriving or not. But you do need to look carefully at your child, and to be aware of how she's changing as the weeks go by. In particular, bear in mind that she should be "filling out" – although this will not necessarily happen very quickly.

It's all relative, however, so don't expect your premature baby to suddenly have rolls of fat. My eldest daughter Rosie, who was born at 29 weeks and weighed just under 3 lb (1.4 kg), was a little scrap of a thing for months. I'm sure that, to the untrained eye, she must have looked severely undernourished and I found my visits to the pediatrician's office to get her weighed were a bit of a confidence-denter. Sitting there surrounded by bouncing cherubs, I'd often meet a baby who was bigger than Rosie and half her age. But what mattered wasn't comparing her with these other babies. It was comparing her with the baby that she used to be – and although I didn't always succeed, I did try to remind myself of that.

Your baby's diapers are a good indication of whether she's getting enough milk. If you are changing between six and eight wet diapers a day, your baby is doing fine.

Look, too, at how active and alert your child is – these are important signs that she is growing and developing normally. For example, babies love the chance to kick their legs, move their arms around, and exercise their muscles when they are lying down on the floor. If she's doing this, it's a good indication that your baby is healthy, happy, and well.

■ **A healthy baby** *is interested in the world around her. She will watch what's going on with interest, and she will turn her head to see what's happening behind her.*

Increasing your milk supply

If you feel that your baby isn't getting enough milk and you're bottle-feeding, it's easy to increase the amount of formula or the number of bottles you offer your baby. If you're a breastfeeding mother, however, you may need to dedicate yourself to making more milk for a few days so that your "supply and demand" system can adjust to the amount of milk your baby needs.

INTERNET

www.breastfeeding-
basics.com
www.obgyn.net

*Two web sites that answer
scores of questions about
breastfeeding and give
advice about how to deal
with problems.*

Breastfeeding an older baby requires energy and calories. Are you eating and drinking enough? You don't need to go overboard, but you do need to drink a lot more than usual, and you shouldn't think of calorie-counting while you're breastfeeding.

To do this, you need to give your baby plenty of opportunity to suck, because this will stimulate your breasts to make more milk. If you can, give yourself a break from the other things you normally have to do during the day. Instead, spend as much time as you can feeding and cuddling your baby in bed or on the sofa in the family room.

It's not necessarily easy to organize this, and it may seem very time-intensive if you don't like sitting around or you've got a hundred other things that you need to do. But if you can give time to your baby in this way, you'll probably find that within a few days you'll be making more milk. In turn, your baby will be more satisfied, she'll be demanding fewer feeds, and she will be settled for longer between feeds.

■ **While you're breastfeeding,** *make sure that you never skip your meals. Even if you're looking after the baby on your own during the day, always make the time to sit down and eat a nutritious lunch.*

DEALING WITH BREASTFEEDING PROBLEMS

You may have a completely trouble-free time breastfeeding. However, if you encounter difficulties, as many mothers do, don't be tempted to throw in the towel just yet. It's crucial not to ignore the symptoms of problems, such as:

a **Cracked nipples:** These are a sign that your baby isn't in the right position when she's feeding. Go back over the positioning information in Chapter 2, and check that your baby is "latching on" properly. Ask your midwife or your doctor for help straightaway. Unfortunately, even when you've got the right position, your nipples aren't going to heal immediately. But you should notice that the pain subsides during feeds, and this is an important indication that you're back on the right track. In the meantime, try wearing nothing on top in bed because exposing your nipples to the air will help. Try rubbing a few drops of milk into your nipples after a feed to help the healing process

b **Thrush:** Check your baby's mouth for the small white patches that can indicate thrush: this could be the cause of your sore nipples. Get help from your pediatrician for this – it isn't serious, but you will both need treatment

c **Engorged breasts:** This means that your breasts are so full of milk that they're painful. The solution is to feed your baby, which will relieve the pressure. If your breasts are very engorged, however, it may be difficult for the baby to latch on correctly. In this case, encourage some milk out of your breasts before you start a feed to help soften your breasts. Do this by massaging behind the nipples – don't squeeze the nipples themselves

d **A blocked duct:** This may show as a hard, painful lump in one breast. Feed your baby from that breast as soon as possible. While she's feeding, smooth the milk from the lump towards the nipple to unblock the duct

e **Mastitis:** Blocked ducts, if they're not cleared, lead to mastitis. You'll notice a red, hot, painful patch in one breast and you might feel a bit unwell. You need to act quickly. Keep feeding your baby, and experiment with feeding in different positions to ensure that the breast is fully emptied. Try the suggestions for relieving engorged breasts and blocked ducts, and get lots of rest. Don't think about doing anything but staying with your baby and feeding her. Ideally, ask someone to be with you who can assist as much as possible. If you don't feel any better within a few hours, go to your obstetrician-gynecologist because you may need antibiotics to clear it up

Introducing solids

YOUR BABY'S FIRST TASTE of "real food" is traditionally regarded as a milestone – but, to use a culinary phrase, it's actually more of a red herring. The fact is that giving an infant a tiny taste of mushy vegetable may be the beginning of "adult" eating, but there are several months to go before she will be getting anything near most of her calories from food other than milk.

Don't expect your baby's eating habits to change overnight just because you've started giving her a spoonful or two of solid food – it really isn't going to make much difference at all to how full she feels.

You'll be nearer the mark if you think of your baby's first attempts at solid food as an experiment in taste. It is important to give your child the opportunity to try out food other than milk, because research has shown that giving babies a range of flavors in their early life can affect how adventurous they are about different foods later on. Don't forget, however, that the baby who's been breastfed will already have had a hint of the flavors to come, because the taste of breastmilk is affected by what a mother eats.

Trivia...

A study of 10,000 babies found that there seems to be a "window of opportunity" at between 4 and 6 months during which parents should try to introduce solid food. If this window is missed, the study found that babies are more likely to grow up with fussy eating habits. In particular, they are more likely to refuse foods like egg, fish, and meat if these are introduced to their diet later than age 15 months.

■ **Let your baby** *join in with family meals. Sit her in a bouncy chair at the table and chat to her while you give her a few tastes of solid foods – be prepared for a messy ride!*

Knowing when to start on solids

For most babies, between the age of 4 and 6 months is the right time to start on solids. In the past, babies under 4 months old used to be given solids, and you may encounter older parents who'll advise you to "try a bit of something solid" for a wakeful 3-month-old. But research suggests that the vast majority of babies aged under 4 months do best on a milk-only diet.

Once your baby is 4 months old, watch her for signs that she's ready for solids. The obvious clue is that she's asking for more food, but she's probably showing an interest in what you're eating, too. Start to encourage this when you feel she's nearing the time to try a bit of solid food. Make sure that she sees you and your partner, and other children if you have them, eating. Sit her up near the table with you so that she can watch. But don't try to force solid food on her if she really doesn't seem willing.

■ **Try tempting** *your baby with a taste of solid foods, but don't persist if she's not interested.*

Don't reduce the amount of milk you're giving your baby in the early weeks of solids. These tastes are just an introduction to proper food, rather than a supplement for her milk intake.

Making a start on solids

My eldest daughter's first taste of real food – at the age of 4 months – was a big event. The food offered was a rice mixture, most of which was dribbled down her new bib, and the proceedings were reported eagerly by telephone to both grandmothers as soon as the "meal" was over. My third daughter's introduction to the world of real food was rather different. Because my life was busier as a mother of three than as a mother of one, I almost always breastfed her while I ate my own food. One day when she was around 6 months of age, she turned from my breast with interest to see what was on my plate. It seemed as good a time as any to start solids, so I offered her a bit of mashed potato, which was her first taste of real food.

■ **For a first taste** *of solids, try sitting your baby on your lap in her usual feeding position. Talk to her while you spoon food into her mouth.*

Comparing approaches

Although I don't think that the way we started Rosie, my eldest, on solids was wrong, it was much easier to just let Miranda, my youngest, pick from my plate as she did for the first few weeks. Babies aren't ready for salt in their diets, and it's best to give them quite watery food in the beginning. But if you leave the salt out when you're cooking, you can give your baby a little taste of the food that you make for yourself.

Most pediatricians recommend rice cereal as the first solid food to feed your baby, because it is one of the least allergenic foods.

The other difference I noticed between the two approaches I used was that waiting until a baby really is ready – which is likely to be nearer 6 months than 4 months – means that she gets the idea more quickly. And when you start giving your baby fruits and vegetables, introduce her to one or two at a time, so that any allergies can be spotted straight away.

■ **Experiment with** *different finger foods. Cutting fruit and vegetables into interesting shapes can make your baby intrigued to try them.*

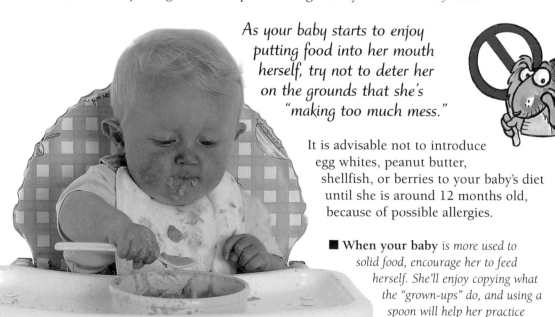

As your baby starts to enjoy putting food into her mouth herself, try not to deter her on the grounds that she's "making too much mess."

It is advisable not to introduce egg whites, peanut butter, shellfish, or berries to your baby's diet until she is around 12 months old, because of possible allergies.

■ **When your baby** *is more used to solid food, encourage her to feed herself. She'll enjoy copying what the "grown-ups" do, and using a spoon will help her practice her co-ordination skills.*

Breastfeeding and working

IF YOU'RE A MOTHER *getting ready to go back to work, and you're currently breastfeeding your baby, you may be thinking about when and how to move her onto bottles. But there is another option to consider: it is possible to combine breast- and bottle-feeding and many mothers do this very successfully.*

Combination feeding

Using a mixture of both breast- and bottle-feeding could be the perfect solution for you, if you're a mother returning to work. It means that although you'll be apart from your baby while you're at work, you can breastfeed her when you get home. This is special time together, and is something that only a mother can do for her baby. Some mothers say breastfeeding is even more precious when they're back at work for this reason.

■ **Juggling a job** *and breastfeeding is demanding for a working mother.*

Getting your baby used to bottles is the key, and the trick is to start early – but not too early. For the first 6 or 7 weeks of breastfeeding, using bottles as a back-up, even if they are filled with expressed milk, isn't really a good idea because they can "confuse" the breasts into thinking that the baby needs less milk than she does. Hence, milk production is cut back.

How do I get my baby used to bottles?

Around the age of 7 or 8 weeks is an ideal time to start giving your baby an occasional bottle, so that she gets used to them before her mother returns to work. Your baby is unlikely to take to bottle-feeding easily after breastfeeding, because there's a different knack involved. Also, you'll probably find that when you first give your baby a bottle, she'll be frustrated that what she really wants – her mother's breasts – are near at hand. If someone other than her mother feeds her, she is more likely to be co-operative.

Don't panic if it takes your baby a while to get used to bottles: she'll get the hang of it soon and it's worth persevering if it's not practical for you to continue breastfeeding.

How to express

If you want to express your breast milk so that you can use it in your baby's bottles, there are a few methods to consider:

a **By hand:** The plus side for this method is that there is no cost involved. You can do it anywhere without needing special equipment. However, you may need help to learn how to do it and you'll need to practice it before you become good at it. The method is also fairly time-consuming

b **Using a hand pump:** Many women find that this is quicker than expressing by hand and the pump is portable and easy to use. It works by creating a suction on the breast

c **Using a battery pump:** The pump is easy to carry around and some people find this method very efficient. However, many women find them difficult to use

HAND PUMP

d **Using an electrical pump:** This is a very efficient method of expressing. The knack to using this type of pump is to keep the suction at a low setting at first, until you get used to the sensation. The downside to them is that the equipment is heavy and cumbersome. They are also expensive, although they can sometimes be rented

If you're hand-expressing, lean over a bowl or basin and use both hands to sweep milk down from the whole breast. You don't need to squeeze your nipples at all – apply a slight pressure behind the nipple, around the darkened skin or areola.

■ **Once you have** *expressed your milk, pour it through a funnel into a sterilized bottle. You can then store the bottle in the refrigerator for a day until you need it.*

Bottle-feeding with breast milk or formula milk

Returning to work after being a full-time mother can be confusing for both you and your baby. Think about what sort of feeding pattern will suit both of you. Some women decide that they do want to carry on breastfeeding even when they return to work, and that they want as much of their baby's milk as possible to be breast milk.

If you return to work while you're still breastfeeding, expressing milk will help you keep your milk supply up.

If this is true for you, then you will need to express milk so that you have a supply of breast milk for your baby's bottles. Some women even manage to express milk while they're at work. For others, breastfeeding isn't so important any more, and they're happy to move on to bottles of formula milk for all or most of their baby's feeds.

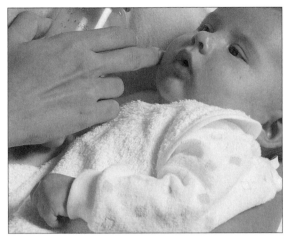

■ **If your baby** *is finding bottle-feeding difficult, try to encourage her sucking reflex by teasing her mouth with your finger.*

A good balance

If you do continue to breastfeed when you return to work, you may find that your baby makes do with less bottled milk during the day while you're at work, and increases her morning and evening breastfeeds. You may see this as a blessing, but it can also be a bind time-wise. Decide which it is in your case, and do whatever suits you best.

If you're away from your baby during the day, and you're still breastfeeding, be aware that your breasts may leak some milk.

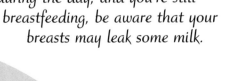

■ **One of the great** *advantages of bottle-feeding is that fathers have the opportunity to feed their baby, too.*

When should I stop breastfeeding?

IF YOU TALK TO NEW *mothers about breastfeeding, the question that always crops up is how long they should continue with it. That seems a shame to me – breastfeeding isn't something that you have to put a time limit on. Your feelings about feeding may change as it becomes easier and you may even find it more efficient as your child gets bigger.*

INTERNET

www.breastfeeding. com

You can find plenty of advice about breastfeeding your baby at this helpful site.

It's your decision

The fact is that how long you decide to breastfeed is up to you and your baby. Some babies decide to stop at 7 or 8 months and their mothers are perfectly happy, other babies feed for a year or more. In the West, breastfeeding a toddler has become a rarity, but in

WHAT IF I CAN'T CONTINUE?

Not every mother can make breastfeeding work. If you decide it's not for you, that's fine. The important thing is that you don't give up simply because you feel you have to or because you're not getting enough support or because you believe your problem is insoluble when it isn't. If you decide that you're not enjoying it, and that you don't honestly feel it's worth carrying on, that's your decision and you're entitled to it. It's far more important to be a happy mother looking after your baby in the way that seems right to you than it is to carry on breastfeeding, feeling burdened by it.

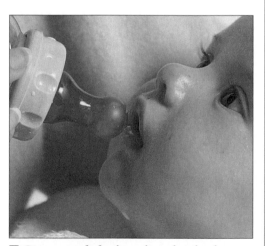

■ **Once your baby** *has adjusted to the change from breastfeeding, she'll be happy with a bottle.*

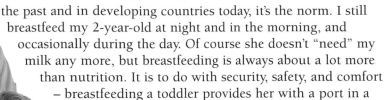

the past and in developing countries today, it's the norm. I still breastfeed my 2-year-old at night and in the morning, and occasionally during the day. Of course she doesn't "need" my milk any more, but breastfeeding is always about a lot more than nutrition. It is to do with security, safety, and comfort – breastfeeding a toddler provides her with a port in a storm, and she's none the worse for it.

■ **If you and your toddler** *are still happy breastfeeding occasionally, there's no reason not to continue doing so. You may find that it helps her settle for the night if you breastfeed her before she goes to bed.*

A simple summary

✔ Almost all mothers worry at some point that their baby isn't getting enough food.

✔ Don't be too hung up on weight gain – your baby's general demeanor is a better guide to whether she's getting enough nourishment or not.

✔ As in the early days and weeks, act quickly to sort out any breastfeeding problems.

✔ Don't start your baby on solids until she's ready. Once you do start on them, don't imagine that solids will immediately make a difference to your child's food intake.

✔ The purpose of giving a baby little tastes of solid food is to introduce her to the world of "real food" gradually – milk will still provide her with her main nutritional intake for many months.

✔ You don't have to give up breastfeeding just because you are going back to work.

✔ Even if you're bottle-feeding, you can still give your baby breast milk by expressing your milk.

✔ It's up to you to decide when to stop breastfeeding; follow your baby's, and your own, instincts.

Chapter 7

All About Routines

NEW PARENTS OFTEN TALK ABOUT "getting into a routine" as if it is an essential aspect of good baby care. But even if most parents find life is made easier by having at least some structure to the day, not everyone feels this way. Always remind yourself that having a routine is your choice. The only limits are the ones that you set yourself, and if you do want a routine, you'll need to work at it. Once there, it can either be a life saver or it can be a chain around your ankles – but if you felt it was the latter, you wouldn't have got into it in the first place, would you?

In this chapter . . .

✓ Do I need a routine?

✓ How to establish a routine

✓ Bedtime routines matter most

✓ The bathtime routine

✓ Being flexible

SETTLING YOUR BABY WITH A BOTTLE OF MILK BEFORE PUTTING HIM TO BED CAN BE A USEFUL ROUTINE

Do I need a routine?

EVEN IF YOU WOULDN'T consider yourself routine-bound, it's likely that having children will more or less force you into doing certain things the same way each day. However, the mistake many new parents make is to think that a routine has to be put into place more or less from week one of their baby's life. In fact, the early weeks – and depending on your personality, the early months – can quite easily be fairly relaxed and routine-free.

Being realistic

Try not to have great expectations of getting into a routine early on. After all, a baby doesn't arrive with a routine: look at how many parents with two or more children fit their newborn into the life they're already leading with their older child or children, with hardly a blip.

If you want structure in your life, however, you've got to put it there, and your baby will probably take a while to cotton on. The good news is that babies are very adaptable. It's true that they can cope easily with changes in their day-to-day lives, but it is also true that they can thrive on routine.

Don't forget that babies will make their own changes to the routines you try to set, particularly when they're small. For example, as they grow, you'll find that their sleep and feeding patterns alter all the time, so you can't depend on things staying the same for long.

Adapting to new patterns

If this is your first baby, you're probably used to a working life with a lot of structure. Perhaps things changed from day to day, but you still got up at roughly the same time each morning, made the same journey to your office, went to the same place or places at lunchtime, chatted with the same people, and left work at a similar time. You had ways of doing things that suited you. Suddenly, all that has gone. Now, if you are at home all day, you might face 9 or 10 hours on your own with the baby. What you do, where you go, and who you see is all up to you, and no one and nothing is going to come along and give you a framework unless you decide to put one there.

INTERNET

www.contented baby.com

This web site is produced by the followers of the child-care guru Gina Ford. She favors routine in the care of babies and young children, and this site contains useful information for anyone thinking about trying to implement and use routines more effectively.

Gaining a sense of order

Unsurprisingly, most of us feel daunted by this. The trend for working later and later into pregnancy means that the transition may be very quick – one month you're living your old life with all its certainties, the next you're on your own. And the neighborhood that you may have known for years seems completely different during weekdays.

Whatever else you do with your time, make a habit of getting out of the house at least once a day.

For this reason, it's often sensible to start getting into a rhythm of doing things. Giving a structure to your day will give you the feeling of being in control, at least to some extent – and feeling out of control is often the thing that new mothers find most difficult to deal with.

■ **Going out first thing** *in the morning will give you and your baby a bright start to the day. Put your baby in a sling and go for a walk to the park or to the shops.*

The problem with rigid routines

The trouble with some routines is that they lock you into the same old way of doing things and don't give you enough flexibility to enjoy life. This is fine if your routine is making you feel on top of things and helping you deal with this new way of life.

But it is not so fine if you're using the idea of "routine" to justify hours and hours spent in the house trying to keep everything perfect and spotless. Basically, what you need is something to get you up in the morning, somewhere to go, and something to look forward to in the day ahead.

You need people to see and a bit of "ordinary life" to dip into. And of course, your baby needs all these things too.

How to establish a routine

THERE ARE TWO BASIC APPROACHES *to establishing a routine.*
The method you choose depends on what feels right for you. Either watch
your baby and follow his lead in when he tends to wake, sleep, play, feed,
and so on. Or, alternatively, impose a regime that seems right for you.

If you aren't too routine-driven and are fairly happy-go-lucky in life generally, the first
approach will probably work well – although you might have to tweak things a bit to
suit you. If you feel you've got to regain control of your life, or if you're a working
parent, you may favor the second approach.

If a routine suits you, it will probably suit your baby. If a routine is
making you feel stressed out, your baby will pick up on it and you'll
find that imposing a structure on your day has been counter-productive.

■ **If your baby has** *an afternoon nap, put him down for his sleep*
and wake him up in good time so that he isn't wide awake at bedtime.

Planning a routine

Make a list of the things
you'd really like to achieve
in a day. Don't be ridiculously
over-ambitious – of course
you aren't going to manage
to polish the silverware, get
through all the washing and
ironing, AND make a three-
course meal for the evening.

The most important thing
is having fun with your baby
and caring practically for
him. On top of this, there
are obviously things that you
want to do in the house for
yourself and for your family.
Take a long, hard look at
what you want, and then
think about how realistic
these aims are and how you
could implement them
into a routine.

Implementing a routine

Whether you're setting a routine based on your baby's daily patterns or creating one that suits you, the key to successfully implementing a routine is to stick at it. You're going to have to be prepared to invest a bit of time and effort into getting it right.

That may mean being tied by your timetable and absolutely not deviating from it. For example, if you always go out at 10 A.M and get back at 11 A.M. when your baby is ready for a feed and a nap, it's no good meeting a friend and deciding to postpone the nap because your baby is happy playing with your friend's child. The routine will quickly go to pot, so you have to decide what matters most – flexibility or knowing what the day ahead holds.

Getting the mornings right is important if you're setting a routine. Always get up at the same time and always wake your baby at the same time, regardless of whether you've had a good night's sleep or not.

Bedtime routines matter most

WHETHER OR NOT YOU'RE *happy-go-lucky or routine-bound by day, the chances are that you will want some semblance of order in your evenings. For many parents, the evenings are the only time in the week when the family is all together, so there are several issues to take into account when you're deciding what's going to be right for you.*

For example, if you or your partner – or both – have been out at work all day, you'll no doubt be eager to see your baby. So as a result, you may not want to have strict rules about putting your baby to bed too early. And if you would like to be able to go out a few evenings a week, then you will need to take this into account when you plan your baby's routine.

■ **If you always** *put your baby to bed at a set time each night, and you have a babysitter at hand, you'll be freer to plan evenings out for yourself and your partner.*

Why have a bedtime routine?

You want a bedtime routine because you need a bit of child-free time in your life, however much you adore your baby and however much you love being with him. You will want a bedtime routine because, however easy-going you are generally, there comes a point in anyone's day when you want to know you can get to bed yourself. And if this is your first baby, you will want a bedtime routine in place before you have a second child, because otherwise evenings will quite probably be hell.

On a good day, the bedtime ritual is a happy, relaxed, enjoyable time of the day. On a bad day, looking forward to the certainty that your baby will soon be in bed can carry you through some difficult moments – a bedtime routine can help to lift your spirits.

How to establish a bedtime routine

You need to decide on what time, roughly, you'd like to get your baby to bed. Think about what you've got to get finished before then, and then plan out a rough timetable that allows you to do everything in the time available.

For example, you might decide 7 P.M. is the time you want your baby to go to bed. Working back from there, it may be that you or your partner always gets home from work around 6 P.M. – and the baby is always pleased to see you, and you enjoy playing

■ **Try to work out** *your daily timetable so that both you and your partner get the chance to spend relaxing, quality time with your baby.*

together. So, it would be useful if your baby has had his supper and his bath, and is ready for bed before you or your partner gets home at 6 P.M. Then the baby can have a bit of playtime. He will then have his bedtime feeding and then it's time for bed. Then, you put him into his crib, read him a story, say goodnight, and then go. Even if he cries, wait a minute before going in to him. As soon as he settles, leave him again. If he cries again, lengthen the time before you go back. Leave it a minute, then 2 minutes, and then 5 minutes. Be firm about this, and your baby will soon find settling down at bedtime easy.

Trivia...

Until the age of 3 months, babies who are submerged in water have a natural reflex that helps prevent them from drowning. A muscle in their throats automatically closes to stop water from entering their lungs.

The bathtime routine

YOUR BABY DOESN'T NEED *a bath every day until he's moving around and getting mucky – topping and tailing will be sufficient most days. But many mothers find bathtime a good routine to get into, because it's a way of drawing the day to a close. Your baby will quickly learn to associate bathtime with winding down before bed.*

Bathtime tips

Always look on bathtime as a fun activity. If you're not in the mood for it, you're better off topping and tailing and doing bathtime tomorrow. Sing to your baby, splash him gently, and give him time to enjoy the unusual sensation of being unencumbered by his diaper and his clothing.

■ **Babies love** *having things to look at and play with in the bath – brightly colored, floating bath toys are a great investment.*

Wash your baby's hair with soap or a gentle shampoo, rinse it, and then brush it through with a soft brush, because this helps prevent or clear *cradle cap.*

Never, ever leave your baby unattended in the bath. Don't be tempted to use one of those inflatable bath-rests to support his head – they are absolutely not a substitute for your presence.

DEFINITION

Cradle cap *is a form of seborrhea of the scalp, common in young babies. The sebaceous glands on the baby's head produce more sebum (oil) than necessary, and this oil collects on the surface of the skin.*

WASHING YOUR BABY IN THE BATH

When your baby has outgrown a small bathtub, he can move on to the big, adult-sized bathtub. This can be a bit daunting for him at first. The sides of the bath are slippery: use a bath mat so that your baby's feet have something to grip against. Be careful not to strain your back when you're leaning over the bath. Sit on the floor next to the bath, carefully lower your baby into the water, and make sure that you're both feeling comfortable before you begin to wash him.

1 Immersing the baby

The water should be shallow; your baby needs to be resting on the base of the bath, not floating. Support his head and gently trickle water over him.

2 Washing him

Talk to your baby and lift his head up so that he can see what you are doing. Once he is wet all over, start to soap his body and shampoo his hair.

3 Rinsing the baby

Make sure that you rinse any soap suds from his skin and hair. Let him enjoy the splashing of the water – he'll enjoy kicking his legs too.

Sharing bathtime

Most evenings, it's more likely that you or your partner will bath your baby without either of you getting in with him. However, it's fun taking a bath with your baby, and it has the advantage that you can get washed at the same time. If you choose to bath with your baby, make sure that you're not in a rush, because it can be a time-consuming event!

When your baby is very small, have someone around who can hand him into the bath to you and take him from you when you want to get out.

INTERNET

www.babybag.com/ parent.htm

This web site outlines techniques for bathing your baby. It covers safety tips, types of bath products you might use, and more.

■ **As a busy parent,** *you'll probably bath separately from your baby most of the time. That doesn't mean that you'll have to wait until your baby is safely asleep before you can take a bath — he can stay with you, but there should be someone else on hand to keep an eye on him too.*

Being flexible

ROUTINES THAT ALLOW YOU to feel on top of things are life-enhancing, but remember that a routine is there to make things easier, not to stop you ever doing anything spontaneous or exciting. Try not to be too inflexible, especially when your baby is young. With a small child, you do have more opportunity to do something unexpected than you will in a few years' time, for example, when he is tied into a nursery school timetable.

Psychologists say people who are too routine-driven lack confidence in their ability to do things, and feel they lack the power to control their life. If you feel this applies to you, think about why you feel powerless – find someone to talk to about it.

■ **Your baby** *will be intrigued and excited about all the new sights, sounds, and sensations when he's in a new environment. Relax and enjoy it with him.*

Coping on vacation

Everyone loves vacations – or do they? Perhaps surprisingly, the more you enjoy your routines, the less you may enjoy your vacation. That's because, according to psychologists, people who "need" routine in their lives fear the loss of structure when they're on vacation, and may even end up pining for what they have at home.

If that sounds like you, letting your routine go to pot on your vacation may be a bad idea. Instead, try and adapt your routine to your new circumstances. You might want to let your baby sleep for longer in the afternoon, for example, if you're somewhere hot, and then let him stay up longer at night. In this way, you are still keeping a semblance of your routine, but without letting it interrupt your vacation.

You may find he sleeps well enough in his carriage or stroller in the early evening for you to take him along when you go out for supper. If it takes your baby a while to adjust back into a bedtime routine when you're home, you can always console yourself with happy memories and a browse through your vacation photos. It really was worth it for such a marvelous time!

Unfamiliar surroundings

Be realistic. Your baby may find it difficult to keep the pattern of his routine when you're on vacation, especially if you are far from home and in a different climate. He may not be settling down to sleep as easily as he does at home, because he's sleeping in an unfamiliar room. And then there are all those new things that he's been seeing and doing. It's not surprising if his routine is unsettled – so don't expect too much of him.

A simple summary

✓ Having a baby doesn't necessarily mean "getting into a routine."

✓ You don't have to radically change the way you've always lived – decide what sort of environment you thrive in, and adapt accordingly.

✓ If you are on your own at home with your baby, it is really worth getting out for a walk or going to the shops at least once a day.

✓ If you want more of a routine in your life, you can either adapt to the way your baby seems to do things naturally, or impose what would be best for you on him. Either way, it's going to work best if you aren't too rigorous.

✓ Bedtime routines are very helpful because they allow you to make a space for yourself in the day. A good bedtime routine includes wind-down time, a bath, a story, and then bed.

✓ If your partner gets home from work at a reasonable hour, make sure that your daily structure allows him to spend time with the baby.

✓ Make sure that bathtimes are fun for both you and your baby, and that your baby associates it with settling down for bed.

✓ When you're away from home, or during a vacation period, don't let routine stop you from doing the things you know you'd enjoy.

Chapter 8

Who Said Babies Sleep All the Time?

Some babies are fantastic sleepers, going through the night from 6 weeks old and taking three perfect naps a day. But most babies – probably yours included – are not fantastic sleepers. There is no reason why they should be, of course. Many of the sleep "problems" with young babies are to do with parental expectations rather than with the baby behaving abnormally. But while you shouldn't have high hopes of your baby's sleep fitting in with yours in the early days, it is important to plan ahead. The habits that your baby is getting into by around the 6-month mark will condition her sleep habits for the months to come.

In this chapter . . .

✓ How much sleep does my baby really need?

✓ Settling her down

✓ My baby cries all the time

✓ While she's awake

JUST BECAUSE YOU'VE PUT HER IN HER COT, IT DOESN'T MEAN SHE'LL SLEEP

How much sleep does my baby really need?

SOME EXPERTS WILL TELL YOU that young babies need as many as 18 hours of sleep in every 24 hours. Others say that they can make do with as little as 12 hours a day. But how much your own baby needs is very individual and is determined by a whole range of factors including your expectations, her size and genes, what kind of person she is, and what's going on around her.

Monitoring her sleep

Some parents feel that they are being kept on the go all day by the demands of their baby. Apart from feeling worn out themselves, they feel that their baby can't possibly be getting enough sleep and rest either.

Your baby's little naps and snoozes during the day all add up to a substantial time spent asleep.

So if sleep is something that you're concerned about, for whatever reason, try keeping a sleep diary for a couple of days.

■ **Babies have** *an amazing capacity to sleep. They don't need peace and quiet to start nodding off; warmth and motion are particularly effective at sending them to sleep.*

Note exactly when your baby sleeps and when she wakes. You'll almost certainly find that she sleeps for longer than you thought, especially if you're the kind of person who tends to use the hours when your child is asleep to do other tasks. Perhaps before she was born, you imagined that you'd be able to use your baby's sleep time to organize the house, but now that she's here it's a shock to find that you only just have time to pile washing into the machine and to wash the breakfast dishes while she's napping. No wonder it feels like she hardly sleeps at all!

Enjoying your baby while she's awake

If your baby is awake a lot of the day, don't feel cheated or frustrated by this. It's probably a sign that she's a bright little button. Certainly it means that she's got lots of time to start learning about the world and her place in it, so take advantage of that.

Play with your baby when she's awake. Of course you need a bit of time to get other things done, but don't begrudge your baby's wakefulness.

Sometimes you need to compromise when you're busy and your baby is wide awake; just put her in her bouncy chair and let her watch you getting on with your tasks.

Your baby's body clock

In the early days and weeks of your baby's life, she probably woke every 2, 3, or even 4 hours for a feeding, whenever her tiny tummy was empty and needed filling up.

Her body clock, in other words, was completely conditioned by hunger and food requirements, and not at all by whether it was day or night. By the time your baby is more than 4 months old, however, she should be starting to realize that life is divided into night and day – and you should be continuing to encourage her to make this connection so that she gets into settled sleeping habits.

Daytime nap tactics

It's often said that keeping the house too quiet when your baby is having a daytime nap is a bad idea. The theory is that you're just building up problems for yourself, because you'll end up with a baby who can't get to sleep unless she can hear a pin drop. In fact, a baby's natural instinct is to sleep when she's tired, not when it's quiet.

Differentiate between daytime naps and bedtime sleep. Put your baby in a carriage in the hall or in a travel basket in the family room for her naps during the day, instead of in her night-time surroundings.

Another plus about this theory is that if a baby sleeps against a background of sound during the day, it gives her another way of differentiating between daytime naps when it might be noisy, and night-time sleep when it's usually quiet when she settles down.

Trivia...

A study at Oxford University found that 1-in-5 children aged between 1 and 3 years old, and 1-in-10 children aged between 4 and 5 years old, had problems sleeping through the night. The report found that psychological approaches, such as having a winding-down period before bedtime, were more effective than sedatives at helping a child sleep. It also concluded that how well babies sleep is a learned behavior that they pick up during the first year of their life.

Settling her down

EVERY BABY IS DIFFERENT. *However many parent groups and baby playgroups you go to, you'll never meet other parents whose stories about their baby's sleep habits exactly mirror your own.*

Sleeping patterns

In very general terms, however, many babies do follow a pattern of having a longer sleep in the morning and being more wakeful in the afternoon. For example, a baby might wake up and feed before dawn, then wake up again, feed and stay awake for an hour or so around 7–8 A.M., before sleeping for 3 or 4 hours. She may then wake for another feed, sleep again for a shorter period, and then wake again with a bit more interest in what's going on around her, ready to play.

Every afternoon, lie her on a towel on the floor without her diaper and let her have some "kicking time" – it will give her some exercise and help tire her out for the (hopefully) long sleep ahead.

This is the kind of "routine" a baby might gradually get into if she's left to her own devices. Never forget, of course, that it's up to you to tweak this pattern to suit your own needs. But it will certainly help if you can work around the sleep patterns your baby seems to prefer, whatever they are, because it's very difficult to get her to stay awake once she's decided that she's tired.

Babies get frustrated if they're lying in a crib and they can't see what's going on. Place your baby in a baby seat where she can watch what you're doing, even if it's just household chores.

Getting to sleep on her own

When you've got a tiny baby, and even a baby who's just a few months old, the easiest thing is to breast- or bottle-feed her to sleep, and then to slip her gently into her crib. This usually works a treat – and as every parent knows, there's nothing quite so marvelous as watching your baby's eyes grow heavy as she sucks, and then falls into

Trivia...

Baby sleepwear should be loose fitting. Although some baby nighties come with mittens attached, ideally, your baby's hands should be left free so that she can look at or suck her fingers. To keep your baby's feet warm, use booties or pajamas with feet; to keep her head warm, use a nightcap.

a contented sleep. It's all very cozy and easy, but the trouble is – so the argument goes – you're storing up trouble for yourself ahead.

If there's one thing that childcare experts agree on, it's the importance of teaching your baby to fall asleep on her own. If you don't teach her, she's not suddenly going to learn all by herself. When she reaches the age when you can't go on holding her every time she needs to sleep, or when you suddenly have something else pressing to do and know she's had enough milk, you won't simply be able to put her down in a crib and expect her to be able to settle down all by herself.

If your baby is finding it hard to settle down at night, try playing a piece of "sleepy" music – something soft and classical is ideal. She'll start to associate the music with going off to sleep.

Finding the right balance

In other words, if you cuddle your baby to sleep when she's tiny, you may be planting the seeds for future problems, because when she's 7, 10, 12, even 18 months of age, she'll still want the same treatment – and you almost certainly won't always be prepared to give it.

Having said that, I've certainly cuddled my children to sleep long after it was "sensible". It did mean that my babies were hard to settle when they were older but, to be honest, I wouldn't have missed out on those cuddles for anything! On the other hand, there comes a time when you do have to try a few ploys to get your baby to go to sleep on her own. In the long run, this will be better for both of you.

Never leave your baby to fall asleep on her own with a bottle, because there is a danger of her choking on it.

■ **Enjoy cuddling** *your baby to sleep: it's one of the joys of parenting. But try not to make it a regular habit that she'll rely on.*

109

Settling her at night

Even if you still enjoy sometimes cuddling your baby to sleep for her naps in the day, let her go to sleep on her own at night. Combine this habit with the good bedtime routine that we discussed in Chapter 7.

Try moving her from your knee to the crib when she's just about to drop off to sleep – when you know that she's really tired but has had enough milk. The trouble with doing this at first is that, assuming that she's been used to being cuddled to sleep, she isn't going to like it, and will almost certainly wake up and start howling. After wallowing in the comfort of your arms, she won't like the cold feeling of the crib sheet.

If you're getting your baby used to going off to sleep alone and you go back into her room because she's crying, try not to pick her up.

Try not to let her make the association that if she makes a noise, you will get her up for a cuddle. Soothe her, but don't pick her up.

Sleep tactics that work

When your baby is around 6 months old, you may be tempted to try a technique known as *controlled crying* or *extinction* to get her settled by herself. This is fine, providing that you're absolutely sure that it's what you want to do, you're determined not to give in, and you've got plenty of energy in the short-term to live with the lack of sleep and rest that are an almost inevitable temporary consequence.

If you're going to try controlled crying, it's a good idea to start at a weekend or to take a few days off work, because you will be awake for longer than usual in the night.

Another thing that you might like to try is feeding your baby on your knee from the breast or bottle, and then starting a song as you prepare to move her to the crib. You then carry on singing the song as you put her down – hearing your voice eases her transition from your arms to the crib.

This tactic is likely to work best with very tired or younger babies. With an older baby, it may have the effect of making her fussy at the breast or bottle: she may be anxious about when the song is going to start, and she won't feed or settle down well in anticipation. If this happens, try something else.

> **DEFINITION**
>
> **Controlled crying** *or* **extinction** *means that you train your baby to get to sleep by refusing to get her out of her crib when she cries. Instead, you go to her and settle her down by rubbing her back or talking to her – whatever it takes to quiet her down. Then leave the room: and if she cries again, you wait a minute or two before you go back in. You then repeat the exercise, leaving a slightly longer interval between the beginning of her crying and your appearance, until she's so exhausted that she gives up and drops off. It does work, and she will learn that crying doesn't have the desired effect.*

My baby cries all the time

FEW BABIES REALLY do cry all the time, but it can sometimes feel like it. There's nothing like hearing your baby go on, and on, and on crying to make you feel like a total failure at parenthood.

However rational or cool and collected you are about parenthood generally, there's definitely something about a crying session that makes you wonder whether you're getting anything right – if you're not careful, it can sap your confidence. But remember, it doesn't have to be that bad.

The first thing you need to know is that all babies cry. They honestly do. It isn't just yours, and it isn't because you're a bad parent or that you can't interpret your baby's needs.

■ **If your baby** *is crying, it could be for any number of reasons ranging from hunger or tiredness, to boredom, discomfort, or pain.*

Understanding why your baby cries

Crying is the main way that a baby communicates. Of course, she can do other things like smile and chuckle and move towards you and babble – but these gestures and noises, on the whole, signal satisfaction with life.

When it comes to dissatisfaction, a baby has only one way to sound the alarm bells. She can't throw herself on the ground and scream and kick, like she will when she's a tantruming toddler in a few months' time. She can't shout at you and tell you that you're useless, like she will in a few years when she's a teenager. All she can do right now is cry: so cry she does.

Don't take your baby's crying personally. Don't immediately think: she won't stop, so I'm useless. You're not, and that's not why she's doing it – look for other reasons!

Coping with crying

How you cope with a baby when she's crying depends on how much she cries and how easily you're able to interpret what's wrong. Staying calm yourself definitely helps, however difficult this may be if the crying goes on and on. The truth is that a baby will easily pick up on your mood, so if you become stressed out you'll build up a vicious cycle in which she's crying because you're stressed, and you're stressed because she's crying.

If you suspect that this is happening, take some time out. Put your baby somewhere safe and leave the room. Try dropping your shoulders and take some long, deep breaths to help you relax. You never know: now that you've left the room, your baby may even have quietened down on her own. Meanwhile, when you're a bit calmer, go back to your baby and see if you can work out what's wrong.

■ **A child can become** *frustrated if you don't understand why she's crying, or she's not getting what she wants. Stay calm and try to soothe your baby if she becomes worked up.*

WHY IS SHE CRYING?

If your baby's crying, and you can't see what the problem is, go through a mental checklist. These are the most common causes of crying at this age:

- Is she hungry? Try offering her a breast or a bottle
- Does she have wind? Try burping her
- Is she too hot or too cold? Feel the back of her neck and her tummy to see whether she's cold or clammy
- Is she lonely? Try giving her a cuddle
- Is she wet or dirty? Change her diaper
- Is she in pain? Watch to see whether she's pulling her legs up towards her tummy (although this may not necessarily indicate pain). Check her clothes to see whether something is too tight or if something is irritating her
- If you have a strong feeling that your baby is crying because of some underlying physical disorder, do act on your intuition and see your obstetrician or pediatrician

Working out what's wrong

When she's older, your child will be able to say whether something is hurting, or if something is uncomfortable, or whether she just wants a cuddle. At the moment, the only way she can signal her problem is by crying.

You might be able to tell a lot from her crying if you listen to it carefully and have a good look at her. Some babies just scream whatever is wrong, but others have a definite pattern to their cries, although usually this is more evident as they get older. Try to interpret your baby's cry if you can from the moment it starts; if her squawks go unheeded, it's likely to turn into an all-out general wail.

INTERNET

www.zerotothree.org
www.cwla.org

These web sites offer plenty of useful information and advice about the health and welfare of babies and toddlers.

Try holding your baby in a different position when she's crying. If she's just bored, or has wind, this may be all it takes to quiet her down.

While she's awake

EVERYTHING YOU DO WITH YOUR BABY, *from the simplest little activity like a meal or a diaper change, to a walk in the park or a shared book, is an opportunity for play, fun, and learning. Your baby is like a little sponge, ready to soak up all the experiences and joy that you're able to give her. And it's more than just fun, too, because she's learning.*

Just as education doesn't stop when we leave school, it certainly doesn't start when we get there. Your baby will learn more from you in her early years than at any other time in her life – and the best bit of it is, she'll learn most if she's enjoying life and having fun.

■ **Let your baby** *spend time playing: she will enjoy grasping and picking up toys, and touching different textures.*

Choosing toys

Cuddly toys are often given to babies of this age group, but in fact they're less useful than many other toys. Apart from being something to look at, they're not the most interesting toys available for babies and they don't make a noise or do anything interesting. The "cute" factor is completely lost on a child of this age – they'll be of more interest when your baby becomes a toddler.

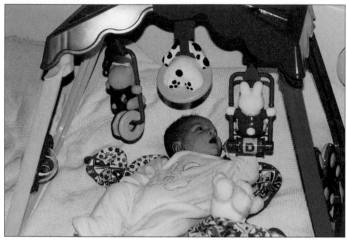

■ **A baby gym** *offers a great variety of toys, shapes, and textures for your baby to look at and touch. It can help keep her occupied and content while you're busy getting on with your own activities.*

Many parents invest in a baby gym or arch from which rattles and other plastic toys can be suspended. The gym is placed above the baby's head while she is lying on the ground, so that she can look up at the toys and reach up to touch them. If you don't want to spend money on a new one, they can be a good buy from a second-hand shop because they're usually very well-made and do endure a lot of wear and tear.

Toys that incorporate a variety of materials to touch and feel are a good idea. Toys that make a noise are another good investment. Choose your noise carefully, however, because you're going to be hearing a lot of it!

Comfort toys

I wouldn't encourage your child to develop an attachment to a particular toy, for the simple reason that you'll be storing up problems for yourself if it's ever lost. But if your child does form an attachment of her own accord, don't discourage it. It can be a psychological crutch for her and may help her, for example, to survive without you at the babysitter's, or go to sleep on her own.

If your baby is becoming attached to a particular toy or blanket, especially if she needs it to go off to sleep at night, invest in at least one identical item as a back-up in case it is lost.

Invest time in your baby

Toys that promise to "aid development" abound, but don't let yourself get too carried away. Remember that at this stage any toy is only as good as the input you're giving as well, so it's better to spend less money and devote more time. Treat any toy that promises to exercise your child's senses with a slight pinch of salt – children are stimulated by all sorts of things around them, but the most important thing for a baby is spending time with her parents, and other adults and children.

Never feel that you're letting your child down if you can't afford to buy her expensive toys. She'll be just as happy with second-hand ones – and remember, her biggest treat is having you there.

A simple summary

✓ Sleep patterns are very individual – some babies sleep a lot, others sleep a little.

✓ If your baby is awake a lot of the time, try to enjoy her company and forget about the chores.

✓ Make sure that your baby recognizes that day is when we are awake and doing things, and that night is when we all go to sleep. Don't expect miracles – this will take time to instil.

✓ Even if you love cuddling your baby off to sleep, try to teach her to settle down on her own. You really will be making life easier for yourself in the long run.

✓ All babies cry – it's their only way of communicating that something is bothering them.

✓ If your baby is crying, try to see things from her point of view so that you can work out what's wrong.

✓ Toys are enjoyable and can also help a baby learn. Look for toys suitable for your baby's age, but don't believe toy companies that tell you that they can add months to your baby's development!

✓ Remember that you're the biggest treat your baby can have – your time is worth more than the most expensive toy.

Chapter 9

Your Baby's Health

I T'S LIKELY THAT EVEN IF YOU WEREN'T the sort of person who spent much time at the doctor's office, you are there quite a lot now. If this is your first baby, and even if it's your second or third, it's easy to get worried about his health and to feel that you need a second opinion about anything that concerns you. Never worry about "bothering" your doctor or any other health professional about your baby's health. Reassuring people is as much a doctor's job as treating them, and any health worker would far rather put a parent's mind at rest over a medical matter than see a sick child whose parents didn't like to trouble them. Trust your instincts; if you're worried about something, get it checked out.

In this chapter . . .

✓ Teething

✓ Considering vaccinations

✓ Using medicines

✓ Seeking medical advice

TEETHING IS OFTEN THOUGHT TO BE THE CULPRIT WHEN A CHILD IS OUT OF SORTS

Teething

AFTER SLEEPING, *teething is the most notorious element of babyhood. Just like sleeping, everyone seems to assume that a child will have problems with cutting his first teeth. And just like sleeping, it's true that while some babies do have problems, others don't have any at all.*

What is teething?

Teething, like colic, has become a catch-all word. Any bout of unexplained crying, any fretfulness or unsettled period, any sign of red cheeks or a slightly raised temperature, and "teething" is likely to be floated as a possible cause. Ask most parents, and they'll swear that teething does go hand-in-hand with real physical discomfort and symptoms like these, but talk to a pediatrician, and you'll hear that there's no evidence to link the appearance of teeth with any ailment whatsoever.

■ **If your baby has** *flushed cheeks and seems upset, you may think teething is responsible. Whether it is or not, be comforting and reassuring.*

Don't be tempted to start using "teething gels" on your baby's gums just because he seems unsettled. These contain drugs, and it may be that there's no new tooth appearing at all.

When to expect the first tooth

Some babies are born with a "natal tooth," which is usually removed because of the risk of choking. However, it is much more common for a baby's first tooth to put in an appearance anywhere between 3 and 16 months.

Sometimes a tiny lump on your baby's gum, which is occasionally bluish in color, heralds the appearance of a tooth — this is nothing to be concerned about.

Every baby is different

That's a wide period of time within which your baby's teeth may start to appear. Don't listen to any old wives' tales, such as that your baby's intelligence is related to the age when his first tooth appears. Tooth growth is very individual – it can vary considerably between siblings, too. My eldest daughter was over a year old when her first tooth appeared, but her younger sisters both had their first teeth by the time they were 6 months of age. Interestingly, however, the pattern does seem to have had a bearing on second teeth: my eldest's teeth have been very slow to come through.

Teething problems

Doctors are divided on whether any real pain accompanies the arrival of teeth in a baby's mouth. Many concede that there may be some discomfort when a tooth is about to break through the gum, but most believe that the problem isn't half as great as parents make out. If you think that your baby is experiencing discomfort because of an emerging tooth, rub his gums with a clean finger to help him to feel better.

THE APPEARANCE OF MILK TEETH

A baby's milk teeth usually appear in a sequence. The central bottom incisors are the first to appear, followed by the central upper incisors. These are then followed by the lower lateral, and upper lateral incisors. The first molars then appear, followed by the upper canines, and the second molars – at the back of the mouth.

Your baby will develop all of his 20 milk teeth by the time he is 3 years old.

His first permanent teeth will start coming through at around the age of 5. By the time he's 14 years old, 28 of his 32 final teeth will be through.

■ **The different** *teeth in a human jaw play distinct roles in the way that we chew our food — incisors cut, canines tear, and molars grind.*

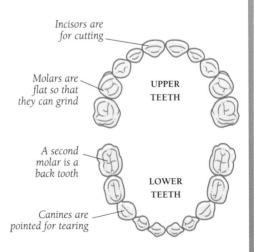

Incisors are for cutting

Molars are flat so that they can grind

UPPER TEETH

A second molar is a back tooth

LOWER TEETH

Canines are pointed for tearing

If it's not teething, what is it?

The fact is that babies aren't able to tell us what's wrong, and because we're usually so eager to find out what's bothering them, we often make assumptions. That's why we often think that our babies are having "teething problems." But don't forget that lots of things can make a baby of under 6 months feel out of sorts. The best way to deal with it, whatever the cause, is to give him lots of love.

Looking after milk teeth

You may be advised to brush your baby's very first tooth and to go out immediately and buy a baby toothbrush and some "infant" toothpaste. If you want to, that's fine – but brushing tiny teeth with your finger will be just as effective at keeping them clean. Creating the habit matters more at this stage than the actual process of cleaning them.

As your baby grows older, and likes to "help" brush his teeth himself – and coat his face in toothpaste at the same time, naturally – it can be a good idea to do his teeth in the bath.

■ **Get into the** *habit of cleaning your baby's teeth in the morning, and then last thing at night. Using a cloth or finger is sufficient.*

What does matter, hugely, is what you're giving your baby to eat. By this stage, your child will probably be able to make very clear to you that he likes (correction: loves) anything sweet. However happy he is to eat sugary desserts and chocolate candies, try to limit his intake of these sorts of foods. As well as getting him into bad habits, these sugary foods could be doing harm to his tiny emerging teeth. Even though these teeth will eventually come out and be replaced by "adult" teeth, they still have a lot of work to do before then!

From the age of 4 or 5 months a baby is able to start using a cup, instead of a bottle, for drinking. If you are giving him sugary drinks, such as diluted fruit juices, get him into the habit of using a cup. This is because research has shown

■ **If your baby** *wants something to chew on, give him something savory, such as a rusk or bagel. Sweet, sugary foods should be reserved for the occasional treat.*

that regular contact with a bottle nipple filled with juice can damage a baby's teeth.

Don't forget that, apart from milk, water is the best drink that you can give your baby.

What can my baby chew on?

Teething babies often like something to bite or chew on. Try a teething ring or a hard, unsweetened cracker. Teething toys that have been put into the freezer are not a good idea because they can harm the gum tissues and cause pain. If you want to cool one down a bit, put it into a mug of iced water for a few minutes before giving it to your baby.

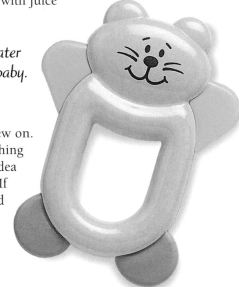

■ **Babies practice chewing** *as soon as they can get their hands or toys into their mouths, so a teething ring can be a good investment.*

Considering vaccinations

VACCINATIONS INTRODUCE a substance into the body that will trigger the production of antibodies and help the body fight a disease if it's later contracted. Whether to have your baby vaccinated is one of the first and, in many ways, one of the hardest dilemmas you'll face about your child's welfare. Like every parent, you only want to do what's best for your child – but there are so many claims as to the rights and wrongs of vaccinations that it can seem difficult to know who to believe.

INTERNET

www.aap.org
www.cdc.gov

These web sites offer scientifically sound and reliable information about vaccinations, which parents may find useful.

Should we vaccinate our baby?

Vaccination does carry risks, as any doctor will tell you. Most doctors argue that these dangers are tiny, but they're talking about the risks that they believe or know to be there.

Leaving a child unvaccinated carries real dangers too; many argue that the risks that your child faces if she contracts the diseases concerned are far greater than any perceived danger from the vaccine is likely to be.

Do your research

Find out as much as you can about immunization. Read about it. Talk to your partner. Talk to other parents. Talk to your pediatrician and your obstetrician. Listen to what all of them have to say, and you'll soon find yourself coming down on one side of the fence or the other.

Don't let apathy or sheer worry about vaccinations prevent you from researching the subject and making an informed choice based on what you've found out.

Early vaccinations

Vaccination schedules change as new vaccines (or combinations of old vaccines) are developed, but most American pediatricians recommend that a baby should be vaccinated at 2 months of age against Hepatitis B, Hib, DTaP (diptheria, tetanus, and pertussis combined), IPV (polio), and prevnar (to protect against pneumococcus, a bacteria that can cause meningitis and blood infections). Some doctors may even give the first Hepatitis B vaccine in the first few days of a baby's life. These vaccines are then repeated at 4 and 6 months old. Sometimes they are staggered so that the baby doesn't get so many shots at one visit, and some immunizations may be given as two vaccines in one shot. Then, at 12 to 15 months, babies receive MMR and Varivax (chickenpox) vaccines. Babies are not routinely immunized against Meningitis C.

PREVENTING DISEASE

Immunization programs have been introduced to help protect children against illnesses and diseases, some of which can be very serious, such as:

- **Diptheria:** A throat disease that can cause breathing difficulties
- **Hemophilus influenza type b (Hib):** A flu-like illness that can cause meningitis
- **Measles:** This causes a fever and rash and it can have serious complications
- **Meningitis C:** A severe illness that carries a risk of long-term damage or death
- **Mumps:** A viral illness that causes neck swelling
- **Polio:** This attacks nerve tissue in the brain and can cause paralysis
- **Rubella:** If contracted by a pregnant woman, this can harm her baby
- **Tetanus:** This disease causes painful muscular spasms
- **Whooping cough:** This infectious disease causes severe spasmic coughing and can lead to serious complications

VACCINATIONS: THE CASE FOR AND AGAINST

Many people have concerns about immunization. Those who have doubts say that, while proponents of vaccinations point to the falling numbers of incidence of the diseases concerned, higher standards of living have played their part, and the merits of vaccination may have been overplayed. They claim, too, that many of the side effects go unreported, and that there may be long-term side effects that will not show up for a generation or more.

If the number of vaccinated people in the population falls below 95 percent, doctors warn that there could be an epidemic of the relevant disease.

Some people believe that childhood immunization starts too early and question whether a baby's immune system is sufficiently developed to cope with it. However, there's no current evidence to back this theory up, while we do know that giving vaccines to young babies protects them from serious diseases from their earliest months. There is also a concern that the MMR vaccine can cause fits. However, official figures suggest that this affects only one child in 1,000. In contrast, a child with measles is 10 times more likely to have a seizure.

Another worry is that giving three vaccines in one jab assaults the immune system. Some people believe that giving them separately would tax the baby's body less. However, authorities say that splitting the MMR vaccine could be riskier because of the danger of catching the disease in between vaccinations. Some reports suggest that the MMR vaccine could trigger autistic disorders and Crohn's Disease. But a recent meta-analysis looking at over 1,000 different studies found no link between MMR and autism or Chrohn's Disease.

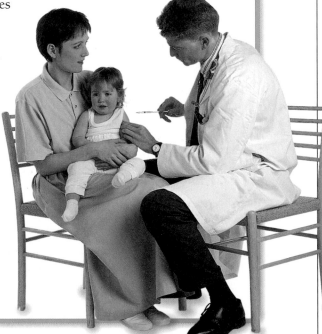

■ **While your child** *is having an injection, be reassuring. If you are squeamish about jabs yourself, don't let your child pick up on this fear.*

Using medicines

IF YOUR BABY HAS A FEVER, of course you are going to be worried and concerned, and you'll want to do everything that you can to bring his temperature down. The temptation to give a baby medicine if he appears fretful or irritable is often great because, after all, he can't tell you if something's hurting – and you don't want to think that he might be suffering. As a result, liquid acetaminophen (Tylenol) has become the children's cure-all in many a family household.

It's important not to become too reliant on the use of drugs in young children. Pain relievers may cover up the symptoms of something that your baby is suffering from, but they won't eliminate the problem.

Children's medicine

Don't automatically go to the medicine cabinet. Liquid acetaminophen can be a great help in bringing down a temperature in a child with a fever – but if you're using it just to treat a general feeling that there's something a bit wrong with your baby, hold off.

Avoid giving medicine in the hope that it will "help him to sleep" because he's been crying a lot during the afternoon, or because he's pulling his legs up to his tummy and you're a bit worried he might have a stomach ache. If he does have an upset tummy, acetaminophen may irritate his stomach further. Always remember that medicines are designed to treat specific ailments and they should be used sparingly.

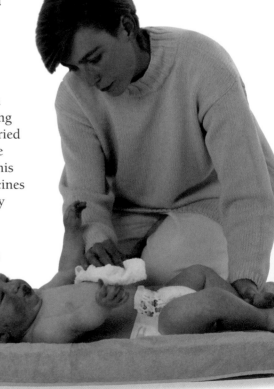

■ **If your baby** *has a high temperature, remove his clothing and sponge him down with cool water.*

DEFINITION

Antibiotics are chemicals used to treat bacterial infections. They work by either killing the bacteria or by stopping them from multiplying so that the body's immune system can then combat them more easily. However, they are not effective against viruses, such as flu.

All about antibiotics

Antibiotics have been much prescribed in the western world, but now concern surrounds their use. The problem is that if antibiotics are used too freely, bacteria can build up resistance to the drug and then these medicines lose their effectiveness.

This, in turn, means that if a person is re-infected with the bacteria, stronger antibiotics will have to be given, and, sometimes, these can be given only intravenously in a hospital. In a wider context, there's also a fear that super-bacteria may be produced that will eventually withstand all antibiotics, putting potentially everyone at risk.

Seeking medical advice

IT'S 2 O' CLOCK in the morning, and your baby seems very unwell. You're faced with a dilemma: should you, or should you not, call your doctor?

Calling a doctor

It's a problem every parent faces at some point, and when you're a new parent and this is your first child, the question seems all the more difficult. The more children you have, and the more contact you've had with young babies, the more experienced you are likely to be at a correct, instinctive diagnosis.

But equally, it's vital never to ignore the voice in your head which says "my baby really is ill, and he does need medical help." Never hesitate if you feel this way; any parent would rather feel a bit silly to be told it's nothing than to regret not calling for medical help sooner.

■ **Your local health clinic** *will have a doctor on call, day and night. He or she will be able to give you advice over the telephone and, if necessary, will make a visit to your home.*

Assessing your baby's well-being

If your baby is unwell but is generally happy and behaving normally, for example, he is feeding and he is producing wet and sometimes dirty diapers, there is probably nothing too much to worry about. It's when your baby's behavior changes, however, that the alarm bells should start ringing.

The condition of a young baby can change incredibly quickly. That's why doctors are always very cautious if they've got any cause for concern. Equally, and happily, a baby who seems very ill can seem much better within an hour or two.

WHEN SHOULD I SEEK ADVICE?

The following symptoms are all valid reasons for calling a doctor at any time of the day or night. It may very well be that your child is not in any serious danger, but it is always better to err on the side of caution. Check for the following signs:

- A temperature of 102.2 °F (39 °C) or higher
- A temperature that doesn't go down after you've tried acetaminophen and you've removed your baby's clothes
- A seizure
- Any difficulty breathing
- Any abnormal discharge from the ears
- Strange body movements or odd posture
- A swelling or a lump
- A strange rash that you can't account for
- Floppiness, listlessness, or lack of interest in his surroundings
- Vomiting or diarrhea, and an inability to retain fluids

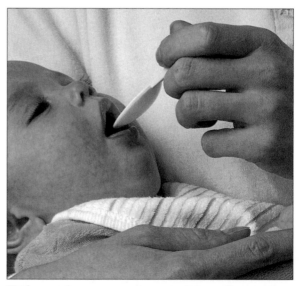

■ **If your doctor** *prescribes a medicine, adhere to the dosage instructions closely. Use a spoon to give your baby a liquid medicine and pour it gently into his mouth.*

All about cot death

Sudden infant death syndrome (SIDS), is something
that all parents fear, but instances of it are relatively rare. In
fact, since a public-awareness campaign in the 1990s, the
number of cases has fallen significantly. SIDS is not an illness.
It cannot be diagnosed in a living baby, and there are numerous
theories about what causes it. However, we do know that some
babies are potentially at greater risk, including: premature babies;
infants of mothers who have had apnoea or stopped-breathing
incidents; infants of mothers who have had little or no antenatal
care; infants of parents who smoke; and siblings of a previous
SIDS baby. But even in these groups, the risk of SIDS is still
as low as 1 per cent.

In Chapter 4, we mention some of the ways you can help reduce the risk of SIDS. It's
also important to ensure that your baby sleeps on his back, unless a doctor instructs
otherwise for medical reasons. However, a contrary medical opinion recommends that
your baby should sleep on his side, so that there is no risk of choking on his own vomit.
Either way, it is important that your baby does not sleep on his tummy. Keep pillows
and large soft toys out of your baby's cot, and don't put your baby to sleep on soft surfaces,
such as a sofa or cushion. Make sure that your baby doesn't overheat in his crib.

A simple summary

✓ Most parents swear that
teething causes fretfulness and
unexplained crying in babies.

✓ If your baby's emerging teeth
are aggravating him, try rubbing
his gums with your finger.

✓ Get into the habit of cleaning
your baby's teeth twice a day.

✓ Sweet foods and drinks can
damage milk teeth.

✓ Vaccination is a thorny issue.
Think through where you stand
before making a decision.

✓ Don't automatically reach for
the liquid acetaminophen if your
child is a bit under the weather.

✓ Sudden infant death syndrome
(SIDS) is relatively rare, but there
are ways you can reduce the risk
of it. For example, don't lie your
baby on his tummy to sleep.

Chapter 10

Don't Forget to Enjoy Life

FOR MOST PARENTS, the first weeks after the arrival of a new baby pass in a blur. It takes time to get used to the new balancing act you've got to perform and, for a while, you'll probably feel as though you'll never get the hang of this parenting business. There will be days when you struggle to get dressed or even make a half-decent meal for yourself. And then, out of the blue, comes the day that you'd begun to believe would never be here: a day when you feel, well, almost on top of things. You've survived the onslaught of early parenthood! Now's the time to start really enjoying being the mom or dad of your gorgeous new addition.

In this chapter . . .

✓ Getting out and about

✓ Making new friends (for both of you)

✓ Having fun together at home

✓ Traveling with your baby

SPEND TIME TOGETHER OUT IN THE GARDEN – YOU'LL BOTH ENJOY THE FRESH AIR

Getting out and about

AT FIRST IT IS DIFFICULT *to believe that you'll ever be organized enough to take up the thread of your normal life and actually go somewhere for part of the day. But you can't stay indoors forever. Getting out and about is an important part of settling into the normality of your new role in life.*

INTERNET

www.gocitykids.com

This web site has lots of ideas for places to go with your baby in several major cities.

Exploring your neighborhood

Now that you have a baby, you'll probably find yourself looking at your local neighborhood in quite a different light. You will be wondering whether there are any baby facilities, such as day care, in your local shopping center, or whether there are any places where you can change a diaper. These are the kinds of factors that you will probably not have noticed before, but you may be surprised by what's out there for children. Get out and explore! Find out where the nearest swings, toy stores, and swimming pools are so that you and your baby can start enjoying them.

■ **Babies love being outside,** *seeing new surroundings, hearing new sounds, and watching other people and children – fresh air is good for them, too.*

If yours is a winter baby, it isn't always easy to get out for a walk – but most days you will have at least a couple of hours when it will be a possibility. Grasp the opportunity. Don't be put off going out by the fact that you haven't washed the dishes, or because you want to clean the kitchen floor. If the sun is out and the baby's fed, now is the moment for getting out of the house.

Meeting other parents

Even when your baby is too tiny for a swing or slide, it's still worth pushing her to the local playground. You may well meet another parent with a young baby, perhaps one who has older children as well.

Seek out places in your local community where parents congregate and see whether you like being there, too.

■ **Playground** *areas are great places for children and their parents to meet. Your young baby won't be able to join in, but she can still feel part of the fun.*

Check out other places, too, where you'll want to take your baby as she grows up into first a toddler and then a pre-schooler. For example, the duck pond, the local zoo, local libraries, parks, playgrounds, or recreation areas

Shopping with your baby

Using the local stores, especially if you can reach them on foot, is often more pleasurable and less stressful than going to the supermarket when your baby is young.

If your carriage or stroller has a good-sized parcel tray underneath, you'll be surprised at how much food you can pile into it. And if your baby cries and needs a cuddle or feed while you're out, it's often easier to make a quick exit from a local store than from the busy supermarket checkout.

■ **Some shopping** *centers are not very convenient for parents with carriages – you'll soon get to know the places where you should avoid taking a baby carriage or stroller.*

Making new friends (for both of you)

PARENTHOOD IS NO PLACE *for loners. Being a parent is a whole lot more fun – some might say, a whole lot more survivable – if you've got other parents with whom you can share your worries, your joys, your fears, your stories. In the past, you might have found all that parent-talk a huge bore. Now, suddenly, you realize why the dads and moms in your office swap stories about their children so much.*

Where to find new friends

The truth is that, despite books like this one, the best way to learn about how to bring up your child is to listen to your own instincts and to talk to other parents. You've got to get out there and find some other people in the same boat as you.

It shouldn't be difficult – in theory. However, bear in mind that the people you most want to know are parents whose children are actually very close in age to yours – age gaps between babies are much more exaggerated than they are between adults. If you are lucky, links may come about as a result of a prenatal class, or even the waiting room at the local clinic. Some mothers get talking on the postnatal ward, and meet up once they've both gone home – lifelong friendships have resulted!

■ **The friendships that** *you made with other parents when your children were babies will often last through the years.*

If you weren't blessed with these kind of contacts, you need to find some quickly. When Rosie (my eldest daughter) was born, I was only 7 months pregnant – so I hadn't started prenatal classes or anything else that gave me links with other mothers-to-be in my area. The first few weeks after she came home from hospital were very, very lonely, and at times I felt I was at rock bottom. There I was, on my own from 7 A.M. until 7 P.M. with a tiny, premature baby who still didn't weigh much over 4 lb (1.75 kg), and none of my old friends could relate to my new situation.

For a while I stuck it out, but that was a mistake. My turning point came when someone from the local branch of Britain's National Childbirth Trust phoned me up and invited me to a postnatal tea around the corner. I went, and only stayed for an hour or so – I didn't meet anyone who became a lifelong friend, but I did realize that there was life out there, if only I could find it. That outing made me determined to find other mothers and, a few more teas later, I'd got the rudiments of a circle of friends – parents just like me with first babies whom I could ask over for tea and who would invite me back in turn.

Don't forget that early parenthood is one of life's major "windows" for forging new friendships. It's a wonderful time for renewing your network and for finding new kindred spirits, some of whom will prove invaluable in the months and years ahead.

Places you can go

If you're a new parent, good places to meet people in the same boat as you might include a postnatal aqua exercise group at your local swimming pool, or a postnatal yoga group: you can usually take your baby along with you to classes like these.

Or you could join a baby massage class, which is great fun and a real treat for your baby – as well as being a good social outing for you, too.

■ **Take your baby** *to the local pool – you'll both get some exercise and you may meet other parents.*

Your pediatrician or local library will have a list of the mother and baby groups (sometimes called "morning and me" groups) in your area. These are mostly aimed at moms rather than dads, but there's no reason why a dad, babysitter, or nanny shouldn't attend! Have a look at these and try to go to a meeting. You may be pleasantly surprised by what it's like and by the other parents you meet there – and if you don't like it, you don't have to go back.

You need to get out as much as your baby does – but remember that joining groups is for her benefit, too. She'll love being laid down on a mat to kick alongside other babies of her own age.

INTERNET

www.huggies.com

Computers are no substitute for real friendships, but the internet has opened up the exciting possibility of global friendships with other parents with whom you can share tips, ideas, and experiences.

Having fun together at home

ALTHOUGH GETTING OUT *together is important, remember that you and your child can have lots of fun at home, too. Some new parents quickly get themselves involved in a busy network, involving lots of social engagements. They race around each morning to get the chores done at home so that they can get out to a playgroup, followed by lunch with a friend, followed by a mid-afternoon coffee at the local café.*

Don't make the mistake of thinking you can't enjoy your baby in the comfort and privacy of your own home.

Spending time at home

Going out is important, but it can be exhausting. Often, a day at home – with a walk or a trip to the store to break things up – is the most wonderful sort of day of all. It gives you the space and time to get down on the floor with your baby and really talk to her and play with her.

■ **Your baby will** *feel safe and loved at home, and this is the perfect environment for play.*

BABY MASSAGE

Massage is a great way to enjoy time together with your baby at home. Choose a time when she's in the mood – if she starts fretting or crying don't push it, just try again another day. You don't have to invest in expensive massage oil – baby oil is absolutely fine. Start with light movements and gradually increase the pressure.

Lie your baby on her tummy and massage her back. This encourages flexibility in her spine and will encourage her to hold up her head and strengthen her neck muscles. Turn her over and massage her chest and feet – these are areas that babies love to have touched and played with.

■ **Massage is a great way** *to keep your baby's muscles flexible and strong.*

Give yourself some treats

Having a home-based day gives you time to talk to your baby, to sit down and enjoy your lunch while she's gnawing on a bit of apple or carrot, or to take the time to marvel over how much she's changing and how much she can do.

If you're lucky, you might also get to have a bit of time to think about yourself. Try lying your baby on a rug while you do an exercise routine: she'll probably be hugely entertained by what you're doing, and you'll feel better for toning your muscles – after all, there aren't many chances for exercise sessions when you're a parent with a young baby.

There are some time savers that will give you more time to play (and relax):

- Order a takeout as a treat once in a while
- Do you REALLY need to iron everything?
- Get your supermarket shopping delivered, or get a friend or relative to get your shopping for you
- For a quick clean up, pile all the mess into a big basket and sort it out later. Obviously this isn't ideal, but at least your home will feel a little less cluttered and chaotic

Toys and games

From 3 months on, your baby will benefit from toys she can try to hold on to. From 5 or 6 months, your baby will also enjoy games that involve gentle bouncing. Try nursery rhymes that involve a bounce on your knee, and you'll probably find her gurgling in delight. A baby bouncer is a good investment, and often good value if you buy it from a reputable second-hand store.

■ **A spinning top** *is easy to hold and will encourage your child to practice balance. The motion of the spinning will entertain her, too.*

Make time for mementos

You'll never believe how fast the first year of parenthood goes. After it's gone, every subsequent year seems to go even faster! Because it's a time of such quick change, it really is a good idea to keep a record of how your baby is developing. You'll have lots of fun seeing how she grows, and it's also a lovely thing to share with her when she's older. My 8-year-old daughter recently did a project at school about herself, and being able to look through the mementoes of her own babyhood with her was an immensely enjoyable exercise – and something that clearly fascinated her.

There's no end to the ideas around at the moment for what to save as mementos. You can buy a kit that enables you to make and frame your baby's footprints, although it's just as easy, and probably cheaper, to get what you need yourself. If you want to splash out, the sky's the limit – an artist will paint your baby's portrait, or you can find someone to dip her first shoes in bronze or hire a professional photographer and do a proper photo-shoot.

Take a photograph of your baby at the same time every month – you'll build up an invaluable record of her as she changes.

Most importantly, however, you should keep a box – a shoebox is great, although a slightly larger one might be more accommodating. Use it to store such mementos as your baby's name-tag from the hospital, a lock of her hair from the first haircut, perhaps the clothes she wore on the day you brought her home, or a favorite pair of baby shoes.

■ **Booties are of** *sentimental value. When your baby's older, it's hard to believe she ever wore them.*

Traveling with your baby

GOING ON VACATION WITH A BABY *may seem a daunting prospect if it's your first child. But in fact, it's far more difficult to travel once your baby is on the move. A baby of between 3 and 6 months is, in many ways, the ideal age for travel. If she's breastfed, this is especially true, as you won't need to pack a lot of formula and bottles.*

Although your friends might say you're being very "brave" by taking her away at such a young age, in fact she'll be easy to look after because all she really needs is you. And you in a relaxed state, happy to just enjoy life with her, could well be the recipe for a perfect family holiday.

At between 3 and 6 months, your baby will probably sleep for most of the time that you're in transit.

Planning ahead

Having children means, for most of us, an end to much that was spontaneous in life. But if you do decide that you want to take off for a break at short notice, it's worth sitting down before you go and making sure that you've covered all the details. Good planning can make a big difference to how much you enjoy yourselves once you're there.

Wherever you're planning to go, it's worth considering whether the location is family-friendly. Places where you had enormous fun before you had children, could be entirely inappropriate now that you have a baby: if possible, ask others who've been there with children. Think about whether you'll want any time just on your own with your partner – if so, look into going somewhere that has child care facilities.

■ **If you'll be sightseeing,** *make sure that you've got a suitable carriage you can take away with you.*

En route

Pack a bag with lots of little treats, just in case your baby is wide awake and needs to be entertained on the journey. You can hide some of her toys a couple of weeks before the trip so that they'll have novelty value when you produce them at the airport, or buy her some new, inexpensive toys.

If you're traveling by plane, remember to feed your baby on take-off and landing – sucking will help reduce the risk of earache.

MUST-HAVES FOR A TRIP

- Sunscreen and sun hat
- Diaper rash cream and enough diapers to see you through the first few days
- Ready-prepared formula and bottles, sufficient to last for at least the first few days
- Plastic bibs
- A collapsible stroller, and some blankets
- Baby wipes and tissues
- Clothes – allow for two outfits a day, in case it will be difficult to do any laundry
- A first-aid kit containing liquid acetaminophen
- A passport for the baby – she'll need her own

■ **Make sure that** *your baby has a hat if she's going to be out in the sun.*

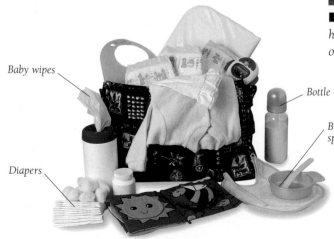

Baby wipes

Diapers

Bottle

Bib, bowl, and spoon

■ **Pack a special bag** *for your baby, containing all the essential daily items that she'll need.*

If you're held up at an airport, or just waiting for your flight to be called, take her for a walk – there's always lots to look at in the airport, and you might as well wait until you're sitting down on the plane to start feeding her if you can: this is when you will be most anxious to get her settled.

Most seasoned traveling parents think that, on an airplane, either the bulkhead seats (no passengers in front; more leg room) or the back seats (near the toilets and flight attendants) are the best option.

A simple summary

✔ Look for places in your neighborhood where parents with young children tend to congregate – you'll meet people to chat with, and your baby will meet new friends, too!

✔ Other parents who are going through the same sort of life adjustment as you right now may very well prove to be a valuable lifeline.

✔ Even if you thought you'd rather die than go to a playgroup, give it a try – you might be pleasantly surprised.

✔ Consider joining a "morning and me" group or going to a baby massage class – these can be fun for both of you.

✔ Start a collection of mementos – your baby grows so quickly, and you will want to remember all those precious early months.

✔ Being out and about is fun, but so is staying at home. Try to build treats and exercise routines into your day at home as well.

✔ Consider going on vacation. If this is a possibility, it could be a good time to travel while your baby is still young.

✔ Pack your bags carefully, so that your baby has everything she'll need to keep her warm, safe, and well-fed while she's on vacation. Keep enough diapers for the first few days in your hand luggage.

Chapter 11

Finding the Right Child Care

WHETHER YOU'RE GOING BACK TO WORK when your child is 3 months old or 3 years old, or you want to make some regular time for yourself a few times a week, finding the right child care is the big question you have to address. Working out what's going to be right for your child and your situation may be a time-consuming and sometimes difficult process, but it's crucial that you put all your available time into getting it right. That's because your child is worth it, naturally. And it's also because, if you're confident that the right person is caring for your child, you'll be able to concentrate on what you're doing while you're away from him. So invest your time now – it will pay off.

In this chapter . . .

✔ What's right for us?

✔ Doing your research

✔ Will child care work?

NOT EVERYONE IS LUCKY ENOUGH TO HAVE A GRANDPARENT ON HAND . . .

What's right for us?

WHEREVER YOU LIVE, *there will be various child care options on offer. But you can save yourself a lot of time at the start if you sit down and begin making a list of what's going to be important to you.*

■ **If you know** *that you will be returning to work after maternity leave, it's worth starting to think about and plan for child care before your baby even arrives.*

TYPES OF CHILD CARE

Nanny: A nanny is a trained or experienced one-to-one carer who looks after your baby in your home, while either living in or out herself. An advantage is that your child will be looked after in his own environment, and the focus will be entirely on him, rather than on a number of children. However, a nanny can be expensive.

You'll need a big house for a live-in nanny, and you will have to be prepared for compromises to your privacy.

Babysitter: This is an experienced caregiver (usually a mother) who cares for children in her home – often alongside her own children. Your child can enjoy a homey atmosphere and the company of other children. This option is usually cheaper than a nanny. However, it may not be very flexible and you will have to adapt to the babysitter's way of doing things. The caregiver may not be able to look after your child if he's unwell, because of the risk of other children catching a bug.

Family member: In this case, the caregiver is often a baby's grandma, aunt, or great-aunt – someone who genuinely loves your child, and this is something that you can't put a price on. You're unlikely to be paying the going rate – and it may be free of charge. However, differences in opinion over your child's care could cause problems. Your caregiver may also be elderly and unable to do as much with your child as you could.

Nursery or day care center: This is a child care center where children aged from 3 months to 5 years are cared for while their parents are at work. The advantages are

Thinking about child care options

Think about what matters to you. Do you think that your baby should be looked after in your own home, in someone else's home, or in a day care setting? Would you prefer your baby to be cared for by another mother, a nanny, or a professional child care provider – or someone who can offer all of these qualities?

Be very honest with yourself when you draw up your list of requirements. It's going to make a huge difference to your life if you can find a form of child care that will fit in with the demands of your work and your life.

INTERNET

www.nccic.org

This is the web site for the National Child Care Information Center (NCCIC), a project of the Child Care Bureau.

that the clear standard of care will reassure you about what's going on when you're not around, and it provides your child with a structured day and playmates. It is a cheaper option than a nanny, although if you have a second child, day care center fees can build up. You may also worry that your child isn't getting enough one-to-one care.

Nanny share: This means that you and another family share one nanny: either the nanny cares for both children simultaneously or, if you work part-time, she looks after your baby for half the week, and the other family's child for the rest of the time. This is more cost-effective than employing a nanny yourself, and your child will enjoy having a playmate. However, arrangements with other families can prove complicated.

Au pair: An au pair is a foreign national, usually a female aged between 18 and 27 years who lives as part of your family and helps out for a maximum of 25 hours a week. However, you will need to have a spare room for her, and you must also be prepared to help her arrange her life and make friends. An au pair may not be suitable for sole charge of very young children and babies, because of a lack of experience.

As well as being the cheapest form of child care, an au pair can provide a kind of "older sister" figure for your child.

Mother's helper: This is an untrained caregiver and is often someone quite young. He or she will provide you with an extra pair of hands. It is a much cheaper option than a nanny, but the help is unlikely to be suitable for extended sole charge and the caregiver may not know how to organize children's activities.

Fitting in with your work

If you're trying to find child care for the times when you will be at work, think about your work and how demanding it is. Do you ever have to work late unexpectedly? Do you work unusual hours? Think about your partner's job, too. Would he or she be able to share the drop-offs and pick-ups, or would it always come down to you? Could you or your partner take days off if your caregiver or your child was ill? In short, how flexible is your job – and how flexible is your partner's job?

Considering costs

Another consideration is how much you can afford to spend on child care. If your job isn't highly paid, you need to look for a form of lower-cost care without compromising your child's happiness or safety. And it's worth thinking about whether you're likely to have more children and, if so, when – child care fees may almost double once you've got two children, whereas a nanny's salary may remain almost the same.

■ **Your baby will enjoy spending** *time in the company of other children, of all ages. Mixing with other parents and their children will help prepare your child for day care or other child care options.*

Doing your research

ONCE YOU'VE DECIDED *which type of child care is going to suit you, see what's available in your area. Ask around – talk to other parents and find out what care they're using and have used. Ask them about the mistakes they've made as well as about their successes, and you'll learn a lot.*

Finding out about child care

Local companies (listed in the *Yellow Pages* under "Child Care Consultants") may be able to provide a list of registered babysitters and day care centers in your area. *Nanny agencies* are also listed under "Nanny Service."

Children's clothing stores and places where parents tend to congregate are often the places where nannies and babysitters advertise their services. Take a look around and see if anything catches your eye, but bear in mind that if you find someone through an advertisement, you'll need to check their references thoroughly (something you should do in any case). If you don't feel comfortable with a particular day care center, for example, that's enough of a reason to rule it out – even if you can't put your finger on exactly why you feel the way you do.

DEFINITION

*A **nanny agency** will charge a fee – often a proportion of your nanny's salary – for finding you a suitable nanny. The agency should have carried out checks on potential nannies, but never assume that they have. Check references yourself. If you take someone on and it doesn't work within a certain amount of time, the agency may help you find temporary cover and help you find someone else at no extra cost.*

Don't forget to consider looking for child care around your workplace or your partner's workplace, but only if the commute isn't too much for your child.

■ **Other parents** *could be the best source of information about child care in your area – and you may be able to share the cost of child care.*

Phoning a potential nanny

The usual starting point if you're hiring a nanny is to talk to her by phone. Maybe she answers your advertisement or gets your number from an agency and calls you; maybe you get her number and call her. Either way, you've got time to think about the call in advance. If, when you speak to her, you feel that she doesn't sound right, rule her out even at this stage. It will save you time in the long run.

Remember that whichever sort of child care you're after, your instincts are the most important thing you've got to go on. If you have a bad feeling about something or someone, don't ignore it.

Keep the call fairly short, but make sure that you get a few details about the nanny. In particular, go over issues that are very important to you. For example, if you really need someone who's not going to mind working until 8 P.M. every Wednesday, mention this now. It may eliminate the candidate from the start.

REGULATIONS FOR CHILD CAREGIVERS

State regulations

State regulations that are designed to protect child caregivers and children exist, but they vary from state-to-state. To obtain information about requirements and regulations in your state, contact local licensing agencies or the state office responsible for child care regulation.

National accreditation

Day care centers can request national accreditation. Although the process is voluntary and several accreditation systems are available, the national accreditation system checks that standards are being met in the areas of health, safety, administration, and programing. It also judges the quality and education of staff, and the quality of interaction between adults and children. To find out your state's child care regulations and additional information on accredited day care centers, check the NCCIC web site: www.nccic.org then go to "directories."

Interviewing a nanny

Make a list of questions before the meeting. This is a real job interview, so don't make it too informal. Take notes during the meeting if you feel it will help. A good ploy is to start with just you, or you and your partner, and the nanny, and then bring your baby in to meet her at the end of your chat. Then none of you will be distracted by the baby.

Spend some time talking to the nanny about her last job and what she enjoyed about it and what she didn't enjoy. Ask her why she left the family who previously employed her. Ask her about why she wants to be a nanny and what she likes about her work.

■ **It can help** *to prepare a list of questions before you interview a nanny – that way you won't forget any important points.*

Discussing care issues

It's a good idea to talk through some of the issues that you feel are important in the care of your child. Bear in mind that most good nannies are not going to want a job where they feel you'll be controlling them while you're out of the house. If this is someone you trust enough to look after your child, she should be someone you trust enough to organize his day and activities.

Of course, you might want to insist that she gives him only organically grown fruit and that she uses "time out" as a punishment if he misbehaves: but it's not reasonable to insist on a regimented timetable of activities.

You've got to give your nanny a bit of space to do things her own way.

■ **If you won't be home** *from work in time to put your child to bed some days of the week, make sure that your nanny will be happy to take on the bedtime routine in your absence.*

A second interview

It's often a good idea to have a second interview for a nanny you're close to hiring. Ideally, this interview should be more like a half day or even a full day with your family.

This gives you a chance to see what sort of a person your nanny-to-be really is, and how she gets along with your child. It also gives her a chance to see you warts and all, while there's still time for her to back out.

Outline benefits with your nanny, such as the use of a car or a cell phone, and what accommodation will be solely hers. Discuss issues such as discipline and television rules.

Once you've found a nanny that you want to employ, draw up a contract. It should cover issues such as pay, sick leave, duties, schedule, and babysitting.

■ **Watch a potential nanny** *to see how she interacts with your child, to get an idea of whether she'll be right for the job.*

Meeting a babysitter (or family day care provider)

If a babysitter or family day care provider has a vacancy and you like the sound of each other on the phone, she'll invite you over to meet her and to see her home. Take your child along with you: remember, you need to see how he fits into the house and also how the babysitter reacts to him. If you think it's going to be too stressful to talk to the babysitter when you've got your baby with you, ask whether you can make two visits – once alone, and once with your baby.

As with choosing any form of child care, first impressions are crucial. Often, you'll know within minutes of walking into a house whether it's the right sort of place for your child, and whether the babysitter or day care provider is someone you can have an easy relationship with.

Be on the lookout for a home in which children seem to be made particularly welcome – remember that a certain level of noise and mess is inevitable when children are having a good time.

Asking questions

Ask about the other children in the babysitter's or day care provider's care. You may have preferences as to whether your baby is the youngest child in the house, for example. Talk to the babysitter or caregiver about the kind of outings she does with the children, such as trips to the park or the library – ask about facilities for children in her immediate area, and remember that any babysitter worth her salt will be a mine of information about these types of things.

Talk about the structure of the day at the caregiver's house. Ask whatever you like about it, but bear in mind that few sitters will take kindly to being told how to run their household. With a caregiver, it's generally a case of your child fitting in with the existing set-up, not the other way around.

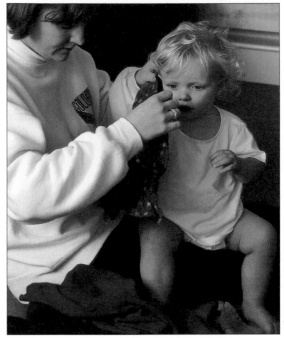

■ **A babysitter or caregiver will** *probably have other children in her care, so supply her with everything your child will need for the day.*

Looking around a day care center

Make your first visit to a prospective day care center a solo one. This is so that you can concentrate entirely on what you think of the place and its staff. If you like it, you will want to visit again – this time with your baby to see how he fits in and is treated.

Pay attention to the children and watch how happy and engaged they seem to be at the day care center. Are they just running around aimlessly, or are they enjoying an activity or playing together?

As with a babysitter's house, you'll often have a gut instinct about a day care center within a few minutes of arriving. At a good day care center, even busy staff will greet you enthusiastically and you should feel that, although there's plenty going on, people aren't too stretched to have a quick word with you.

Look at the work up on the walls of the center. Does it feel like a purposeful place with plenty of stimulating activities? Can you imagine your child in this environment?

Talking to staff

Ask about issues such as staff turnover and adult to child ratios. Ask, too, about the level of training of the people working at the center: What professional qualifications do they have?

You'll need to talk about attitudes to discipline and what the day care center's stance is on television and videos. Safety is of paramount importance. If you have any nagging doubts about any safety issue at all, however obscure, do ask – it's horrible to leave your child somewhere with even a shadow of a doubt about whether he'll be safely cared for.

Opening and closing times are another crucial issue: most centers have heavy penalties for late pick-ups, and you should talk about these. Some day care facilities, especially those in big city centers, have "additional services," which may be a help if you and your partner both lead very busy lives: some will take care of your ironing and dry-cleaning, for example, and others can even supply you with prepared meals if you're going home late from the office and won't have time to cook!

Trivia...

Some day care centers are offering parents the chance to watch their babies through the day via a secure internet site and web cam. Day care managers say it helps parents feel in touch with their children even when they're at the office – cynics suspect it's a gimmick to help anxious parents over the hurdle of leaving their child.

■ **A day care center** *will have a variety of toys on hand, and your child can learn from playing with other children and copying the things that they do, too.*

Will child care work?

REST ASSURED THAT NO PARENT
goes back to work leaving their child in someone
else's care without a few worries. Some mothers
remember crying through their first few days
back at the office: others say they were completely
convinced, in the early weeks, that they'd never
get used to leaving their child with someone else.
You're not alone in the way you feel!

INTERNET

www.dmoz.org

*The Open Directory Project
is a comprehensive,
well-researched site.
Go to "Child Care" to
find child care agencies
throughout the U.S.*

Work and parenthood

Hard on the heels of getting used to
being a parent, you've now got another
role to learn quickly: that of being a
working parent. It's not going to be easy.
You might feel guilty; you will worry
about what your child is up to when
you're not around; you may worry that
you're missing out on time with him. But
life isn't perfect, and none of us can have
everything. Okay, so you're not with your
baby 24 hours a day. But on the plus
side, you enjoy your work (hopefully);
you're better company for your child
when you are with him; and you're
building up a career that is for the future,
as well as for now.

*There's plenty of research to
support the claim that the children
of working parents can fulfill
their potential, and
reap the benefits of the
experiences that their
working parents bring
to bear on family life.*

■ **Just because you're working,** *it doesn't
mean that you have to sacrifice spending quality
time with your baby.*

Settling in

Don't imagine that, even once you've found your perfect child care set up, you can simply dump your baby and run. Settling in is crucial, and you have to think ahead about this: build in plenty of time for your baby to get used to his new child care arrangements before the day when you have to leave him to go to work for real.

In fact, "settling in" sessions can be a real help when you're preparing to go back to work. You'll probably need to go shopping for new clothes, or may have organized a few hours back at the office ahead of your formal start-date to catch up on what you've missed. These are obvious opportunities to try out your new nanny, babysitter, or day care center. And these trial days will also give you a chance to deal with the feelings of guilt and grief that you may well experience when you leave your child with a caregiver for the first time.

The first time you leave your child will be the hardest: you'll probably feel as though you've left a bit of yourself behind as you close the door on the nanny, babysitter, or day care center.

Keeping things stable

Finding the right child care is only the start of it – now you've got to keep things on an even keel. That means keeping to your side of the child care bargain: delivering your baby with the things you've agreed you'd bring (such as diapers and toys), picking him up when you've said you would, and making sure that you have enough time to chat with your caregiver at least once a week.

Catch-up times, also called review sessions, are the cornerstone of a good parent-caregiver relationship. Your caregiver is now partnering you in the essential business of bringing up your child, and you owe it to her to spend a bit of time once in a while talking to her about her life as well as, of course, about your child.

■ **Build a good** *relationship with your child's caregiver – chat to her about herself, and listen to what she has to say about your child's progress. Otherwise, you may feel that you're losing touch with his development.*

If you think a quick doorstep handover is the only contact you need with your child caregiver, you're wrong. It won't be enough. And if there's anything you're not happy about to do with your child's care, don't let the situation fester: talk it though at the earliest possible opportunity.

INTERNET

www.icomm.ca.daycare/

This web site is for day care providers but also has useful information for parents.

Don't underestimate the importance of remaining in touch with your child care provider: show her respect for what she's doing for both you and your child.

A simple summary

✓ Start your child care search by thinking about your needs and your budget. Think about what's important to you regarding your child's care.

✓ Look at the pros and cons of the different sorts of care, and investigate what's on offer in your area.

✓ Don't take anyone else's word about a particular day care center or babysitter. Make up your own mind and go with your gut instincts.

✓ If you use a nanny agency be prepared to follow up references yourself – for your own peace of mind.

✓ The interview process or day care visit is very important, so allow enough time for it. Leave your child with someone else so that you can concentrate fully.

✓ If you're employing a nanny, try to organize a day with her before making up your mind about whether she's the right caregiver for your child.

✓ Don't expect to feel confident about leaving your child on day one. However lucky you've been in finding great child care, it's never easy to leave your child.

✓ Be ready for some anxious days at work – see how things go for a set number of days or weeks.

153

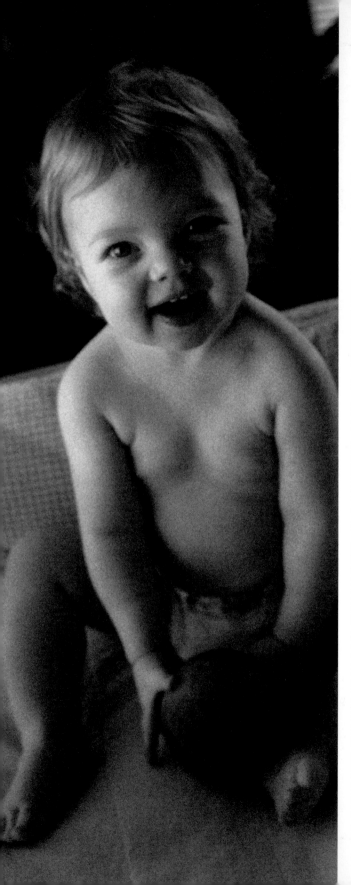

PART THREE

SHE'LL "TALK" BEFORE SHE CAN FORM REAL WORDS

Chapter 12

Speak to Me!

HEARING YOUR CHILD say her first word is one of the high points of early parenting – a real milestone, something to tell the grandparents about. It is exciting because your baby, so recently a helpless newborn, is now able to verbalize her own thoughts. More than anything else, the development of communication and speech turns your baby into a "real person." It's also, of course, the crucial building-block to finding out about the world, and she can start to learn from you and others once she has the basic tools.

In this chapter . . .

✓ **When do babies start to talk?**

✓ **What to expect**

✓ **Offering encouragement**

✓ **Is everything okay?**

When do babies start to talk?

WHEN MY BABIES WERE TINY, *I often wondered what their voices would sound like. It seemed impossible to imagine that each of my babies would turn into a talking person – and in so short a time, too. The truth is, of course, that a baby starts to communicate long, long before she begins to talk – you could say she starts even before she's born.*

Early communication

Remember when your baby used to kick inside the womb? When you were convinced that she would move in response to your partner's voice or to a particular piece of music?

■ **When your baby** *kicks in the womb, it can feel as if she's communicating with you.*

Trivia...

Scientists in Texas have been studying babies' early sounds. They believe that the noises babies make may be very similar to the language spoken by our ancestors, one million years ago! Research shows that there are four basic sounds common to all babies wherever they are in the world. This could mean that there was once a mother tongue that evolved into all the languages now used around the world.

Then, after she was born, she looked into your eyes for the first time, and you looked into hers – wasn't that communication? Not to mention the countless times since when she's cried and you've responded with a bottle, a cuddle, a diaper change. Babies, it's fair to say, are pretty skilled at the communication game: our role as parents is to encourage them to realize that communicating is fun, that it's something enjoyable, and that it enriches our lives and adds to our possibilities.

From the earliest days, make talking to your baby a priority – and make sure that you enjoy it too. Communicating this enjoyment is what many psychologists believe is the key to inspiring your child to learn to speak.

How speech and language develop

There is some amazing research that shows that babies are starting to listen and make sense of what they hear from the very day they're born – and maybe even before. Researchers have discovered that newborn babies can tell the difference between the sounds "ba" and "pa."

What they believe is that, even in the womb, a baby is listening to what's going on outside. Imagine hearing a stereo playing through a thick wall in the house next door, and you get some idea of what a baby can hear from inside a mother's body. They are able to pick up frequently-heard noises and intonations. This is the beginning of "making sense" of these sounds – a first stepping stone to communication.

What to expect

IT'S CLEAR ENOUGH that babies are communicating beings long before they're talking ones. What research seems to show is that babies are born "programed" for communication – just as their parents are conditioned to understand them and respond. We interpret their cries, their facial expressions, and their body language all the time.

One of the biggest frustrations of parenting is not being able to second-guess your child's attempts at communication. At these times, you may feel as though you are failing your child, because you can't interpret what she is "saying" long before she can actually speak.

Studies show that children take a statistical approach to words they hear – they have the innate ability to spot combinations of words that are more likely to be spoken together.

■ **When you talk** *to your baby, watch her facial expressions – she can convey a surprising range of responses.*

DEFINITION

Babbling is your baby's first means of verbal communication. Often, it's one sound – bababa or gagaga – that is repeated. Although it sounds as though a baby is copying adult conversations, this isn't the case. Research shows that even babies with hearing problems babble too.

First attempts

There's no sound quite so sweet as a baby's early *babbling*. That's why they're so often used in heartstring-tugging television advertisements. Babbling is almost always a happy, chirpy sound, because if a baby is unhappy, she will usually cry instead.

Don't let anything come in the way of enjoying "chatting" with your baby. Babies learn from communication with anyone, it's true – but at this stage they learn most, and are at their happiest, when they learn from you.

Babies start babbling from around the age of 3 months – but don't worry if your 3-month-old isn't doing this yet, because some children may not start "chatting" until they're 8 or 9 months old. What your baby is doing when she starts to babble is looking for a reaction – so make sure you react! Getting a response that is fun and enjoyable is an enormous incentive to a baby to babble more – and no baby is going to speak who hasn't spent a good few months babbling first.

How much does my baby understand?

Babies can understand you long before they can speak. As early as 4 to 6 months old, your baby will have learned the signs that mean a feeding is imminent, and she'll look around when she hears her name. She'll certainly know when you're talking about her!

By the ages of 6 to 9 months old, she'll understand the meaning of "no." When she hears words like "mommy," "daddy," "dog," or the name of one of her siblings, she'll know who's being talked about and will often look at them. She'll also understand simple requests too, for example, "clap hands" and "wave bye-bye."

■ **Babies learn a lot** *about communication from other children – especially when they play with their older siblings.*

The meaning of words

Before she starts to speak any real words herself, your baby will be learning what they mean. Sometimes, of course, she will get words wrong. But on the whole, when she starts to use a word, she'll have a good idea already of what it means.

It's estimated that a baby hears a word around 550 times before she starts to use it herself. This is a good reason to include your child in conversations long before she's ready to speak.

The exciting breakthrough

At somewhere between 10 and 14 months old, some of your baby's babbling will sound like actual language. It may be that everyone else in the room finds it impossible to pick out the word you've identified, but that doesn't matter: you are convinced that your baby is, at last, using a real word. The chances are that it's "mama" or "dada" – and a great milestone has been reached.

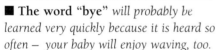

■ **The word "bye"** *will probably be learned very quickly because it is heard so often – your baby will enjoy waving, too.*

SIGN LANGUAGE

You don't have to wait until your baby can speak to get her to tell you what she wants: you can use sign language. Many parents are convinced of the benefits of teaching their child simple signing to indicate when they want something – a drink, a cuddle – or when they see something that they want to point out – the cat, a duck. Baby sign language all started with a book called *Sign with your Baby* by Joseph Garcia, which comes with a training video. Garcia noticed how keen babies are on songs such as *Itsy Bitsy Spider* and *The Wheels on the Bus*, which use hand movements. He claims that teaching your child to use signs can reduce both her frustration, and yours, in the pre-verbal months. Some parents who've used it believe that it's helped their child learn to talk more quickly. For more information, see www.signingwithkids.com which is an internet web site for parents who want to use sign language.

Being enthusiastic

Your reaction to your baby's first word is a perfect example of how important your role is in helping your child to learn to speak. Make a big fuss over your baby when she uses her first word. The next time someone else is around, make another huge fuss over her, and try to get her to repeat the word. Your baby will love all the attention and lap it up. When she realizes how delighted you are with her use of the word, she'll use it even more. This is exactly how her language skills grow in the early weeks and months of word usage: and your delight in her advances will egg her on to greater goals.

Speaking more and more

In the first few weeks of using "real" words, your baby probably won't add more than a word or two a week to her repertoire. They will be words that you and your immediate family can understand, but they probably won't be easily understood by people who don't know her well – in effect, they are "pre-words." But the fact that others can't quite pick up what she's saying isn't important at this stage: the vital point is that she's showing you that she can both understand what's going on around her and that she can imitate and use a word correctly. Pronunciation will come later.

Don't correct what your child is saying. She'll learn the correct rules of speech and grammar later from listening to you. But for now, just go on talking to her, and enjoy this great new skill she's acquiring.

Initially, a lot of her words will be baby versions of adult words. That's fine, and there's no need for you to correct them or not to use them yourself. What your child is demonstrating is her truly amazing skill for learning and understanding communication.

■ **When your child** *picks up an object, tell her what it is and explain what it is used for – the more you tell her, the more she'll learn.*

Offering encouragement

The first 4 years of a child's life are the time when she picks up the important building-blocks for good communication – and within those 4 years, the stage of most intensive learning is between the ages of 6 and 18 months.

INTERNET

www.cbcbooks.org

Find out about reading groups and events for children.

At this time, your baby is ready to make sense of the world and start talking to you about it and about herself. Your role is to light the match, to fan the flames of early interest in speech and language, and then to keep the fire burning even when language expands her world so that she is learning new things all the time, from everything and everyone around her.

Keep talking to your baby

As we've already discussed, speaking to your child and having conversations with her from the earliest days is vital. Always remember that enjoyment and having fun are the crucial elements in learning speech and language.

Don't prioritize your other commitments – your job, your housework, other relationships, your older children – above spending time talking to your baby.

Try to set aside a little time each day – even 10 minutes is better than nothing – to focus solely on your baby and to talk to her about anything and everything. Show her things as you talk to her, because her natural curiosity is one of the most important factors in encouraging her to learn. There's lots of evidence to suggest that the sing-songy way that we recite nursery rhymes actually helps babies understand the use of speech and language. They like the soothing rhythm of the words. And of course, nursery rhymes also often involve simple actions that reinforce the meaning of the words being used – and are fun to do.

Picking out words

When you're talking to your baby, remember that she's just learning the words you're speaking. Speak more slowly, slightly more loudly, and more clearly than you might do with older children or adults: this will help your baby pick out words and help her to understand their meaning more quickly. According to a report, children learn to speak more quickly when their parents use and emphasize single words in isolation rather than in complete sentences.

When she "tells" you something, make sure that she realizes that you have heard and understood her. If she drops her teddy out of her crib and says "teddy," say "Oh, you've dropped teddy. Let's pick him up and give him back to you." This helps reinforce the words she already knows, but it also lets her realize that she has been able to communicate (a great deal) in her use of this one word, "teddy."

Reading to your baby

From as soon as she's old enough to be propped up on your knee, find a book with lots of simple, bright pictures and look at it with her. It doesn't have to be "reading" yet. In fact, some of the most effective baby books at this stage are books with pictures only, where you decide what to say as you leaf through. This enables you to move on from just labeling words – such as "ball" or "apple" – to more complex ideas, for example: "Here's a ball. We saw a little boy playing with a ball in the park, didn't we?"

■ **Being able to express** *her needs is a real spur to a child's ability to speak; for example, if she has a teddy that she likes to carry around, she will soon learn to ask for it.*

A study found that babies who had been given books at 9 months of age achieved better results in school tests when they reached age 7 years than children who had not been exposed to books at an early age.

Don't have high expectations when you share a book with your baby at this age: of course she'll want to chew it and she won't realize for a while how to turn the pages. Don't let this put you off. Libraries, all of which have baby and toddler sections, expect some of their junior titles to come

■ **When you're at the library,** *let your child be in charge of choosing a book, holding it, and turning the pages.*

back slightly the worse for wear. Some of the best-loved baby books in our house are battered and torn, but that's a testament to how much they've taught my three daughters over the years.

Over the long term, reading helps your child learn to concentrate, even though she won't be able to pay attention to a book for long periods in the early years. It also helps her to realize that print on a page goes from left to right, and that we turn the right hand page to find out what happens next in a story. These are all essential pre-reading skills that have to be learned long before a child can start recognizing the letters of the alphabet.

Sharing books with a child is one of life's most pleasurable activities. If you make time for it now, you may find that learning to read comes more easily later.

Turn off the television

All babies, especially those with older siblings, see a little television from time to time – and that's absolutely fine. In fact, they're not very likely to be interested in what's on the television at the moment anyway because, once they've got used to seeing the bright colors and images, they don't have sufficiently developed language skills to make much more sense of what's going on. What's damaging to babies who are learning to talk is the constant background noise from the television, the radio, or even the constant blaring out of music from the stereo. Remember that speech is something new for your child, and picking it up and understanding it is a hugely complex skill that can become almost impossible if it's got to compete against other noise as well.

INTERNET

www.familyplay.com

This web site contains lots of suggestions for activities that will help to keep your baby or young toddler entertained.

The best environment for your child to be introduced to the use of speech is a quiet one.

Your child is not yet able to make a lot of sense of words that spill quickly from a television set or a radio, so they won't be of any help to her. Turn any background sounds off, and start talking yourself. It doesn't have to take up all your attention: sit your baby in her infant seat close to where you're washing the dishes and describe what you're up to.

Is everything okay?

SOME BABIES PICK UP LANGUAGE and speech very quickly and are able to say quite a lot of words and to understand almost everything by the age of 18 months. Others are slower, and are just starting to get the hang of what it's all about by the age of 2 years. Often, whether a child is quick or slow to learn isn't important: by the age of 4 years, the differences will have leveled out.

Monitoring progress

Babies go through phases when they "concentrate" on one area of their development, so it may be that your child isn't learning lots of new words because she's making a lot of progress in mobility right now, and can't do everything at once. At the same time, however, problems with learning speech and language are relatively common, and if your baby has a problem with either hearing, understanding, or speaking, there's a lot that can be done to help.

Research shows that the earlier a child with a speech problem gets speech therapy, the quicker her problem can be resolved and the less she'll be held back.

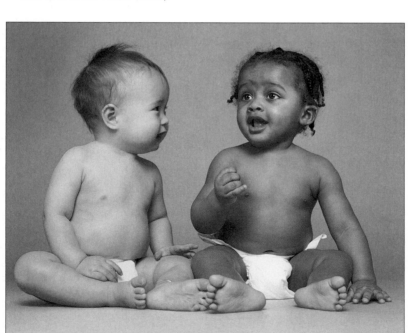

■ **Even before babies** *can speak real words, they will practice "talking." Sit your child down with another baby – it will encourage them both to chat.*

Some of the smartest people around seem to have had speech therapy as young children, so don't ever see a problem with learning to speak as a sign that your baby isn't going to do well when she reaches school age.

Look for signs that your child can UNDERSTAND a lot of what's going on and being said by around 18 months. That's a more important indicator of whether there's a problem than the number of words she's actually using.

If you suspect a problem, need reassurance, or just want someone to talk to about your concerns, don't hesitate to see your pediatrician – it's better to get some expert advice rather than spend time worrying.

A simple summary

✓ Communication and speech don't start with your baby's first word – she is starting to learn from the moment of her birth, and even before.

✓ Your baby communicates by the noises she makes, the body language she uses, and her facial expressions long before she starts to speak "for real."

✓ It's vital to make time to talk to your child – speak slowly and clearly, and turn off any background noise so that she can concentrate on listening to individual words.

✓ Enjoy "pre-talking" activities, such as sharing a book together and singing nursery rhymes.

✓ Sharing books with your baby encourages her communication skills now and for the future.

✓ Your baby's first word will probably come at between 10 and 14 months – and don't worry if you're the only person who can understand it!

✓ Every baby learns to speak at his or her own pace, but get an expert opinion if you have any concerns.

Chapter 13

Safe and Well-Behaved

ACCORDING TO SAFETY EXPERTS, we parents don't always do the wisest thing when it comes to keeping our children safe at home or on the road. So take the time to reduce the risks as much as you can. Discipline is another subject we should pay attention to. The shift from yesteryear's authoritarian styles of bringing up children to today's liberalism has left many of us wondering which methods make the most sense.

In this chapter . . .

✓ Childproofing your home

✓ Basic first aid

✓ Safety on the road

✓ Encouraging good behavior

✓ Dealing with tantrums

ALWAYS KEEP A CLOSE EYE ON YOUR BABY WHEN HE IS NEAR WATER AND NEVER LEAVE HIM UNATTENDED

Childproofing your home

HOME IS WHERE WE THINK *our children are safest – the irony is, it's where they're most at risk. Statistics show that home is where children under 5 years old are most likely to be when they have an accident of some kind.*

Think about childproofing your home before your child is crawling. Don't wait until he's mobile before you get around to it, or an accident may happen first.

Fires, burning, suffocation, choking, and drowning are the main causes of death in youngsters – and it's children aged between 1 and 4 years old who are most at risk. Children in this age group are also likely to suffer injuries caused by accidents such as falling. The reason that toddlers are so vulnerable to accidents is that they are mobile and curious, but they don't yet understand how to steer clear of dangerous situations.

■ **Young children** *have no real sense of the danger that they can get themselves into – and this can lead to some precarious situations.*

INTERNET

www.childsecure.
com

Detailing various aspects of child health, plus information on safety items.

Being safety-conscious

Making your home safe for a baby, and the toddler he's about to become, means looking at your surroundings from a different perspective. Things that you haven't considered to be hazards before – such as electrical outlets or medicine cabinets within easy reach – could be life-threatening dangers now that your baby is about to become mobile. And if there are general safety issues that you may have neglected – such as installing smoke alarms and keeping a fire extinguisher in the kitchen – now is a good time to deal with them.

Assessing risks

You don't want to compromise your child's safety, but you don't want to get paranoid about it either. Look around your home for dangerous areas and figure out how to deal with them.

To find out what's going to be dangerous to your crawling baby, get down on your hands and knees yourself and explore your home. Then you will be able to see what's visible, tantalizing, and grabbable.

■ **Once your child** *becomes mobile, a stair gate will prevent him going upstairs and having a fall.*

Being realistic

Statistics show that the most common times for accidents to happen are when parents or caregivers are stressed, when a usual routine has been discarded, or if a parent or caregiver is distracted and not able to focus his or her full attention on supervising a child. If you ever witness a near-accident, take immediate measures to rule out the possibility of a potentially more serious repeat episode.

Keep reassessing what you can do to make things safer. But once you've done all this, try to be realistic. Don't feel that you've got to buy every safety device on the market.

Vigilance is the watchword with child safety. However much safety equipment you've got in your house, nothing is more important than your presence to make sure that your baby is safe.

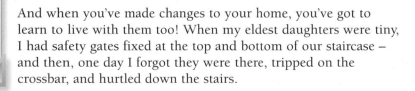

And when you've made changes to your home, you've got to learn to live with them too! When my eldest daughters were tiny, I had safety gates fixed at the top and bottom of our staircase – and then, one day I forgot they were there, tripped on the crossbar, and hurtled down the stairs.

Safety at home – a checklist

There are a number of basic safety rules that all parents should be aware of:

a **Prevent choking:** Don't leave peanuts, hard candy, grapes, or other small objects around. If your baby has access to an older child's toys, especially those that include small pieces, be vigilant and put them out of his reach

b **Prevent drowning:** Never leave your child unattended in or near water, including the bath. Don't rely on buoyancy aids: these are not a substitute for your presence

c **Prevent burns:** Don't leave your child unattended near fire, hot liquid, or other sources of heat: make sure that he can't reach kettle or pan handles. Don't leave hot drinks where your child can tip them over – and always run hot and cold water into the bath at the same time

d **Prevent falls:** Invest in safety gates where appropriate. Don't ever put your child in a seat on a work surface or a table. Make sure that windows are locked or out of reach. Some cities, such as New York, require window guards in all households with young children. Landlords are obligated by law to install them

e **Prevent poisoning:** Keep all medicines, household cleaning products, alcohol, garden chemicals, insecticides, and any other dangerous fluids locked away. Your medicine box should be high up and well out of reach, and all medicines should be kept in it. Don't rely on childproof or child-resistant bottles

■ **Children are fascinated** *by bottles of pills – they look enticing and too much like candy. Although medicine bottles usually have childproof lids, always keep them out of reach of children.*

Basic first aid

LEARNING SOME *first aid won't be wasted once you're a parent. If there's an emergency to deal with, it's very likely that there won't be time for you to refer to a book, and it could be crucial that you know how to react in a potentially life-threatening situation. Many local colleges run evening courses in first aid – it's often better to do something participatory than to buy a manual you'll probably never read.*

■ **If your child** *has been hurt, keep calm, assess the problem, treat the injury to the best of your ability, and, if necessary, seek medical advice.*

General first aid

Learn as much as you can about first aid so that you can do your best when your child has an accident – whether it's minor, or more serious. You're going to be around your own, and other people's, children a lot for the next few years, and any knowledge you have will be useful. If your child has cut his hand, for example, apply pressure on the cut and hold his arm above his head – this will help slow down any bleeding. A cut may not need medical attention – but always make sure that you wash a wound with water and also check that there are no foreign objects or dirt left in it.

Dealing with choking

Every parent should know what to do if their baby is choking. If your child is choking on an object, but is able to cough and is not turning blue from lack of air, give him a series of sharp pats between his shoulder blades – the object should soon be dislodged. If your child is struggling to breathe, hold him upside down supporting his chest with one hand and pat him sharply between the shoulder blades.

■ **When you take a first-aid class,** *you will be able to practice the technique of how to deal with a choking baby on a dummy – this will help you remember what to do if you're ever faced with the situation in real life.*

If this doesn't work after several slaps, give your child's stomach a short, sharp squeeze – this should push the object out of his windpipe. Don't try this unless it's absolutely necessary. For a baby under the age of one, and if back blows do not work, place two fingers over his breastbone and carry out chest compressions.

If your child is choking and not turning blue, you should allow the child to cough. Do not try to remove the object with your fingers.

WHEN A CHILD STOPS BREATHING . . .

In a situation in which a child has stopped breathing, call for medical help and start *rescue breathing* immediately – every second counts. Persevere – you may have to try for a long time before the child will start breathing alone. As you're carrying out rescue breathing, watch the child's chest to see whether it's rising and falling – it should be rising with each breath you give him. If it isn't, tilt his head further back and try again. The following steps apply to toddlers and babies – although, with a baby, it is more effective to cover both his mouth and his nose with your mouth.

> **DEFINITION**
>
> **Rescue breathing**
> *means that you're doing
> the breathing for your child –
> you're putting the air he
> needs into his lungs so that
> his body is oxygenated
> during the period he's not
> breathing for himself.*

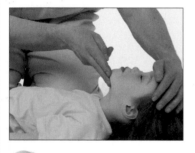

(1) Getting into position

If your child has stopped breathing, lie him on his back and tilt his head back, with his neck arched.

(2) Mouth-to-mouth

Place your mouth over his mouth, pinch his nose, breathe out gently. Repeat until he starts breathing.

■ **Once your child's** *breathing has resumed, place him in the recovery position: lie him on his left side, with his right knee raised.*

Safety on the road

MOST BABIES ARE BORN IN THE HOSPITAL so, for the majority of newborns, a car trip when they're just days or even hours old is almost mandatory. So vital is it that babies of this age are safely strapped into a child seat that some hospitals won't discharge babies unless their parents have a car seat. In fact, some helpful hospitals even offer seats on low-cost loan.

A child car seat could have prevented death or serious injury in two out of three cases where unrestrained children have suffered as a result of a car accident.

Buying a car seat

Remember: your baby can sleep safely without a crib; he can go for walks without a stroller (you can carry him or use a sling); he can have a bath without having a tub of his own (the sink will do). But he absolutely cannot travel in a car without an appropriate car seat – it's the one piece of baby equipment you must, by law, invest in.

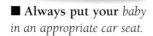

■ **Always put your** *baby in an appropriate car seat.*

Despite an increased use of child safety seats and restraints, motor-vehicle accidents continue to be the leading cause of death among US children under the age of five. In a study of automobile-related deaths, the Fatal Accident Reporting System (FARS) reports that 500 to 700 infants are killed each year in car accidents and among those killed, 70 percent are not restrained. FARS estimates that the use of child safety seats would reduce fatalities by 69 percent for infants and 47 percent for toddlers.

If a car seat has been involved in even a minor accident, it can be damaged. Be wary of second-hand car seats and only accept a gift of one from someone you know so that you can be sure that it hasn't been involved in an accident.

What seat will be suitable?

The general rule is that tiny babies and those who weigh under 22 lb (10 kg) are safest in a rear-facing portable car seat. However, these must never be used in the front passenger seat if there is an airbag on that side, because this could in itself be dangerous to the baby if an accident occurred and the airbag was activated.

Older babies and toddlers should be transported in a conventional child seat that fits into the back of the car, and older children can be given booster seats so that the adult seat belt fits correctly across the chest. If you've got an existing seat that you don't know how to fit, contact the manufacturer and ask for instructions.

Try to buy your car seat from a shop or store where you'll be given help with fitting, too.

If you know you will be traveling in someone else's car, for example, on a trip to a playgroup, think ahead and ask them to borrow a seat – or, if possible, bring your own. Never hold your child on your knee as an alternative option to using a car seat, even if it's just for a short ride.

■ **As your child grows,** *you'll need to invest in a larger seat that can be fitted in the back seat of a car and used in conjunction with a seat belt.*

Encouraging good behavior

THIS SECTION OF THE BOOK *could have been called "preventing bad behavior," because in encouraging the good, you go a long way to discouraging the bad. This is the basic foundation of effective discipline.*

Introducing good discipline

Dealing with naughtiness is a whole new ballgame in today's climate. Over the last couple of generations, our attitudes towards our children's misdemeanors have changed dramatically. The approach isn't so authoritarian, in most families at least; fear and retribution are no longer a big part of the message. Today, discipline is all about ground rules, such as talking to a child rather than shouting at him. The emphasis is on understanding why a child is behaving as he is, rather than on stopping him from misbehaving no matter what.

■ **Giving your child 5 minutes** *of "time out" can be an effective punishment.*

Praising good behavior should always be your front-line of defence against bad behavior. It's easy to forget to do it – but make the effort, because giving your child attention for being good means he won't have to be naughty to attract your interest.

Setting and enforcing rules

Even from the early days with a baby who's just starting to move around and get into things he shouldn't, you need to be clear about the behavior you will and won't tolerate. Clarity is important in getting your message across, even to a young child, because he will pick up whether you really mean what you're saying or not. Don't change your mind from day to day. For example, if you don't normally let your child play with your CD player, don't let him fiddle with it just because you're on the phone. These kind of mixed messages confuse young children and aren't fair to them. Similarly, it's important that you, your partner, and your childcarer have the same ideas about what is and isn't allowed.

When you make a threat, follow through. If you've told your toddler he won't get an ice cream unless he gets down from the bench, then don't give him an ice cream if he doesn't.

Dealing with punishments

The rule about punishments, especially for young children, is that they need to be quick, short, and appropriate for the misdemeanor. Using the time-out chair has had some success in my house – especially for our 2-year-old, who hates above all else to be removed from the center of attention.

Don't delay punishment of a misdemeanor by threatening to keep a child from getting candy tomorrow or next week, because you'll never remember. And even if you do remember, you won't have the heart to do it because your child won't have a clue, so long after the event, why he's being punished.

If your child damages something, get him to "help" fix the item or clean up – it will show him the consequences of his actions. Research shows that hitting or slapping children doesn't work – it doesn't make them stop the behavior you don't like, and it gives them the message that it's okay to hurt someone if they're doing something they don't like. Most parents hit their children because of the stress they feel, not because of what their child is doing. If you feel you're going to "lose it" and strike your child, try counting to 10 or leaving the room for a minute to regain control of yourself. Remaining calm is far more effective.

Dealing with tantrums

TANTRUMS ARE OFTEN LINKED *with the "terrible twos." You can see why, because toddlers of this age are often frustrated, and frustration does fuel the dreaded tantrum. But tantrums aren't solely the province of the 24- to 36-month-old, as many a child who's younger or older sibling will demonstrate. Some children as young as 14 or 16 months have them – and in some cases, repeat performances continue into old age!*

The toddler tantrum is a truly terrifying sight to behold. Terrifying, especially, if you're the toddler-in-question's parent and the setting is – as it so often is – somewhere very public. Like, say, the busiest aisle of your local supermarket. Your toddler says he wants to get out of the cart and you know it would lead to chaos if you let him out. So you resist: you open packet after packet of candy in a desperate attempt to deflect the brewing storm.

If deflection fails, you've got three choices: you can give in to the child's request, produce a bribe, or get out of there (with your child, unfortunately). If you're going to give in, bear in mind that the important thing is to give in right away. There's no point fighting for 10 minutes and THEN giving in.

■ **A child can** *become very worked up, frustrated, and upset during a tantrum.*

Don't hold out over something trivial: these days when we go to the local store, I say "yes" right away to the request for chocolate and I tend to save the real battles for bigger issues. And on these things, it's important not to give in.

Bribes are a tactic that almost every parent will confess to having used at one time or another: some of us never leave home without a box or two of raisins secreted somewhere on our person, just in case. It's the third option, removing yourself and your child from the scene, that causes the most difficulty: who wants to be the parent who has to leave the playgroup or birthday party with a screaming, out-of-control son or daughter? Even though you know every other parent in the room has been through the same thing, it's still a very, very difficult moment to have to deal with.

Understanding what tantrums are about

The bottom line is that tantrums are about control. They come in two types: type one is the frustration tantrum, where your child loses control because he can't work something out. This is the easier kind to deal with, because you can look out for the triggers and deflect a brewing storm. Type two is the one that is hard to deal with: the "I want that" tantrum. Make no mistake: this is the frontline of responsible parenting. Let your child walk all over you once and he'll expect to be able to do it again (and again, and again), and in no time at all your honeykins is everyone else's brat of the year. So, when you think it matters, just say no. It's easier to say than to do, but children do learn fast.

A simple summary

✓ Keeping your child safe is the main priority in childcare: everything else pales in comparison.

✓ We all care about our children's safety, but there are ways that we can be more vigilant.

✓ Childproof your home before your baby becomes mobile – it's better to be well prepared.

✓ Learn about first aid so that you can act quickly in an accident – whether it's minor, or serious.

✓ Safety equipment can help you look after your baby, but it's not a substitute for a vigilant parent.

✓ Praising good behavior is the foundation of good discipline.

✓ Resist getting angry with your child for minor misdemeanors: keep rules to a minimum, but be firm about enforcing the things that really matter.

✓ Once in a while, you'll have a big showdown. Keep your resolve and carry through your threats.

Chapter 14

My Baby's Growing Up Fast

To you, of course, your baby has always been a very definite "separate person." To the rest of the world, however, she's probably just been "the baby." Friends and relations will have cooed over her, but without really knowing a lot about what she's really like. But now it's becoming clear to everyone that she is a little person with a distinctive personality and pronounced likes and dislikes. This isn't a "milestone" in your child's life, but it is an indicator that she's moving on through babyhood and getting to the point where she'd probably enjoy some activities that are a little more stimulating than simply watching you peel the potatoes or having a rattle shaken in her direction.

In this chapter . . .

✓ Toddler gym classes

✓ Swimming babies

✓ The toddler social circuit

✓ Make time to be together

YOUR TODDLER WILL BE CURIOUS ABOUT EVERYTHING AND WILL WANT TO COPY THE THINGS YOU DO

Toddler gym classes

GYM CLASSES FOR TODDLERS are very popular. They usually
cater to babies of 6 months or over, and some groups have classes for up to
7-year-olds and beyond, so it can be the start of an ongoing commitment.

Attending gym classes

The classes concentrate on children's motor skills and coordination. The babies are
encouraged to roll over and kick their legs, and as they get older they also learn to
balance, run, jump, hop, and climb. No one is forced to do anything, and until they're
3 years old or so, a caregiver stays with each child, guiding her through the activities
– there are usually plenty of paid helpers on hand.

*Signing up for a gym class can be expensive, so make sure
that you're free to do the class each week, and that
it's somewhere you'll be happy to get to,
whatever the weather.*

Play centers

A cheaper option than a gym class, if you think your baby will benefit
from doing some kind of gym, is to go to a local play center. These are
usually pay-as-you-go, so they are less expensive than paying for a whole
gym class upfront. Like a gym class, play center programs, such as
Gymboree, usually involve singing and hand-clapping as
well as movement. Play leaders will be on hand to encourage
and help your child. Sessions
can be great fun and
children tend to enjoy
feeling part of a group.

■ **Practice hand-clapping**
games with your baby.

Don't think that your child will miss out if you don't want to sign up for a gym class. Go to one or two play or activity centers instead and then try the things you learn at home – preferably, with a few little friends as well as your own child.

Never sign up for a gym class – or any other kind of class – without a trial lesson. That way you can check that your baby is going to enjoy the class – and that you will, too.

Swimming babies

JUST A FEW YEARS AGO, *almost no one took a baby swimming. Today, most swimming pools have a program of classes and groups aimed at even the youngest customers and their parents. These classes are enormously popular. Just as more and more women are choosing to use water during childbirth, so more parents are choosing to introduce their babies to the joys of water and swimming at an ever-younger age.*

Trivia…
It's sometimes said that babies shouldn't go to a public swimming pool until they've had their initial immunizations: this isn't true. If this was the case, babies whose parents decided against immunization wouldn't ever be able to go swimming!

Should I take my baby swimming?

Is it a good idea? Well, a lot of claims are made for the long-term benefits of early swimming. A German study found that babies who swim have more advanced motor development, social skills, and intelligence, while a Finnish study found that it helps babies to talk earlier. Swimming instructors often claim that babies who swim regularly tend to sleep more soundly, and that they are less likely than other babies to suffer from colds, sniffles, and even asthma.

The first few times you take your baby swimming, take some of her familiar bath toys along too – they might help her feel at home.

While beneficial effects are all well and good, the most important considerations when thinking about taking your baby swimming are: will she enjoy it and will you enjoy it?

Is it a good idea to start early?

Enthusiasts of baby swimming classes say that the earlier you start taking your baby to the swimming pool, the better. This is because she's less likely to develop a fear of water, and also she'll get used to the techniques taught at the class from early on.

However early you take your baby swimming, make sure that the pool is chlorinated, and heated to at least 89.6° F (32° C).

Under the age of 6 months, babies don't possess the mechanisms for regulating their own temperature; after 6 months they do begin to have it, but you still have to be very careful that they don't get too cold in the water.

Toddler swimming classes

Parent and toddler classes are usually taught in small groups of five or six parent and baby couples (it is usually mothers, although most classes are more than happy if it's the dad rather than the mom who goes along).

Often, there's nursery rhyme singing and children's music in the background. Lots of the exercises are aimed at getting your toddler used to the idea of being in the water. Some classes involve submerging the baby's head under the water for a second or two – young babies have what's called a **diving instinct** that will automatically kick in when this happens.

> **DEFINITION**
>
> *The **diving instinct** means babies will naturally hold their breath when they are underwater. This tends to disappear at 6 months, but can last longer in a child who's used to being dunked underwater.*

■ **Let your child** *have fun in the water, and don't have unrealistic expectations about her progress: children under the age of 3 or 4 years can't learn to swim properly because they haven't got enough muscle control.*

Of course, you don't have to join a formal class to enjoy a trip to the local pool with your baby – although it is often more fun for both of you if you team up with another parent and baby. Try finding a pool with some sort of child care so that you can swim for a while on your own before or after going for a dip with your toddler.

Don't be surprised if your child loses interest in swimming at around 1 year of age – it's a common phenomenon. But do continue to take her to the pool from time to time anyway – it may take a year or so, but eventually she'll start enjoying it again.

Try taking a brightly colored inflatable ball along to the pool with you, to give your baby something to look at and play with in the water. Let her lie on her back, with your hands supporting her, so that she can kick. And when she's happy to go on her front, glide her through the water so that she gets used to the feel of "swimming" through the pool.

The toddler social circuit

SOME TODDLERS HAVE SCHEDULES *that make you feel tired just looking at them! Monday it's music group, Tuesday toddler gym, Wednesday playgroup, Thursday swimming, Friday massage class – not to mention weekends packed with social activities.*

Getting the right balance

The truth is, it's all too much – if it sounds too much for a 30-something mother like me, it's got to be too much for a tiny tot who still needs daytime naps and is still learning how things work and where she fits into the world.

That, in fact, is the essence – your toddler still has a lot to learn, and almost any situation, properly used, has learning opportunities for her, whether it's a specially designed activity or not.

You don't have to be part of a group or class for your toddler to be taking things in and learning from them.

INTERNET

www.parentcenter.com

This web site has lots of information on where to go and what to do with your older baby and toddler.

Having said that, a baby of 6 or 9 months plus does gain from inclusion in some sort of group from time to time. It doesn't have to be a formal thing – you might just dip into a playgroup of a local church or temple when you can find the time, and that's as good a start into the world of socializing as anything, and it's usually inexpensive.

One or two group sessions or classes per week are ample for a child in this age group. Schedule lots of time for one-to-one fun at home or at the park, too.

Your baby's social life with her caregiver

Babies who are looked after by a caregiver sometimes have the busiest social lives of all. It's worth taking stock with your caregiver from time to time if you think your child is being taken to too many activities. It's easy to see why it could happen – unlike you when you're at home, your nanny or au pair doesn't have to run the house, so the chance to go out and mix with other people has a big appeal.

Initially, you may be eager to have your caregiver signing your baby up for a lot of activities. But keep in mind that your child needs lots of one-to-one care as well. Try to discourage your nanny from having friends over or going to a group every day of the week – suggest that some days are just for "chilling out" at home.

PLAYGROUPS

One of the most rewarding ways to connect with other parents and children your child's age is to join a playgroup. These are informal affairs that take place as often as two or three times a week and last for a couple of hours or more; moms (or dads) take turns inviting the group into their own home or backyard, although some groups choose to meet in more public places, such as parks, playgrounds, or the local church or synagogue. "Neutral" spaces like these can be good choices for 2- and 3-year-olds, who are often very possessive about their toys!

A playgroup can be extremely beneficial for parents as well as children because it gives them an opportunity to share their concerns and worries about parenting, as well as to enjoy a little socializing themselves. If you're a newcomer to the community, joining a playgroup is an ideal way to break the ice and get to know your neighbors.

Make time to be together

WHETHER YOU WORK IN OR OUTSIDE *of the home, you need down time with your toddler, too. It doesn't have to be time when you're just sitting around doing nothing – but it should be a time when your life isn't being ruled by the clock, and when you don't have lots and lots of other demands pressing in on you all at once.*

Playing at home

Some of the happiest times with my current toddler, Miranda, have been the days when we've both been lounging around at home while her older sisters were at school. The school day is amazingly short when you're trying to get things done: you only get around 5 hours before it's time for the children to come home. I found that it helped to downsize my expectations about what I could achieve in a day. I still usually managed to straighten up the bedrooms, Miranda in tow. And as we wandered around making beds and putting teddies back on their shelves, we had lots of time to sit around reading a book, or singing along with some nursery rhymes on her tape machine.

■ **Relaxing with your baby** *is just as important as getting out and about. Quiet time spent together gives you the best opportunity to talk to your baby while your mind is focusing on her alone.*

What shall we do?

Talking to your child, reading with her, and singing to her are the three basic essentials of spending time together. You don't need lots of equipment or to be part of a group to be able to do this – you just need to have time, and one or two of your child's favorite books on hand.

Picture books are excellent at this stage. I've always particularly enjoyed sharing the kind that have large color photographs of things children are familiar with – a cup, a swing, a television set, and so on. Babies enjoy looking at and recognizing the items pictured. Try repeating the names and talking a bit about the different things on the page – this will help with your baby's early language development.

Small children love photographs of people they know. Buy a cheap photo album with plastic see-through slots for the pictures, and give your baby her own picture book to fill with photographs.

Outings and expeditions

Going on outings together is another way to have fun. Of course, trips with another parent and child are very rewarding, too. But do reserve some trips for just the two of you, as you'll find you're more likely to talk to your baby if you're alone with her.

There are lots of things you can do out of the house with a baby or toddler. Don't assume that you have to leave everything until your child is older. Art galleries, for example, can be great at this stage, but the trick is not to be too ambitious. Go to a gallery where you know children are welcomed, and concentrate on looking at just one or two areas. You can plan your trip so that your baby has a sleep while you're there, giving you some free time to walk around with the stroller.

■ **Children who were** *introduced to animals at an early age are far more likely to be comfortable with them as they get older.*

Make time apart, too

Fun as your baby is, you'll find your relationship with her is actually strengthened if you manage to spend at least part of the time away from her.

Try to find another mother with a child the same age as yours, who'll do a child care swap with you for a couple of hours each week.

A baby of 6 months plus is old enough to be left with another mother or caregiver for short periods – you don't have to invest in formal child care. If you have a regular evening babysitter, it can be a good idea to get her to look after your child occasionally during the day, too. This will help to strengthen the bond between her and your baby and increase your confidence about leaving them when you go out at night.

■ **Making time** *for yourself is beneficial for you and your baby – catch up with your friends, and enjoy some exercise.*

A simple summary

✔ At this age, your baby is old enough to enjoy some sociable activities such as playgroups, play centers, or toddler gym.

✔ Consider joining a baby swimming class – the benefits are worth the effort.

✔ Time spent relaxing at home with a parent or caregiver is still vital for a child.

✔ Keep an eye on the number of group activities your baby is involved in, and make sure that she's receiving plenty of one-to-one care.

✔ Plan a few outings with your baby, either just the two of you or with another parent and child. Do something you'll all enjoy.

✔ Remember that it's important to plan some time for yourself, too.

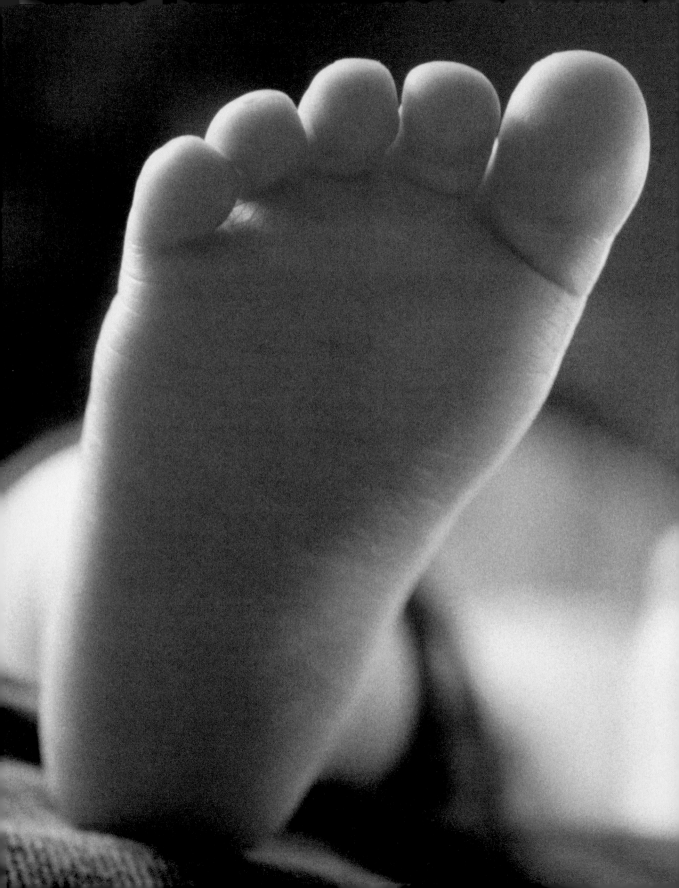

Chapter 15

He's On the Move

WHEN YOU HOLD YOUR TINY BABY in your arms in the early weeks and months after his birth, it's truly astounding to think that in a year or so this little person will have control of all his limbs and be able to take himself wherever he wants to be (often, that's precisely where you'd rather he wasn't!). The way a baby learns to be mobile, and the speed with which he achieves it, is astonishing. Between the ages of 6 and 18 months, your baby will go from sitting propped up, to crawling, to walking around holding onto the furniture, and then – before you know it – to walking around independently.

In this chapter . . .

✓ Mobility and how it develops

✓ Helping him learn to walk

✓ Don't expect too much

BY THE AGE OF 10 MONTHS, YOUR BABY HAS GOOD CONTROL OF THE MUSCLES IN HIS FEET

Mobility and how it develops

AS YOUR BABY GROWS, he will begin to understand the boundaries of his own body. At the same time, his muscles will start to strengthen so that he has the ability to control his head and limbs. This muscle control usually starts to happen from the head downward.

In the first few weeks and months of his life, your baby will concentrate first on strengthening his neck, so that he can hold up his own head; strengthening his back, so that he can manage to sit by himself; and learning to use his hands and arms.

As he grows stronger, he will be increasingly eager to flex his muscles and he will become more and more fidgety and restless when he's put in a sitting position.

Give your baby regular opportunities to practice moving around on his own – without the restriction of a diaper.

CHECK OUT THOSE HIPS

Babies are checked for hip abnormalities or "clicky hips" at birth and at every checkup until they are walking (usually 2, 4, 6, 9, and 12 months.) This condition – developmental dysplasia of the hip – means that the hip joint is in the wrong place, or that it moves too easily in and out of its ball socket. The earlier dislocation is picked up, the more successful treatment is likely to be.

Clicky hips affect three or four babies in every 1,000 – it is more likely to occur in newborns, and girls are 7 times more likely to be affected than boys. There are some predisposing factors to the disorder, and if they affect your baby, point these out at checkups. These include low levels of amniotic fluid while your baby was in the womb and a family history of childhood hip disorders. Even though your baby will be checked at birth and at 2- or 3-month intervals, some hip problems may be missed until the baby starts to walk. If your child seems to have a limp when he first begins to walk, don't hesitate to consult a doctor.

INTERNET

www.steps-charity.org.uk

If your child has any kind of lower limb or hip abnormality, or you're worried he might have, this web site is full of useful information.

Learning to move

Once he's got the basics of controlling his upper body down, your baby's attention will turn to the possibility of whole-body movement. Between the ages of 4 and 6 months, your baby will probably show an interest in rolling over – first from his belly onto his back, and then from his back onto his belly.

Creeping and scooting

The next stage is often *creeping*. You'll find your baby can move a surprising distance in this way – often (as with most new movement) he's attracted to some object across the room and literally makes a move for it.

By the age of 9 months, most babies are eager to move around on their own. When they're sitting up, they're often very frustrated at not being able to reach an object they want. Some will cry to be picked up or to be given something, but others take matters into their own hands – or, more literally, bottoms – by starting to scoot along on their buttocks. This turns out to be a surprisingly efficient way of getting around, and many babies are content to scoot along for some time.

> **DEFINITION**
>
> **Creeping** is the unfathomable process by which a baby manages to move himself halfway across a room even though you know he can't crawl yet. When the baby is left lying on his front on a blanket, he may inch himself forward, bit by bit. It can give a parent quite a surprise to find their child isn't where they put him!

There is evidence that babies who scoot to get around are slower at learning to walk than those who crawl, but this isn't a cause for concern. The reason for this may be that a scooting baby finds he can move pretty quickly, and still enjoy a relatively upright position. Crawling babies find it frustrating that they have to raise their heads to see and, as a result, they tend to move on to walking as soon as possible.

■ **Crawling babies** *can find it awkward to hold their heads up to see where they're going – this is a good incentive to start walking.*

■ **Babies love** *the freedom that crawling gives them, and the chance to explore everything.*

Starting to crawl

Think of a baby and you often think of a crawler. Crawling, to many people, sums up the stage of mid-babyhood – no longer a babe in arms, but still a little way off from becoming a toddler. However, even though the majority of babies crawl, many bypass this stage altogether. You can encourage crawling by lying your baby on his stomach for a short time, while you're there to supervise. As your baby gains strength in his upper body, he will begin pushing up with his arms. Eventually, his legs will be strong enough to get him onto his knees. Often his attempts to get going are stimulated by something across the room that he'd like to get his hands on!

As soon as your baby is mobile, you need to review safety around your home. Even if you thought you'd made everything childproof, check again.

TO CRAWL OR NOT TO CRAWL

The "back to sleep" campaign was launched in the 1990s, and its aim was to encourage parents to lay their babies on their backs to sleep, rather than on their stomachs, to reduce the risk of crib death. New research shows that this may be a factor in why fewer babies are learning to crawl. Because babies are spending less time lying on their stomachs, they are not using their arms and legs to start crawling as they did in the past. However, this does not seem to affect a child's development – whether a child crawls or not, the average age for starting to walk is still around 12 months of age.

■ **Research shows that** *significant numbers of babies are no longer crawling, and are moving straight on to walking instead.*

And they're off!

Once a baby is up, he's off – although, frustratingly for the child who's got an object he wants in view, early efforts at crawling can often result in the child feeling more despondent than ever about reaching his target!

A variation on crawling is "bear walking" – a baby gets onto his hands and feet and walks like a bear. Sometimes this is a stage between crawling and walking, but for other babies it is the main means of mobility for some weeks.

Standing up and "cruising"

Human beings are built to stand up and see the world biped-style so, not surprisingly, your 9-, 10-, or 11-month old baby is desperate to get up there and see how it all looks! The first stage will involve pulling himself upright by holding on to a coffee table or chair – once his legs and back are strong enough, he'll be eager to stand up.

Investing in soft corners to stick on tables may be a good idea – your child will be clinging to furniture a lot at this stage, and table corners can cause injuries if babies fall against them.

From this stage, it's a short hop to "cruising," or moving around the room with the help of furniture to hang on to. When he finds that he can do this, your baby will be delighted. Not only is he able to look at the world from a standing position, but he has found that he can get around like that, too.

■ **Your baby** *will start pulling himself up to a standing position, using furniture that is within his reach.*

Trivia...

Your baby's feet will carry him on average 70,000 miles during his lifetime – that's the equivalent of five times around the globe.

While your baby is learning to walk, look around your home for pieces of furniture he may try to use to pull himself up on, but which won't be strong enough to support his weight. Put these away for now, because if he tries hanging on to them and then falls over, his confidence will suffer a set-back and he may hurt himself. Don't start panicking because you hear other parents saying that their babies are walking already and yours isn't. Remember that all babies learn to walk in their own time.

Learning to walk

A baby's first steps are a huge milestone – definitely something to get the camera out for and put in a few calls to the proud grandparents! But no baby just suddenly stands up and walks – in fact, it's often difficult to establish exactly when the first independent steps took place. That's because, like everything your child is learning, walking is achieved as a process. First, he learned to pull himself up on furniture; then, to walk a step or two between a table and a chair. Do you count these as his first steps, or do you wait until a few weeks later, when he's confident enough and strong enough to walk toward you when you put your hands out?

■ **A walking toy** *can be a good buy at this stage – but make sure it's sturdy enough for your child to pull himself up on and that it won't topple over while he pushes it along.*

Helping him learn to walk

WHILE THERE'S A LOT YOU CAN DO to encourage your baby to enjoy learning to use his body and to find out what he's capable of, babies learn to walk whether they're given lots of stimulating exercise or not. So if your baby isn't the first in his group to learn to walk, don't blame yourself for not doing enough to help him. And remember that it isn't possible to make a baby walk before he's ready.

Don't purchase a "baby walker." There are fears that these devices can harm a baby's muscles. They are also dangerous near stairs. However, the stationary devices that allow a baby to bounce in one position are fine.

Have fun!

There are lots of games you can play that encourage your baby to move on his own. One you can try from his early weeks and months, and continue until he's quite big, is to lie him down on his back on a bed or on a blanket on the floor, and push your hands against the soles of his feet. As his strength grows, he'll enjoy being able to push you away, and you can gradually push a bit harder yourself to make the game a little more difficult. Baby massage is also a good way to strengthen your baby's muscles.

A golden rule that applies throughout parenthood is to consolidate what your child already knows, rather than move him on to something he isn't ready for yet.

Build on his confidence – when he's confident he can do one thing, his natural instinct is to move on to the next. Conversely, if you try to move him on to something he's not ready for yet, he's likely to lose some confidence and may even go back a stage in his development. When he is able to hold on to furniture and move between tables and chairs around the room, it can be great fun to set up a kind of "adventure course." He can then cruise from one piece of furniture to the next. If he's ready for it – but only if – move a table just that fraction further away from where it was last time, and see if he'll take a shot at reaching it.

Don't worry if things slow down

Children don't make constant progress in every area of their development, and that certainly includes mobility. Your baby might be crawling at 8 months, but still not walking at 13 months. If it's causing you real concern, it's worth getting a check-up from your pediatrician – but it's unlikely that there's anything wrong. Don't forget that at this age your baby is making huge strides forward – metaphorically speaking – in all areas of his life. Sometimes, he concentrates on some other aspect of his development and doesn't appear to make any progress in his mobility for a few weeks.

If your child has an illness, even just a sniffy cold that lays him low for a day or two, he may regress and go back a stage or two while he's getting better. For example, a child who's started to walk may become a crawler again, or hold out his arms to be carried all the time until he's well again.

■ **Encourage your** *child to learn to walk by playing "walking" games together. This will help give your child an example of the kind of movements to make, and it will also show your toddler that walking is fun!*

195

Don't expect too much

JUST BECAUSE YOUR BABY has learned to walk, don't expect him to be able to use this new skill to walk long distances. This won't happen for a long time – he's likely to be 3 or more before you can expect him to hold your hand and walk somewhere with you.

To a toddler, walking is an exploratory exercise, not a practical means of getting somewhere. Even when your toddler is 2 years old, walking still means the chance to explore up and down people's driveways

■ **When you're a toddler,** *walking is about having fun, rather than actually getting to a destination – let your children walk at their own pace, and let them stop and look at things.*

THE FIRST PAIR OF SHOES

While your baby is still sitting and crawling, shoes are largely decorative, although it's important that they are not too small. When children start to walk, however, they often curl their toes, so it's better for a child to go barefoot or wear socks or padders for as long as possible. The bones in a child's feet are very soft and can be easily damaged – this can lead to posture problems. Wait until your child is walking unaided, or ready to walk around outside, before buying him his first pair of shoes. Always take your child shoe-shopping when he's alert and happy, not tired and cross. Ask the fitter to point out the shoes that offer the best fit for his feet, and choose a shoe that will allow your child's feet to "breathe" – leather uppers are the best option. You need to get his feet measured by someone who's properly qualified. The length of the child's foot isn't enough – you need to check how wide his feet are too.

■ **Before your child** *is walking, material shoes are fine for him to wear when he goes out in his pram. But once he's on his feet, his shoes should be soft enough to allow movement, but sturdy enough to provide proper support.*

and to look in wonder at the leaves that have fallen from the trees. You'll be making life difficult and frustrating for both of you if you expect a walk to actually get you somewhere. Wait until your toddler is old enough to make a decision about walking himself, otherwise you may not get very far.

Reining in

Some parents invest in a pair of reins so that they can keep a close watch on their child. Reins can certainly be a lifesaver, especially if you've several children to look after, and need to walk along a busy street. If you do use reins, however, take care not to rely on them too heavily. As he grows older, your child needs to learn about road safety and about the importance of staying close to you when you're out. Also, when you're away from busy roads, he needs the freedom and space to stray a little from your side.

■ **Always take** *a stroller with you on any walks, so that you can put your toddler in it when he gets tired of walking.*

A simple summary

✔ There are various ways that babies find to get around before they start toddling. Some crawl, some creep along on their tummies, and some scoot around.

✔ You can encourage your baby to crawl by lying him on his stomach for a few minutes each day while you're around to supervise him.

✔ There are games that you can play to encourage your child to start walking and to be more ambitious in his mobility skills.

✔ When your baby has learned to walk, remember that it's still a new experience for him – don't expect him to walk everywhere with you now.

Chapter 16

Childhood Illnesses

A BIG WORRY FOR PARENTS is that their children will get ill with something serious, and they won't recognize it or act quickly enough. This is an understandable fear. Babies and small children can get very sick quite suddenly, and you need to be vigilant. On the other hand, having a new baby doesn't mean an inevitable string of illnesses. Many children get through their early years without much in the way of illness. The important thing is to be ready to drop everything and to move quickly if you suspect your child is ill, but to have confidence that your baby is probably quite healthy and likely to remain so.

In this chapter . . .

✓ Natural immunity

✓ Is it serious?

✓ Types of illnesses

✓ Taking care of a sick child

✓ Talking to medical staff

THE PRESENCE OF A FAVORITE TEDDY BEAR CAN HELP COMFORT YOUR CHILD WHEN SHE'S NOT FEELING WELL

Natural immunity

ONE IMPORTANT REASON to breastfeed, if you can, is that your milk will provide your child with immunity to help fight off diseases. In the past, breast milk used to be referred to as "white blood" because, like blood, it is a living tissue. In particular, it contains leucocytes – cells that contain important antibodies.

Immunity from disease

Studies have shown that breastfed babies may be protected by any immunity the mother has to various viral diseases – including measles, mumps, polio, herpes, hepatitis, some kinds of pneumonia, and some respiratory infections.

This immunity lasts for around 3 months, although it doesn't necessarily end as soon as you give up breastfeeding. But it does "protect your baby" while her own immune system is developing. You may notice that, even if you and the rest of the family come down with an infection, your baby either escapes altogether, or only gets a mild form of it.

If you are breastfeeding in the early months, you will be giving your baby a kind of "invisible shield" to help ward off some illnesses.

The risk of infections

But this protection doesn't mean infections are unknown in breastfed babies, and bottle-fed babies are vulnerable too. It's over-cautious to try to protect your baby from infection with too much vigor, but it isn't paranoid on your part to avoid obvious sources of infections – it's a good idea to keep her away from someone whom you know has got flu, for example.

If you are bottle-feeding, the most likely source of infection is the nipple. Be scrupulous about sterilizing bottles and nipples.

The likelihood of your child getting sick increases, depending on how exposed she is to infection. If you have older children, socialize with other people a lot, or if your baby has been in daycare for the last 3 months because you had to go back to work, then you should expect some early colds and infections.

Is it serious?

MOST EARLY CHILDHOOD ILLNESSES *have similar symptoms: your child may have a raised temperature, be lethargic and out-of-sorts, cry a lot, and not eat as well as usual. It's a horrible feeling to know that your baby is under the weather. As well as wishing you could do more to make her better, there's always the suspicion at the back of your mind that something might be seriously wrong.*

Recognizing serious symptoms

If your baby has a good color, is alert, eating a little, and breathing normally, she's probably fine. If she has a high fever, however, and is over 6 months old give her acetaminophen or ibuprofen. Bathe her in tepid (not cold) water while waiting for the medication to take effect. A low grade fever may require no intervention if your baby or child is not particularly bothered by it. Fever in and of itself is not usually dangerous, but depending on the age of your child and how high the fever is you may need to call the doctor.

Sickness and diarrhea are obviously indications that your child is ill. This is of more concern when your child is very young, although even an older child can become dangerously dehydrated once she starts losing fluids – especially from both ends. If this is happening, seek advice from a doctor straight away.

Always consult a doctor immediately if you see signs of dehydration, such as sunken eyes, loose skin, or sunken fontanelles (soft part of a baby's skull).

Older children can help you determine how ill they are by giving a description of how they're feeling. However, don't take what your child tells you too literally. If your 3-year-old tells you that she's got a tummy ache, for example, she may just mean that she's got a pain – it doesn't necessarily mean it's in her stomach.

■ **To check your child's** *temperature, place a mercury thermometer under her arm and hold it for a few minutes. Alternatively, use a tympanic (ear) thermometer.*

FEBRILE SEIZURES

Very occasionally, a young child with a high fever will have a convulsion, known as a *febrile seizure*. She may lose consciousness, her body may go rigid, her eyes may roll, her teeth clench, her skin turn pale, and she may stop breathing.

Don't try to restrain a child who is seizing: stay calm, turn her head gently to one side, and put something soft under her. When she recovers from the seizure, she's likely to be confused. Take off her clothes to reduce her temperature, give her ibuprofen, and sponge her with tepid water. If there's another fit soon afterwards, or if the fit continues for more than 10 minutes, call a doctor immediately.

> **DEFINITION**
>
> A **febrile seizure** *occurs when the brain cannot cope with a sudden rise in temperature. It's the suddenness of the rise, rather than the temperature the body reaches, that's the problem.*

Types of illnesses

MOST BABIES WILL HAVE at least one cold in their first year. A child who's in contact with a lot of people will tend to have a greater number of colds and sniffles – so if your baby is in daycare or at a busy babysitter's, for example, or if you have an older child in school, be prepared. On the other hand, preventing colds is virtually impossible. The best thing you can do is to be there for her when she's feeling sick.

A baby with a cold

Babies panic when they get a cold because they can't breathe through their noses. Although they aren't seriously ill, dealing with a baby who can't breast- or bottle-feed because of a cold can be a traumatic experience. It's terrible to be sitting with breastfuls of milk while you're holding a hungry baby who'd love to nurse but can't. The baby will keep breaking off and crying piteously because she simply can't understand why her beloved breast or bottle isn't the comfort it usually is. You can help by clearing her nose with a suction bulb that you can buy at the drugstore – the process of sucking out the mucus is sometimes helped by putting a few drops of saline solution, also available from the drugstore, into the nose first.

My child gets everything!

Some children seem to fall prey to every bug that goes around. Sometimes it's because they have a "weakness" in a particular area – it might be that they have recurring throat and respiratory tract infections, ear infections, or eye infections.

If your child seems to get sick with high temperatures or vomiting more often than other children, it is worth going to your doctor to ask about a blood test for anemia. If she has low blood iron, this can be treated with supplements. You might also want to look at your child's diet, and think about whether she's eating enough fresh fruit and vegetables.

■ **It's very important** *to see your pediatrician about any recurring problem, however minor, because repeated infections can cause long-term damage.*

Asthma in children

This is a respiratory disorder that causes difficulty in breathing. Some say asthma is like coming up from being underwater for a long time and then having to suck air through a straw. It's most likely to strike a child who has two parents with the condition. The prevalence of asthma among children in the U.S. is estimated at 3.6–9.5 percent (depending on the study and the questionnaire used.) This ranges from 12–16 percent of inner city children to 5–7 percent of suburban children.

Technically, it isn't asthma if your child is under 18 months because she doesn't have the muscle control to squeeze her lung airways closed. This action is what causes asthma.

A persistent cough or wheezing are common symptoms of asthma – often the wheeze is triggered by an allergen (common ones are dust, pollen, or a cold). Pediatricians deal with many cases of mild asthma without referral to a specialist, but children with more severe cases are usually referred to a pediatric pulmonologist. The more specialized the medical staff who deal with your child the better, because the usual method of dealing with asthma is to prescribe steroids, but these can be harmful if taken over time. They are most effective when they are used in an inhaler, since they are then taken straight to the lungs. Oral steroids are generally only given for short periods during an acute asthma attack. If your child has to take steroids, make sure that your doctor is giving your child the least amount of the drug in the most efficient way.

COMMON CHILDHOOD ILLNESSES

Croup

The symptoms are a hoarse or lost voice, followed by a dry cough that leaves a child fighting for breath. There is often a "whoop" on breathing in. Keep your child calm – the calmer she is the easier she'll be able to breathe. Fill the sink or bathtub with hot water or turn on the shower full blast to create steam – this makes breathing easier. If breathing difficulties persist for more than 10 minutes, seek medical help.

If it's night time and your baby's breathing has improved, put her in her crib. Prop the end up so that her head is slightly raised.

Impetigo

This appears as small blisters that turn into areas of pus covered by thin skin. It is a highly infectious bacterial infection that requires a prescription for antibiotic cream or antibiotics from your pediatrician. The infection spreads like wildfire so keep your child away from other children. Keep your infected child's wash cloth and towel separate from yours and anyone else's in the family.

Chickenpox

This illness is not commonly seen in the U.S. anymore, due to vaccination. It starts with a raised temperature and your child may feel generally out-of-sorts; red spots will then appear on the face and body. These will turn to blisters and burst, crust, and dry before healing. Try to discourage scratching of blisters, because this can cause scars. Your child will generally feel better, although still uncomfortable, after a day or two. There is no need to go to the doctor unless you have particular worries. Chickenpox is infectious until the blisters have stopped forming and have dried and crusted over – usually this takes a week or so from the first indication of illness.

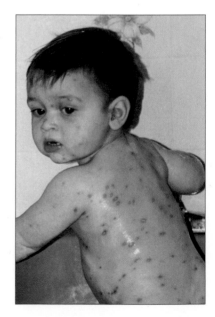

■ **Lukewarm baths** *help soothe the skin when your child has chickenpox. After a bath, apply calamine lotion to reduce itching.*

Conjunctivitis

The main symptom of conjunctivitis is a sore, inflamed eye – often, both eyes are affected. Take your child to the doctor for eye drops or ointment – don't use over-the-counter treatments because they often don't work and you end up delaying a visit to your pediatrician. Get your child to lie down to insert the drops. If you have a baby or a very young child, ask someone else to help. Keep your child's wash cloth and towel separate from the rest of the family, because conjunctivitis is highly contagious

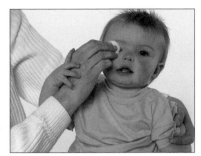

■ **Wipe any** *crusty discharge away from the infected eye – use a fresh cotton ball for each wipe.*

Molluscum contagiosum

This appears as little whitish yellow, pearl-like spots that can occur singly or in clusters. They should go away on their own, although this may take some months. If your child has an extensive breakout, see your pediatrician.

Pinworms

Symptoms include an itchy bottom or a tummy-ache. A doctor can prescribe a drug to treat them. Pinworms are so common it's thought that half of all children under the age of ten get them at some time: prevention is the best defense. When your child scratches her bottom and then puts her hands near her mouth, this can transfer eggs and start the cycle again, so scrub your child's fingernails and put her to bed at night in pants.

Head lice

If your child keeps scratching her head, she may have head lice. These are passed from child to child and are unpleasant but not dangerous. However, they can eventually take their toll on your child's system because lice are parasites, so you need to be vigilant. Chemical lotions and special shampoos will get rid of them, but contain fairly strong ingredients. An alternative is to "nit comb" the lice out using a special comb and conditioner – this is time-consuming and you'll have to repeat the process every third day until there's no sign of the lice at all. Prevent lice taking hold by inspecting and brushing the hair regularly.

INTERNET

www.cps.ca
www.canadian-health-network.ca
www.medicinenet.com

These web sites offer information on health issues, including childhood illnesses and diseases.

Taking care of a sick child

LOOKING AFTER A SICK BABY *or child takes time; often, it takes all your time for several days or until she's well again. If your child is slightly sick, it may be possible for someone else – your babysitter or nanny, for example – to care for her. But if she is really sick, it's likely that only you or your partner will do.*

Bedside tips

It can be really difficult to suddenly drop everything to be with your sick child, but do make every effort to devote yourself to her while she's feeling really bad. You may be giving her medicine and following the prescribed way of caring for her, but at the end of the day your presence will be every bit as important in making her well again.

If your child doesn't like taking her medicine, lie her down with her head slightly raised, or if she's a baby put her in her high chair. Then, use a syringe to feed the medicine to her.

You can help your child to swallow her medicine if you gently lift her chin up so that her mouth is kept shut as she swallows the liquid. Stroking your finger along her throat lightly will usually encourage her to swallow.

There may be periods of 1 or 2 hours when she's asleep and you can do other things, but if she's drifting in and out of sleep you really need to put her first. Once she starts getting better, your nursing role will be made easier if you have a stack of interesting books and audio or video tapes to keep her occupied. Keep a special book or video on hand for just these occasions – illness can catch you off guard, so it's good to be prepared.

■ **When your** *child is sick, put her to bed and keep an eye on her. If she is feeling nauseous, leave a bowl by her bed. Encourage her to drink water so that she doesn't get dehydrated.*

Talking to medical staff

GOING TO A HEALTH PROFESSIONAL *can be daunting at any time. And if you have a sick child with you and you're very worried, it can be difficult to remember all the questions you want to ask. Afterwards, it can be even harder to remember everything you've been told.*

Asking questions and explaining symptoms

Your doctor won't think it's silly if you're armed with a list of questions – and it helps to write down the points he or she makes about your child's illness. Don't worry about "taking up too much time" – the doctor is there to deal with people like you and your child, so take the time you need to get the information you want.

Don't feel that a concern is "too small" to ask your doctor about; if it's worrying you, it's worth consulting a professional about it.

One of the most important ways of telling that there's something wrong with a young child is when she's "not herself." The doctor, of course, doesn't know what your child is like when she's "herself," so it's important to explain what's different from the way she usually is. If you're concerned about an underlying medical condition that you feel should be investigated, don't let your doctor dismiss you. In fact, most doctors I've come across give a lot of weight to the intuitive feelings parents have about their children's health. If you don't think your doctor takes your views seriously, maybe you should think about changing your doctor.

ALTERNATIVE THERAPY

Two reliable sources of information on complementary and alternative medicine are the National Institutes of Health web site (www.nih.gov) and the National Center for Complementary and Alternative Medicine (www.nccam.nih.gov). If you're thinking of taking your child to an alternative practitioner, make sure that he or she has had experience with children – try to go to someone who has been recommended. And always get an estimate of the cost before going ahead with any treatment. Alternative therapies can be expensive and they may not be covered by your medical insurance or health plan. More and more pediatricians, however, are aware of alternative therapies, so it is always worth asking your doctor about them.

Hospital visits

If your child is referred to a hospital, try to take your partner or someone else with you for at least the first visit. Having moral support to get a sense of what's involved in whatever treatment is planned can help. Some of the best parenting advice I've ever received was from a pediatrician when my daughter had to go to the hospital. "Never forget," he said, "that she's YOUR child. The doctors might know about the illness she has, but you're the expert on your baby."

Undergoing surgery

If a surgical procedure is suggested, ask what will happen if you decide NOT to go ahead with it – it may be possible to put it on hold and see how your child gets along. Two years ago, it was recommended that our daughter's eye be operated on, because she had a slight squint. We weren't convinced that surgery was in her best interests. We discussed our concerns with the consulting physician and he agreed that there was no hurry. So we waited another year, and when the squint didn't show any signs of improvement by itself, we decided to go ahead with the surgery. No harm came to our child's eye in the meantime (she had regular check-ups), and when the operation eventually came around, we were convinced it was for the best.

Don't remain silent if you don't understand something. ASK for clarification – and if you still don't understand, ask again. It's your right to know what's happening to your child.

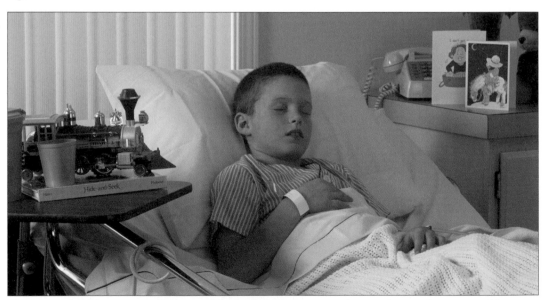

■ **If your child** *has to go to the hospital for treatment, try to spend as much time there as possible. Make sure that you take along favorite books and toys, too.*

Longer stays in the hospital

Having a child in the hospital is a very stressful and worrying event – but a surprisingly common one. Figures show that one in four children under the age of five goes into the hospital each year. If your child has to spend some time in the hospital, you can make the experience less frightening for her. For example, if you know in advance that your child will have to go to the hospital for a procedure, find out all you can about the operation and tell her all she seems interested in knowing. It can help if you "play" at being in the hospital before her admission, so that your child becomes familiar with the idea of doctors and nurses and won't find the experience too new and intimidating.

Try reading her children's stories that involve a stay in the hospital before she goes in for any treatment

While you're on the hospital ward with your child, concentrate on her rather than on what's going on around you. It's interesting to meet other parents, but don't let your thoughts stray too far from your own child. And try and take a break for an hour or two every day – it will be better for both of you if you take some time to refresh yourself.

A simple summary

✔ Most children are robust and healthy – and if you breastfeed, you're passing on antibodies that offer protection to your child.

✔ Vomiting and diarrhea (at the same time), dehydration and listlessness – all these are signs that your child is seriously ill and you should seek medical help immediately.

✔ There are a number of illnesses that are common in young children.

✔ Asthma is a lot more common than it used to be among children under the age of five. If your child is showing symptoms of asthma, seek medical advice.

✔ Dealing with health professionals can be daunting, but remember: a parent's intuition is often right, and good doctors appreciate this.

✔ If your child is really sick, drop everything to be with her. Your cuddles and presence will be the best comfort for her.

PART
FOUR

YOUR CHILD'S PERSONALITY SHINES AT 18 MONTHS

Chapter 17

It Just Gets Better and Better . . .

O VER THE LAST YEAR OR SO, you'll have seen amazing progress in terms of your baby's mobility and abilities. Over the next year, you'll see an explosion in his thinking, talking, and comprehension. This is a time when he'll sometimes be incredibly frustrating, but he'll also be an endlessly interesting little person to be around.

In this chapter . . .

✓ The ups and downs of parenting a toddler

✓ A real little talker

✓ Dealing with independence

✓ Concerns about development

✓ The arrival of a sibling

The ups and downs of parenting a toddler

"IT JUST GETS BETTER AND BETTER."
That's what I've often heard parents say about their child in this age group – it's as though the fascination of watching the early days and weeks of life has just gone on getting deeper as the months have rolled by. And the unexpected part of it, for a lot of people, is that children do become more and more fascinating as time goes on. They're picking up new skills almost daily and are only too happy to show them off.

Developing self-expression

On the other hand, this is also the stage where self-expression starts to surface, and one result of this is that your toddler will start getting cranky when things aren't going the way he wants. No longer is he a little baby, happy to sit where you put him and to do as you want, looking at you adoringly all the while: your toddler is quite capable of screaming and throwing his arms around if he isn't getting his own way.

This stage can be hard work for you, but don't lose sight of how confusing all this can be for your toddler, too.

Your child is discovering that he isn't just a part of you; he's a separate person and he has his own ideas about the way things should be done.

■ **Your toddler is eager** *to experiment with everything. He will want to copy the things you do, and to feel like a real "little adult."*

If this is your first child, you may worry from time to time that you've suddenly got a little monster on your hands. This isn't the case, so don't go out of your way to tell other people that's what he's become (it might turn into a self-fulfilling prophesy!). Difficult, demanding, bratty behavior is part of what being a toddler is all about: and the good news is that, like everything else about childhood, it's only a phase.

Toddling is the least of it

It's funny that this part of childhood is named after a form of walking, because this is probably the least significant factor of a child's development at this stage. Learning to walk, after all, is something your child achieved during the last 6 months or so – by now, he's refining his physical abilities all the time, but he is also just as busy concentrating on his speech and understanding.

A real little talker

BY 18 MONTHS, MOST CHILDREN are able to say at least a few single words. These are almost always labeling words: children tend to learn words that refer to the people and objects in their world – mommy, daddy, dog, book.

INTERNET

www.google.com

The World Wide Web has thousands of sources for speech and language therapists. Visit a search engine like google.com, then request "speech and language therapists" in your region.

Building on vocabulary

When your child is learning to speak, he'll start to use a few words, and he might stick with them for a while. And then, suddenly, a whole new set of words will spill out. Soon, you can no longer count the number of words he uses. The next thing he'll do is start to put the words together.

This is a fascinating process, too, because it's the beginning of real conversations. For a long time, however, your child will only learn words he needs to use. Don't expect him to use words such as "the," for example, because he'll be able to make himself understood without them and at the moment he's far too busy coming to grips with the general principles of speech to be bogged down in the niceties.

Write down the funny things he says in a book you can keep for ever. You think you'll remember them, but you won't – and it's lovely to have them to look back at.

Encouraging conversational skills

The main way you can help your child develop language skills is simply by talking to him, and talking to him with enjoyment. Spend quality time chatting together, making sure that it is just as much fun for both of you. And remember, talking to your child doesn't just help his language and communication skills; it helps build your relationship with him.

Give your baby enough time to express himself verbally – even if he's not very fast. Don't be tempted to finish sentences for him, because this may result in him stuttering and stammering when he begins to put sentences together.

The other thing to remember is that it's only when your child is a toddler that he'll regard the chance to have a talk with you as the thing he'd most like to do in the world. How often I wish I could entice my 9-year-old away from the many other pressing concerns in her life just so that we could have a few minutes to chat! When she was a toddler, of course, she craved my attention, as all young children do – treasure this time, because it doesn't last forever.

SHOULD I LET HIM WATCH TELEVISION?

A lot of parents worry about television viewing, and this is the age when some children first get a taste for it. A limited amount of television won't harm your child – in fact, research shows that under-fours actually benefit from age-appropriate programs – but be careful not to use the television as an unpaid babysitter. If you watch television with your child, discuss what you've seen. This makes the program much more educational for him. Don't keep the television on as background in your house; make it clear to your child that the television goes on for specific programs, and then off again.

■ **It's "safe" to allow** *your child to watch a limited number of appropriate TV programs.*

Concerns about language development

We all know children who learned to talk way ahead of our own youngsters, and it is important not to become competitive with other children. But if you have real concerns about your child's progress, talk to your pediatrician and see whether he or she thinks you should take him to a *speech therapist*.

DEFINITION

Speech therapists *assess communication and speech problems and suggest treatment. These usually involve one-to-one sessions, although some therapists recommend "talking playgroups" for young children who need help with speaking.*

If you're at all worried about your child's developing language skills, seek expert advice as quickly as possible.

Speech therapy tends to work more effectively if it starts early – so don't hesitate to get a referral just because you don't want to face the fact that your child might need help. It doesn't reflect badly on you, it doesn't mean that your child is a slow learner or has other problems, and it isn't something to be embarrassed about. The sooner a problem is treated, the better it will be for your child.

BUT WHY WON'T HE SHARE HIS TOYS?

Being able to share is a relatively advanced social skill, and a toddler doesn't have any concept of it yet. That doesn't mean you have to give in and never encourage him to give a toy to another child. But it does mean that you have to understand that, from the child's point of view, he isn't being mean. He just doesn't have the skills to empathize or think through the consequences of his actions.

Sharing things with him yourself is one way to make him aware of the importance of being generous and giving. Also, when your child is playing with others, be on hand to mediate if there is a fight. Don't get angry: just be clear and consistent in the message that sharing is best. Sometimes, it's best to take a toy away from both parties rather than let one child "win" – usually, they can be pacified with other toys almost at once.

■ **Children learn** *to share by example. When your child is with friends, point out to him how the other children share their toys when they play.*

Dealing with independence

THIS IS THE AGE WHEN *independence really kicks in. Don't be surprised if your toddler spends an hour learning to put on his own jacket rather than "letting" you show him how. It's as though, having just about mastered the ability to do something, it becomes imperative for him to try out the new skill again and again until he gets it right.*

Being patient

It's tricky to remain patient when you're a busy parent. It's a lot easier to put the jacket on your child yourself and get out of the front door when you want to. But you know this will lead to a tantrum – so your blood pressure goes up as you watch your determined little 2-year-old trying and trying to get his arm through the arm-hole, knowing that any offer of help will be rejected.

■ **Let your child** *choose the clothes he wants to wear in the morning – within reason – and dress himself if he wants to.*

Start everything as early as possible so that your child gets a chance to "do it himself." For example, tell him to get his coat on half an hour before you need to be out the front door.

Slow down!

If your life tends to be rush, rush, rush, this is a stage in your child's life when you will probably have to slow right down so that he can get a chance to try things out for himself sometimes. Always being too busy to take things slowly will be a cause of frustration for both you and your child; toddlers aren't equipped yet to do things in a hurry, because they simply don't have the skills.

Of course, there are occasions when you can't help but be in a hurry. This is when you need to bargain with your child: "You can't do it this time, but when we get home you can take your coat off on your own and show grandma because she'll be here by then."

Concerns about development

BOASTING IS AN ENDEMIC *and rampant infection
in the parent population: however reticent a person might
be about his or her own abilities, for some reason having
a child unleashes the desire to let everyone else know
how brilliant his or her little one is. And then there are
the comparisons: we know we shouldn't, but we can't
help ourselves.*

Plenty of toddler behavior seems "odd," so what's normal? Most "odd" or anti-social behavior is simply a phase. Biting, for example, is something a lot of children do at this age. It's difficult to deal with because many people take a very disapproving view of it and you can sometimes feel like a bit of a pariah.

*If you have a "biter," the best way to deal with it is to exclude him
from a game or the children he's with for a short while. Tell him
firmly and gently that it's wrong. But never, ever bite him back.*

> ## Trivia...
> By the age of two, the
> average girl is able to
> say 52 words, while the
> average boy can say 47.

Avoiding comparisons

The culture of comparing and boasting leads, inevitably, to worry and fear on the part of some parents that their child isn't progressing as well as he should be. Often these fears are completely groundless: children don't develop uniformly, after all.

Your child's speech might not be as clear as that of the child up the street, but your child might be better at climbing and concentrating on physical skills right now. That said, there's no point in burying any nagging doubts that you may have; and you certainly don't want to transmit any worries to your child. Talk to your pediatrician about your concerns.

■ **Concentrate** *on your child's
new skills and abilities, rather
than making comparisons with
other children you know.*

217

■ **Children should be** *cautious of things that can be dangerous, such as deep water, but don't let fear spoil their enjoyment of the world around them.*

Dealing with phobias

Phobias and fears are another common feature of toddlerhood. Dogs are the number one favorite phobia, followed by other animals and insects. These fears are irrational, but that doesn't mean that you can deal with them by forcing your child into contact with the creature or object he is scared of: indeed, this is likely to be counterproductive, so don't try it.

Instead, stay calm yourself – don't get flustered by his fear, and don't transmit any worries you may have yourself if you can help it. As with so much else in parenting, your example will be the best way to teach your child that a dog isn't something to be scared of (although it's right to be wary of them). Children with phobias usually grow out of them, but don't expect it to be a quick turnaround – they can persist for some time.

What to do if you're worried

As we've already discussed, many parental concerns about young children are groundless. But if a child does have a problem, be it developmental or physical, a parent is often the first to spot that something is wrong. When my eldest daughter was about a year old, I thought I noticed something a bit funny about one of her eyes. I took her to the pediatrician for an examination. He said he couldn't see anything wrong, but he'd err on the side of caution and refer us to an eye specialist. The specialist confirmed my suspicion, and it was indeed helpful to have the problem picked up early.

If you're completely convinced that there's a problem, don't be talked out of it. Ask to see another pediatrician, or insist on a referral to a specialist.

Most pediatricians, like mine, will treat any concerns you have seriously, even if a problem isn't obvious or evident. If your pediatrician has the attitude that "all parents are worriers" and that there's almost certainly nothing wrong however concerned you seem to be, think very seriously about getting a new doctor. This attitude is frankly outmoded in today's healthcare system and you need to find a pediatrician who can empathize with where you're coming from.

THE FUNNY THINGS THEY DO (AND WHY)

Your child may never go anywhere without a particular teddy, old blanket, or another "comfort object." Why? Because he's worried about facing the world without you there by his side, and this "comfort" or "attachment" object has become invested with the idea of "safety." It's like taking a bit of your love, or part of home, or all that he holds dear, with him wherever he goes. As he becomes older and more confident, he'll be able to leave it to one side as he plays. Eventually, he'll be able to go out without it.

Perhaps your child asks for the same story over and over again. Why? Because children learn through repetition, so in asking you to read that story again, although you've just read it twice, he's asking you to reinforce what he's learning from it. Of course, it can be a bore for you – but when you understand that it's your child's thirst for knowledge that's driving him on to ask for more, you realize it's worth humoring him! As your toddler gets to know the story, he'll love filling in little bits of it himself. Look out for sequels or other books that feature the same characters that you know your child enjoys.

Some children worry that they'll fall down the toilet. Why? Because although they're learning about the world and about what can and can't happen, they don't have the confidence yet to rely on what they know. Fear of what can happen to their bodies is often very strong at around 2 years of age, and you just have to be patient. Explain to your child that he's quite safe – but don't expect him to believe you just yet!

You may find that your child wanders up everyone else's driveway when you let him walk along the sidewalk. Why? Because toddlers love to explore and they're learning as they go. They love to poke around at things and to touch plants, bricks, and anything else they encounter (including dog poop, which can be harmful, so beware!). Toddlers can't walk that quickly, and they're inevitably going to want to take a lot of detours, so don't let them walk anywhere unless you've got time to accompany them at their speed.

■ **Many children have** *a favorite toy that they carry everywhere with them. As they gain in confidence, they'll grow out of this habit.*

The arrival of a sibling

TWO YEARS SEEMS TO BE *the most common age gap, especially between baby number one and baby number two. If yours is an "only" who's about to become an "eldest," this can be a worrisome and sometimes difficult time. You're going to need a lot of patience to get you through the months when you have a small baby as well as a toddler to take care of.*

Tell your child what's happening to your body, and why you're getting fat, and answer his questions as clearly and simply as you can. A book about babies and where they come from might help, but don't overload him with information.

Looking back on my 9 years of being a parent, I can honestly say that the most difficult period for me was when my two older girls were about 6 months and 3 years old. Basically, I had two babies to look after – both at a demanding phase, and neither was capable of doing much in the way of give and take.

Learning to cope

We got through it, of course, but it was tough-going. There were times when we just had to hang in there and believe it would get easier (it did). Preparing your toddler for a new sister or brother is hard. There's a limit to how much a young child this age can take in, and the truth is they don't really know what it's all about until the baby is actually on the scene. And by then, he'll probably be confused and this is where many problems arise.

Even when life is stressful for you with a toddler and a baby, try to see that things are also stressful for your

■ **Let your older** *child feel involved in the arrival of a new sibling. Let them spend time getting to know one another – but make sure that your older child is gentle with the baby.*

older child. That doesn't mean that you have to treat him with kid gloves and always put him first. The adjustment your child is having to make in realizing that the universe doesn't revolve around him will, in the long term, be very good for him. But you need to be sensitive to your older child's needs and his understandable confusion about the huge upheaval in his life.

Don't tell your child you're having a baby to give him a playmate. Firstly, because that's not why you're doing it, and secondly because the new arrival won't be a playmate for quite a while.

A simple summary

✓ For the first 18 months or so of his life, your baby has been developing in leaps and bounds. Over the next year, you're going to see huge changes in his ability to speak and communicate his wants and feelings.

✓ This is a fascinating time in your child's life, but it can also be frustrating. Prepare yourself for the fact that your toddler doesn't like being told he can't do something if he's made up his mind he wants to do it.

✓ He'll already be using a few single words; over the next few months, he'll increase his vocabulary tremendously, and start putting words together.

✓ It's really important to talk to your child as much as you can, one-to-one.

✓ If you're worried about your child's progress, seek expert advice early on. Health professionals will take your concerns seriously, and most know that a parent's hunch is often correct.

✓ If a new baby is due in your family and you've already got a toddler, try to understand how stressful this will be for your older child. Try to prepare him for what's ahead, while knowing that the full impact of what's involved won't hit him until after the birth of his sibling.

Chapter 18

Potty Training

WHEN YOUR CHILD IS AROUND THE AGE OF TWO, you'll find yourself talking to parents of other toddlers about whether their children are potty trained, how long it took, and whether they had any problems. You'll wonder whether it's easier for girls or boys, and whether you're starting too early or too late. You may worry about whether your child is a little behind, or you might feel smug that she's so far ahead. This is all perfectly normal parenting behavior; the irony is, as most parents will confirm, potty training is 10 times easier if you can just relax, take it or leave it, follow your child's lead, and avoid comparing your child with others.

In this chapter . . .

✓ When to potty train

✓ How to get it right

✓ Dealing with problems

✓ Staying dry at night

YOUR CHILD WILL LEARN TO USE THE POTTY IN HER OWN TIME

When to potty train

ONE MISTAKE A LOT OF PARENTS *make is to start potty training too late, or to introduce it too early. How so? Well, they start too late by failing to talk to their child about it until it's time to embark on the process itself. Or they start it too early by expecting their child to learn how to use the toilet when he or she is not really ready.*

Try not to see potty training as a phase that begins when your child is around 2 years old. View it instead as a whole process that starts much earlier – you should really begin explaining about potties when your child is around the age of one. Nor is the training phase "over" when your child starts to use a potty of her own accord.

Even when your child has successfully used a potty once or twice, continue to encourage her to use it and reward results with interest and praise.

Introducing the idea

Buy a potty and leave it in the bathroom long before you expect your child to actually use it; the fact that it's there will remind you to talk about its use. This in turn will get your little one ready for the idea of using it herself. Let her see you using the toilet, too – and, if you have older children and they don't mind, let her accompany them to the bathroom (especially if they still use a potty). As with everything else in the early years, children learn best through imitation.

Your child must be comfortable on her potty, so get her to try sitting on one in the store before you buy it.

Some children enjoy using small-scale toilet seats, but many feel insecure on these because they can't put their feet on the floor.

■ **Show your child** *her new potty and put it in the bathroom. Talk to her about it so that she gets used to it and starts to understand what it's for.*

When's the right moment?

Some books suggest that you should look for signs that your child might be ready to use the potty at the age of 18 months, but I'd say hold off until at least the age of two. Very few children find potty training easy until they're that age – and why make it hard for yourself? As someone once said, there are two ways to potty train: the easy way and the difficult way – and the difficult way is when your child is not ready.

The two crucial elements in successful potty training are your child's readiness and your state of mind. If you're anxious about it or you're having a busy, stressful time at the moment, it's not going to work. That's because you are going to have to deal with the odd accident or two, and if you react by being bad-tempered and put-out over it, you'll only succeed in setting back your child's attempts.

Don't start potty training if you're under any stress, for example if you're about to have a new baby (or have just had one) or if you're moving, or starting a new job.

Summer is a great time to potty train; the living is easy, and the clothes your child will be wearing are lighter and easier to do without. If your child is playing in the yard, it's as good a place as any to start using the potty. Another advantage is that the sun will dry any extra laundry in no time. My advice is to wait for the good weather if you can.

KNOWING WHEN THE TIME IS RIGHT

You may have a hunch that your child is ready to cast diapers aside, but if you're not certain, check the following list to make sure that all the signs are right. Be honest with yourself about your child's capabilities – it really isn't worth putting yourself through the difficulties of trying to potty train a child who isn't ready:

- Your child talks about, and takes an interest in going to the toilet
- She has regular bowel habits and sometimes has dry diapers
- She seems to want to copy you and even asks to sit on the toilet
- She's around 2 years old

Trust your own instincts about whether your child is ready to potty train or not — if she is, you won't have any doubts.

Preparing for potty training

Once you decide to go for it, stop a moment to think about the kind of clothes your child wears. Will they be easy for you – and her – to get off and then on again? Buttons are bad news for toddlers trying to be independent on the toilet: zippers can be easier, but elastic waistbands and Velcro® are even better.

Helpful tips

There are quite a few gimmicks around to help make potty training easier for parents and their children. Don't get your hopes up, however, because nothing is going to work miracles – patience is your best ally. But if you think your child deserves something to encourage her efforts, consider investing in a book or a video, or even a potty that plays a tune when something lands in the pot.

■ **Skirts or trousers** *without fastenings or buttons make life easier for your child during potty training.*

INTERNET

www.jpma.org
www.cpsc.gov

The Juvenile Products Manufacturers Association gives advice on shopping for baby gear. The U.S. Consumer Product Safety Commission's site gives details about recalls on products for children.

A book, a video, or a potty that gets your child interested in moving on from diapers is a step in the right direction – with the added advantage of making it all seem like fun!

Introduce a story book or a video about potty training slowly, and don't expect immediate results just because your child has heard or seen the story once! Remember that this is just part of a process. Talk about the characters in the book or video and how they learn to use the potty. Then start suggesting that your child might like to try out the potty too, just like that little girl in the story. Explain to her that she could go to the toilet on her own, too. Talk about how proud the parents are of the little girl in the book or video, and about how pleased she is with herself.

If you're worried about splashes on your carpet, place a plastic sheet under the potty.

How to get it right

TRY INTRODUCING YOUR CHILD to potty training by suggesting that her teddy or doll needs to go to the toilet or potty. This gives your child the feeling that she is in control over what's happening and lets her rehearse what's going to be expected of her in a fun way. Don't expect your child to understand about potties right away, however – the whole picture will only dawn on her slowly.

■ **Let your child** *get used to just sitting on the potty for a short time each day while you chat together. She'll slowly become more and more comfortable with the whole idea.*

Be on hand to help

You'll need to help when your child first uses the potty or toilet, but don't do more than necessary. Your child will be more enthusiastic about using the potty if she can do it by herself, so let her. Encourage her independence so that she gets the idea that this is something that she needs to do for herself. After all, she's the one who will need to recognize the signs that she's ready to go to the toilet.

My youngest daughter started off by sitting on the toilet for 30 seconds or so each evening before getting into the tub. She didn't actually use it for a while, but she obviously enjoyed doing something "grown up," and she especially enjoyed using the toilet paper and flushing the chain afterwards.

Don't mock your child's early efforts on the potty if they don't produce anything. It's great that she's just trying it out – so tell her.

If you want, you can suggest that she might like to try using the toilet or potty another time – but really, don't push it. The fact that she's sitting there means she'll soon get the idea about actually using the potty.

Training stages

In general, children learn the toilet routine from the end first – they start off by just sitting on the pot or toilet and then flushing it, washing their hands, and so on. Next, they might learn to take off and then pull up their pants again. Actually doing something is usually the very last thing, and for some children it only happens when they feel confident that they've mastered the other stages. So don't push them to get on with producing something – you could set back their very competent efforts and undermine their sense of how well they're doing with the routine as a whole.

If you feel too pressurized and tense at the idea of your child's potty training, YOU'RE the one who probably isn't ready – and the most likely reason for that is that your child isn't either.

Praise, praise, and no comment

Whatever you do, be prepared to show interest and to praise any reasonable efforts that your child makes to get clothes on and off, sit on the potty, wash hands etc. Don't try to dramatize efforts to get to the toilet by racing off at the mere mention of a need to pee, or announcing it in a loud voice to everyone at dinner. At the end of the day, your child is learning to go to the toilet in the way grown-ups do, and most of us tend not to tell everyone exactly what we're about to do. Also, getting over-excited about it will add to your child's sense of anxiety.

Many parents wonder whether rewards are a good idea when a child is learning to use the potty and toilet. While they can be helpful, it's best to use rewards that aren't candy and chocolates – stickers are a good idea, and are probably better than a chart at this age. Building a collection of colorful stickers can be a good incentive to keep your child persevering in her efforts!

■ **You can reward** *your child with a sticker for every successful attempt she has at using the potty.*

However, other than stickers, rewards are probably not necessary. Most children of potty-training age are excited about becoming independent, and that's their main incentive for wanting to use the potty or toilet.

Your child is inevitably going to have the occasional accident while she's getting used to the potty. When this happens, don't make a big deal of it, however inconvenient and annoying it is. Simply clean up without comment, say "never mind, let's try and do it on the potty next time" and leave it at that.

Don't use trainer pants. Most parents agree that they don't have any place in potty training; they give the message that it's okay to go in your pants sometimes, and this is very confusing to a toddler.

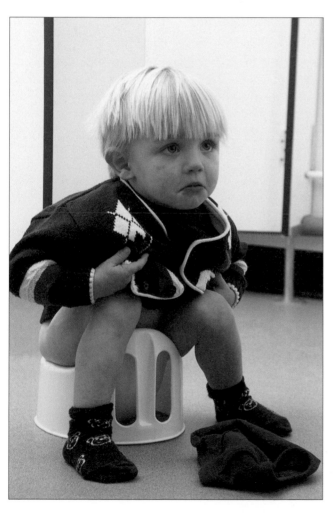

Don't keep asking!

Another mistake parents can sometimes make, if they're a bit anxious about potty training, is to ask a child 10 times an hour whether she needs to use the potty. Resist the temptation to do this, however difficult it seems. An occasional reminder is fine, but the important word here is "occasional." If you keep on and on at your child, she'll find it boring and will start saying "no" automatically.

Also, remember that what you're trying to do is teach your child to take control of when she wants to go to the toilet. She needs to start noticing when the time is right, not you, and she should make the decision for herself.

■ **Some parents worry** *about whether to teach their sons to pee standing up or sitting down. Leave it to your child to decide; some prefer to do it "like daddy does" – others feel more comfortable sitting, and that's just fine.*

Dealing with problems

HAVING SAID POTTY TRAINING can be a breeze if you choose the right time, you should have already guessed that – like so much else to do with parenting – it certainly isn't always easy.

Don't be afraid to put it on hold

No sensible parent is going to expect potty training to be easy, but it certainly shouldn't be a total pain. If your child wets her pants once or twice a day in the early days, you may decide to persevere. If, on the other hand, she soaks every pair you put her into, and only once or twice seems remotely interested in using the potty, use common sense. This really isn't the moment to be potty training, and it's going to be a lot easier on both of you if you put it on hold, at least for a short time.

If you've already told the doting grandparents or your friends that your little darling is about to potty train, it can be difficult to then back out. The moral of the tale, of course, is to keep quiet about potty training until it's almost complete – don't tell everyone your 18-month-old is on the verge of being out of diapers because you'll only put pressure on yourselves to achieve the (unrealistic) target you're setting.

A halfway house

You may find that your child is ready, but not for the whole nine yards. She might be ready to stay dry through the day, for example, but is unwilling to use a potty or the toilet for bowel movements. This, in fact, is a very common phenomenon encountered by parents of toddlers – it happened to me with my eldest daughter. I don't know why I worried about it at the time. After all, a child who always makes sure she's got a diaper on before she takes a poop, isn't really being so very difficult.

■ **There are bound** *to be some accidents even after your child has been toilet trained. Be reassuring and patient.*

Needless to say, the problem resolved itself within a few weeks – and that, to be honest, is the situation with almost all problems that are associated with potty training.

Try not to get wound up about toilet-training problems, even if they take you off guard just when you felt you'd got it beat. They're almost always short-term, and they're exacerbated by you getting upset about them.

Regressing to wet pants, even some time after potty training has successfully been completed, is a common problem. It is often associated with worries in a child's life, such as the arrival of a new sibling or moving to another house. So, too, is a refusal to sit on a toilet even when, in your opinion, your child is too old to be using a potty.

Staying dry at night

BY THE AGE OF 3 YEARS OLD, *9 out of 10 children are dry most days. But learning not to wet the bed at night often takes longer, and some 5-year-olds still wear diapers or "pull-ups" at night.*

A night-time routine

It's often difficult to know when to make the break from night-time diapers or pull-ups – you don't want to try it too soon and risk undermining your child's confidence if there are accidents (not to mention the inconvenience for you, of course). On the other hand, you don't want to make your child dependent on diapers or pull-ups when she doesn't need to be.

Some parents swear that getting their child up to use the toilet, before they go to bed themselves, is a good way to ensure a dry bed.

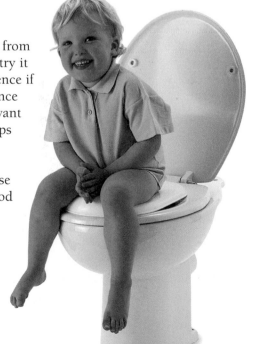

■ **Make sure that your child** *always goes to the toilet just before going to bed at night, so that the chances of a night-time accident are reduced.*

I'm dubious about this method because it seems to me that if the child doesn't really wake up, you're not teaching her anything. And if she does wake up, you could have a whole different set of problems! My motto is, let sleeping children lie.

Some children get confused if they're wearing underwear during the day, but a diaper at night. If your child asks you whether she's wearing a diaper or not, it's time to at least try her without a diaper overnight.

Look for the signs that your child isn't wetting the diaper she's wearing overnight; try taking her to the toilet or potty the moment she wakes up and, if you find the diaper is still dry, get her to use the toilet immediately.

Some parents worry that their child has **enuresis** long before a medical professional would make a diagnosis of that sort. In general, a child has to be having problems with bed wetting after the age of 5 or 6 before a pediatrician might check for urinary infection, diabetes, or abnormalities of the urinary tract. Try not to be too concerned, and don't let your child notice any anxiety on your part – it will only make it more difficult for her.

> **DEFINITION**
>
> *Enuresis is the inability to control the bladder voluntarily, particularly during the time when you are asleep.*

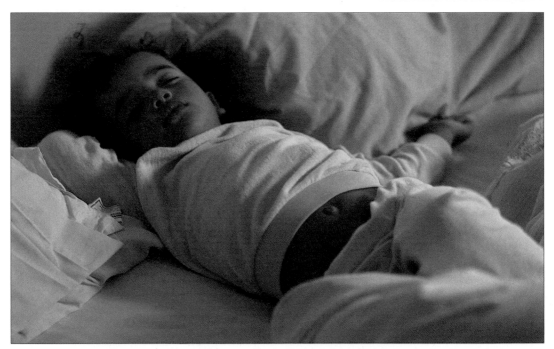

■ **If you're worried about** *your child wetting the bed, particularly when you're away from home, put a waterproof pad under her bottom sheet so that the mattress doesn't get wet.*

A simple summary

✓ Don't consider starting potty training until your child is at least 2 years old, and shows signs of being ready for it.

✓ Start introducing your toddler to the idea of potty training a few months before you start putting it into practice – let her see other people using the toilet so that she starts to get the hang about what is involved.

✓ Buy a potty and put it in the bathroom before your child is ready to use it so that she becomes familiar with it.

✓ Make sure that you're potty training because your child is ready for it, rather than because you think she ought to be.

✓ In general, children learn the routine backwards – they start by flushing the toilet and washing their hands; then sitting on the toilet (without doing anything) and wiping themselves; and, finally, they sit there one day and produce something.

✓ Praise her efforts, and be casual about any mishaps – making your child anxious about the process will be detrimental.

✓ If things seem to be going nowhere, don't be afraid to put your child in diapers or a pull-up again and put the whole thing on hold for 3 weeks. There's no point in changing nine pairs of wet underwear a day!

✓ Resist broadcasting the fact that you have started potty training your toddler – this will put you both under unnecessary pressure to succeed, and fast!

✓ Even when your toddler is successfully using the potty during the day, she may still need a diaper or pull-ups during the night – for some time to come.

✓ Whatever problems you have, try to keep things in perspective. Your child will get the hang of using the toilet eventually, and it really doesn't matter if it takes her a while.

Chapter 19

Choosing Preschool Care

Preschool, or nursery school, is the educational environment in which your child can be cared for before he starts school. Most children don't start at preschool until they're at least two-and-a-half, but you need to be thinking about it well in advance, especially if you live in an area where waiting lists are long. Going to preschool will be an important stage in the life of your little one, so you need to be sure that you choose the preschool care that is right for him. Of course, you might decide to keep your child at home until he's old enough for "big" school – whatever suits you and your child.

In this chapter . . .

✓ **What are the options?**

✓ **Finding the right preschool**

✓ **Getting a place**

✓ **Alternative preschools**

PRESCHOOL WILL HELP YOUR CHILD DEVELOP SKILLS AND LEARN INDEPENDENCE

What are the options?

OVER THE LAST FEW YEARS, *the number of preschool options has mushroomed. It can be tricky, however, to understand the differences between programs, before you even get around to deciding which one would be best for your child! Preschool options are known by a confusing variety of names, but it's safe to say that the ones you're most likely to hear are nursery school, pre-K, and kindergarten. Meanwhile, some day care centers provide many of the same educational and social advantages of preschools, too.*

Weighing the alternatives

Over the last few years, a lot of study has gone into establishing what the best early learning environments are for young children between the ages of three and six, and the picture is confusing. Some studies seem to suggest that young children learn better when they are at home with a parent; others, that a well-rounded preschool setting gives them the best start in life. Research has also suggested that too much of an emphasis on learning at this early age can have long term negative effects on a child's academic career, while there is another view that early learning is the backbone of all future achievement. What's a parent to make of it all?

However much you'd like your child to do well in later life, don't be swayed by promises that a nursery school will teach your baby to read by the age of three. The most important thing is that he'll be happy there.

The truth probably lies somewhere between the diametrically opposed pieces of research: good preschools can give children important experiences of being with and learning how to live with other people. On the other hand, it's crucial that young children have a strong sense of security and spend as much time as possible with their parents. Getting out and about and having new adventures is very exciting and opens up new horizons for children over the age of two and a half. But the security of their own home, or a caregiver's home, still has plenty to offer in terms of a big enough and busy enough environment for early learning.

Several factors will affect your choice of preschool: your child's personality and level of social maturity, your work schedule, and your income.

Learning at home

Never underestimate how much a young child can learn at home. Don't make the mistake of relinquishing your responsibilities just because you are sending your child to preschool or day care. You will still need to take the time to share books with him and talk about the alphabet and numbers. On the other hand, educational concerns shouldn't dominate your relationship with your child either.

■ **Spend time with your child.** *Talk to him and take a lively interest in what he tells you. Develop his enthusiasm and curiosity for life, because this is the best basis for learning and sound academic achievement later on.*

EARLY LEARNING GOALS

Certain criteria underpin the teaching at good quality preschools, whether they go under the name of kindergarten, nursery school, pre-K, or day care center. The aim is for the following set of goals to be achieved in the 3- to 6-year-old age group:

● **Personal, social, and emotional development:** Your child will learn self-confidence. He will understand his own needs, take an interest in the people and things around him, and be able to tell the difference between right and wrong

● **Communication, language, and literacy:** He will learn to speak confidently and clearly. He will enjoy stories, songs, and poems, and he will get used to hearing, saying, and linking words to the alphabet

● **Mathematics:** He will be introduced to mathematics through stories, songs, and games. He will be encouraged to use numbers and to understand concepts such as "heavier" or "taller," and he will build an awareness of shapes and space

● **Knowledge of the world around us:** Your child will explore how things work and how to share stories about events in his life and his family's life

● **Physical development:** Your child will learn to move confidently and develop body coordination skills through a rich variety of physical activities

● **Creativity:** He will explore colors, shapes, and music. He will learn to dance, create things, and make up stories

Finding the right preschool

THERE ARE MANY WAYS to find out about good preschools in your community. Typically, many early childhood schools are associated with churches, synagogues, YMCAs, and YMHAs, but pediatricians, friends, and colleagues are also excellent sources of information. Call your local school district to find out about public pre-K programs and check the yellow pages of your phone book under "Schools – Nursery Schools and Kindergarten." In the end, no matter how much your friends praise a particular preschool, the best way to determine whether it will be right for your child is to visit it yourself.

Location, location, location

Living close to the school your child goes to can make all the difference in the world, especially for very young children. For one thing, getting out of the house in the morning is a lot easier if you don't have far to walk or drive, and it may also be more convenient for your child to participate in after-school programs and playgroups. And, if your child becomes sick over the course of the day, you won't have far to travel if he or she needs to be brought home.

If both you and your partner work, or if you are a single parent who works at a distance from home, you might want to look for options near your job. In fact, some employers provide onsite centers that supply high quality care, including a variety of educational materials and staff who have had training in child development.

Half day? Full day?

There are as many options for how long your child can spend in preschool as there are preschools. Some offer part-time programs – a few hours several days a week. Others offer the equivalent of a regular school day

■ **Caring staff** *give your child guidance and help spark his interest in books or toys.*

five days a week, and still others offer all-day programs that begin as early as 7 A.M. and extend until 7.30 P.M. Some preschools and day care centers give parents an even more flexible range of options depending on their schedules. It's always worth making enquiries about what's available.

Don't think of preschool merely as another form of childcare; it is, in fact, a very important stage in your child's educational and social development. Take the time to find the right environment for your child.

Which option is best for your child largely depends on the social maturity of your child and his or her previous experiences. Some children thrive in a full-day program, while others tire more easily and are better served by a morning or afternoon session.

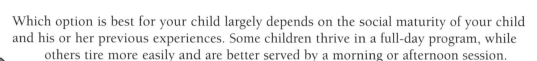

Don't feel pressurized to enroll your child in a nursery or kindergarten if you don't feel he's ready for it. Children mature at different rates, and there's nothing to be gained from pushing them into school before they're ready.

If your preschool child feels comfortable staying at his day care center, and it offers educational opportunities that are similar to those in public or private nursery schools or kindergartens, there's no reason to uproot him. However, he might eventually find the same level of comfort at a "big" elementary school, especially if he stays there through the upper grades. Bear in mind, though, that the school may not be able to guarantee him a place after pre-K or kindergarten.

Trivia...

According to an Oxford University study, children who have less structure and more play in their early education are more likely to stay married, to vote, and to read newspapers as adults.

Teachers and class size

Two very important aspects of your child's preschool experience will be the size of the class he is in, and his teachers. Both these factors vary widely from one setting to the next. Preschoolers in the four-, five-, and six-year-old group seem to do best in classes of up to eighteen children, but the number in the group should not exceed twenty. Equally, your child's classroom should provide him with access to age appropriate activities and opportunities to build on his language and social skills.

If your child qualifies for either Head Start or Early Head Start, the government will pick up the tab for your child's preschool fees. To find out more about the program and to determine if your child is eligible, call your local Head Start agency.

There's no question that good teachers are at the core of happy and successful early childhood learning. There are as many different teaching styles and personalities as there are teachers, but it's safe to say that a good teacher should be interested in and genuinely enjoy the company of children. He or she should also be perceptive and patient.

Philosophy

One of the most important things to consider in choosing a preschool is finding a good match between your values, priorities, and general philosophy about education and that of the school's. For example, does the school play down competition, or is a team approach to problem-solving emphasized? If your child is used to a more competitive environment at home, and thrives in an environment where individual achievements are championed, he may feel uncomfortable with the lack of continuity.

Have a plan before you start visiting preschools. Make a list of your family values and educational goals beforehand, and be prepared to ask lots of questions.

Is your child's home-life very structured, or is it very relaxed? What kind of atmosphere makes him feel comfortable, happy, and eager to learn new things? The best way to make this assessment is to observe how your child prefers to function at home and look for similar conditions in the preschool you choose.

■ **Preschools** *should give children plenty of access to outdoor areas, where they can be active and learn to play with each other as well as share equipment and toys.*

Getting a place

IF YOU THINK THERE'S A DIZZYING ARRAY *of terms that describe early learning options, just wait until you start navigating the deep and changing waters of preschool admissions. Yes, they vary widely from school to school and even from year to year. The best policy is to start looking into preschools well ahead of time so that you'll know exactly which ones require applications, fees, an interview, or tuition – and which ones don't.*

Admissions

Some preschools admit children according to age or date of application, on a first-come, first-served basis. Application dates vary from place to place, so be sure to establish when your application is due. Also, find out how early you can apply and how old your child should be in order to qualify for admission. For example, some preschools require that a child should have reached the age of three by June 1 in order to be accepted in that year's class; others may accept children with September birthdays.

If you really want to get your child into a particular preschool, find out exactly what its admissions procedures are and how decisions are made.

Admission to some public school programs may be limited to a certain number of children and may involve quotas for low-income families or children with special needs, while admission to some private or exclusive nursery schools may be limited to those who can afford steep tuition costs.

In some places, your choices may be affected by the school district you happen to live in, and there's no denying that some communities have more choice when it comes to quality public schools.

■ **It's important to get into** *a preschool that will serve the interests of everyone in your family. If your schedule prevents you from picking up your little one before 6 P.M., you need a school that has a reliable after-school program.*

Some private schools are located in churches or synagogues, while some large businesses have onsite facilities that combine early childhood learning with basic day care for a reasonable fee. Admission to these eagerly-sought programs can be difficult, so always get as much information as you can, as early as you can, no matter what kind of preschool you have in mind for your child.

Alternative preschools

IF YOU ARE INTERESTED IN FINDING an alternative to the *traditional form of preschool (sometimes referred to as "academic," "cognitive," or "formal"), be prepared for another raft of confusing terms. "Progressive," "informal," "total child," "whole child," "open," "unstructured," and "child-centered" are just some of the terms used to describe the alternatives. Of course, there are differences between all of these approaches to early learning, and the only way to find out what they are is to do a little research.*

■ **No matter what kind of preschool** *your child goes to, take the opportunity to participate in classroom projects and field trips as often as you can.*

Different strokes

A good place to begin your research is with friends, family, and neighbors whose children are currently attending an alternative preschool. There's nothing better than an insider's view, but if none of your friends or neighbors can give you one, the next best thing is to attend an open house. On these occasions, you'll have the opportunity to meet administrators and staff and to learn something about the school's curriculum, resources, and schedules. Most importantly, you'll have enough information about whether or not the school will be a good match for your child before it's time to make a decision about enrollment.

Before you enroll your child in any preschool, be sure that you understand its overall philosophy, methods, and approach to early learning.

Libraries are another good source of information about alternative schools, and many schools, especially private and alternative preschools, have web sites. Many of them will also send you a brochure and arrange for a meeting with the school's admissions staff. Don't discount public schools, however, many of which have special non-traditional programs for preschoolers.

Look in your local yellow pages for school listings and call for information about alternative programs. "Walk-ins" are not discouraged by some schools, so don't hesitate to visit one unannounced. You can learn a lot by simply observing alternative programs in action. Seeing how the children relate to teachers and to each other, and getting a sense of what the curriculum and social environment has to contribute, can help you decide whether or not an alternative school will best serve your child's growing intellectual, creative, and social needs.

DEFINITION

Montessori schools *were founded by Maria Montessori (1870–1952), an Italian doctor. The fundamental aim of her approach is self-education by the children.*

INTERNET

www.amshq.org
www.awsna.org/awsna/

If you're interested in the Montessori or Waldorf (Rudolf Steiner) approaches to education, check out these web sites for more information.

Two popular alternatives

Two of the most popular choices for preschool are **Montessori schools** and Waldorf Schools, also known as Rudolf Steiner schools. Both of them have something special to offer.

Montessori schools are the best-known alternative to traditional preschools. Although not every Montessori school adheres to all the original principles, most emphasize self-directed learning, because classrooms are made up of children ranging in age from three to six. The teacher's role is to direct the child to appropriate materials and demonstrate their correct use. The framework covers activities that a child can recognize from daily life.

Waldorf or Rudolph Steiner schools, started by Rudolph Steiner in Germany after World War I, are based on the belief that young children can and do suffer stress and anxiety if they are pressured into too much learning too soon. This belief holds that childhood is a precious time and that it's important for each stage to be enjoyed and unhurried, instead of rushing the children on to the next stage of learning. Each element of development is fully experienced so that it can be properly absorbed and built on.

■ **Playing outdoors** *is an important part of a preschooler's day, even if there's a drop of rain or two.*

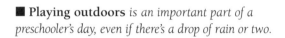

PRE-SCHOOL CHOICES – PROS AND CONS

a **Traditional Nursery Schools, pre-K, and kindergarten:** Trained staff follow an eclectic curriculum to give children a sound introduction to education, while fostering a warm and friendly environment that soothes and invites curiosity, builds self-esteem, encourages respect for others, and promotes a love of learning. Be aware that some private nurseries can be expensive

b **Day care center:** A good option for working parents, some day care centers provide childcare, flexible hours, a permanent staff and, sometimes, early education opportunities for children in an environment they already know and trust. It can be ideal for a child who is not emotionally or developmentally ready for the transition to preschool

c **Alternative schools:** For a more holistic approach to learning, there are alternatives such as Waldorf (or Rudolph Steiner) schools, which emphasize creative activities instead of academic ones – these are not taught until a child is six or seven. The goals and objectives of some schools that bill themselves as "alternative" can be poorly defined, so be sure to do your homework and know what you want for your child before you enroll him

A typical preschool day

Regular features of a preschool day include lots of playtime, story-reading, an introduction to numbers, letters, shapes, and basic words, as well as snacks and a nap.

Most children attend preschool between 9 a.m. and 3 p.m.; others attend morning or afternoon sessions only; and some children stay as late as 5 p.m., in an after school program. Children who attend day care centers can arrive as early as 7 a.m. and stay as late as 7 p.m.

Most children don't learn in a subject-based way; they learn through their senses, through asking questions, and through interacting with teachers and peers. Find out whether your child's potential preschool is geared toward encouraging independence, curiosity, and self-respect.

A simple summary

✓ Typical preschool options are nursery school, pre-K and kindergarten, although day care centers offer similar educational and social advantages.

✓ Make the effort to visit a preschool before you enroll your child, no matter what your friends have told you about it.

✓ The best preschool for your child is the one that matches his temperament and level of social maturity, and which works for you in terms of your philosophy, budget, and other commitments.

✓ Admission to preschool can be tricky unless you start looking early and find out exactly when applications, fees, interviews, or tuition are due.

✓ Before you enroll your child in an alternative preschool, make sure you understand its philosophy and methodology.

✓ There is a lot of flexibility in the preschool day. Be assured that you will find one that satisfies both your schedule and the needs of your child.

PART FIVE

Chapter 20
Developing in Leaps and Bounds

Chapter 21
Your Child's Expanding World

Chapter 20

Developing in Leaps and Bounds

YOU MIGHT HAVE A CHILD who sleeps from the moment her head hits the pillow each night, who eats everything you put in front of her, and who plays nicely with other children. On the other hand, if you do, you're probably in the minority. Young children in the preschool years are nothing if not individual. At this stage of their lives, they're temperamental, picky, and expert at defying what you expect of them. On the other hand, they're interesting, amusing, curious, eager to learn, and they love you to bits!

In this chapter . . .

✓ Sleep patterns

✓ Why do I bother to cook?

✓ My, how you've grown!

✓ Play's the thing

✓ Different sorts of play

Sleep patterns

WHEN I SAY "PATTERNS," I'm using the word loosely. Many parents say their young children don't have a sleep routine they can rely on. And if they do, it's usually one that's less than ideal, such as the inability to get off to sleep or disturbed nights.

Part of the problem for children who are around 3 years old is that they're still likely to need a daytime nap – on some days, anyway – which means bedtime is a moveable feast. I try to cope by letting my daughter of this age have a 15-minute "power nap" on days when she seems too tired to make it through. It always takes a bit of tact and a lot of cuddles to wake her from this siesta. But the advantage of the nap is that it has the effect of re-energizing her for the afternoon without affecting the time at which she'll go to bed at night.

■ **Some children** *go through a phase when they can't get to sleep – this is especially common in the summer, when it stays light until later at night.*

Don't let your child take a nap after 3 P.M. because if you do, she won't be tired at bedtime.

Like so much else in parenting, dealing with daytime naps and their effect on bedtime is all about juggling. You can't have things both ways; your 3-year-old can't be expected to go to bed at 7 P.M. if she's slept from noon until 2 P.M. From your point of view, which is easier: a child who naps in the day, or one who goes to bed early at night? Decide what will work best, and then stick to a pattern.

My child still wakes up at night

By this stage, you might expect to have put sleepless nights behind you – indeed, if you also have a new baby, you might be surprised to find that your older child wakes you just as often as your little one does. It's not unusual for sleep problems to continue into the fourth year of life, and if you have a child who sleeps consistently well, you're one of the lucky few.

However frustrating you may find it, try and remember that night-time waking is only a problem in so far as it upsets or makes life difficult for you. My youngest daughter wakes every night at around 3 A.M.; I go into her room on automatic pilot, and carry her back to our bed, where she sleeps for the rest of the night. By the next morning, I don't usually remember having been woken up at all. If I told you I was awakened every night, you'd probably think it sounds awful, but in fact it's not an issue at all and I don't find it even mildly annoying. Like her older sisters, our youngest daughter started life in our bed. This is her transition stage before sleeping through the night on her own.

WHAT IS A SLEEP CLINIC?

Virtually every parent is going to encounter sleep problems with their child at some time or another. But if, by 30 months, your child is still experiencing significant sleep problems you may want to consult your pediatrician. If he or she is unable to help with the problem, your child may be referred to a psychologist or other mental health professional with experience in sleep problems. Sleep clinics are sometimes the next point of referral, and are worth investigating if your child has persistent sleep problems.

At the very least, a sleep therapist can be an understanding listener who'll sympathize with your woes, at a time when family and friends may be sick of hearing about how your little one is up half the night, every night.

Most clinics don't see children under the age of one (much older children are generally more likely to have problems). A child usually attends with both parents, so that the psychologist or therapist can get a better sense of the family dynamic. You will also be asked to keep a sleep diary for a week before your first appointment, which will provide the therapist with a record of when and for how long your child is sleeping. After you've discussed your concerns, the therapist will suggest specific ideas to put into practice for a couple of weeks or more. You may also be given a hotline number to call if things get difficult between appointments.

■ **After a couple of weeks** *of following the suggestions, you'll be asked to report back on how things are progressing.*

How can I reinforce a routine at this stage?

If your child is making the transition from a crib to a bed at the moment, you have the perfect opportunity to reinforce her sleep routine now. Tell her that big beds are for big girls who sleep in them all night.

It might help if you explain to her that, if she wakes up, she should have a sip of water and then turn over, cuddle her teddy, and then go back to sleep. That's what grown-ups do, and that's what she can start doing now that she's old enough to have a big bed of her own.

Early risers

Many children at this age get up early in the morning – sometimes at 5 or 6 A.M. – ready to start the day. Not surprisingly, they'll need a nap later on to make up for the early start. If this isn't ideal (and let's face it, it rarely is), start by looking at things you could do to deter your child's early waking. Is there a noise you could do something about, such as the hiss and clank of the heating system as it comes to life?

If your child is waking up at dawn, think about hanging thickly lined curtains or blinds at the window to help block out the morning light.

Maybe your child is waking up because her bedclothes have slipped off and she's cold. If this is a possibility, buy her a pair of extra-warm pajamas. And if your child's daytime naps are long, think about shortening them.

Some simple tactics

If early waking continues, devise ways in which your child can keep herself happy without disturbing the rest of the family. Try putting books, a cup of water, a tape player and storytape, and a basket of toys by her bed. Tell her that when she wakes up, she can have a drink, listen to a tape, read her books or play with her toys, but that she shouldn't come into your bedroom (unless there's an emergency of course!).

Try putting a light on a timer switch and telling her she can't come in to mommy and daddy until that light has gone on.

Why do I bother to cook?

APPARENTLY AROUND HALF *of all children between the ages of 2 and 6 years old have limited food preferences, and one in five families with preschool children admit that there is a squabble about food at almost every meal. The thing that surprises me is that these figures aren't higher. Ask any parent about their young child's eating habits, and the chances are that you'll hear a tale of woe.*

My experience with all three of my children has been that eating has been a very low priority until around the age of four. With my first daughter, I worried about the fact that she never seemed to consume more than a morsel, and that at every meal she seemed to skip the main course and wait for dessert. She's not exactly a strapping 9-year-old now, but she is certainly healthy and active. So fear not; providing you offer a range of "good" foods to your child, she isn't going to starve.

Don't torture yourself with endless ways of enticing your child into taking a bite of something healthy. Offer it, and if she doesn't want it, take it away.

Preparing food

One of the problems with preparing food for a child who doesn't want to eat much is that after you've invested so much time and effort in making the meal, you want her to eat it so you don't feel that you've wasted your time! It can be very frustrating when your 3-year-old sniffs one forkful of the lasagne you've slaved over and announces that she doesn't like it and won't be eating any.

■ **Prepare simple meals** *for your child, rather than presenting her with a dish that took you hours to make.*

The answer, of course, is simple: don't invest time and effort in a meal that only your toddler is going to eat. Cook regular meals when she's eating with you and the rest of the family. Then, if she refuses to eat, your work hasn't been in vain. But when it's just lunch or supper for her, or for her and some equally finicky friends, go for simplicity. Miranda, my toddler, is just as likely to eat a baked potato with cheese, peanutbutter on toast, or a tuna fish sandwich as anything else, but any of these meals can be made in about 2 minutes flat. No appetite? – no problem!

Coping with picky eaters

Actually, it's easier to write about picky eaters and how not to cope with them. Basically, what you shouldn't do is worry and cajole and threaten and coax your child into eating. This approach is not only a total bore, but it makes meal times a chore for both of you. The simple way to deal with a picky eater is to keep calm about it. Have family meals as often as possible or invite other children to eat with your youngster. The main message is that you should make meal times enjoyable. It doesn't actually matter that much whether your child actually eats or not. At least she's making the connection between food and fun, and this is a lot healthier than eating something in a gloomy and threatening atmosphere and coming away with the idea that food equals problems and guilt.

Trivia...

Research shows that 9 out of 10 young children will eat bananas and potatoes. The most detested vegetable is the Brussels sprout, although many children grow to like these in later years, when their taste buds have become more developed.

Don't bother bargaining with your child: "Just two more spoonfuls and then you can have dessert." Those two spoonfuls won't make much difference to her nutrition, but they could ruin the meal and cause an argument.

Desserts can be healthy too!

If your child perks up for dessert and shows an interest in sweet food, great. Never punish a child by refusing dessert. You can be much cleverer than that by making the dessert as healthy as the main course. Fruit, yogurt, custard, pancakes, rice pudding – so many sweet courses contain their fair share of healthy foods. And don't start torturing yourself with the thought that if she doesn't eat savory food now, she never will. This is just a difficult phase.

It's very tempting when you have a preschooler to see the time when she eats as a chance for you to "catch up with things." Instead, sit down, have a cup of coffee and a chat with her; make meal times a pleasant occasion for both of you.

Making meals simple

If you know your child's eating "problems" are getting you down, think about why you're so worried. Do you honestly think that your child is going to starve? If so, see your pediatrician and talk about your fears. If your child is not eating enough fresh fruit and vegetables, maybe she's anemic and needs to supplement her diet with a multiple vitamin. Maybe, if she's very thin, she has some kind of absorption problem. If you are really worried that there's an underlying cause behind her apparent lack of interest in food, check it out.

But it's unlikely that the cause is physical. It's much more likely to be, on her part, a simple case of being a stubborn preschooler, and on yours of being too much of a worrier. Many "fussy" children seem to particularly like food that looks straightforward – in other words, a piece of meat, a potato or two, some peas. Pasta with butter or olive oil and parmesan cheese and ham or bacon on top, has always been a big winner in our household. If you have picky eaters, they can easily remove the ingredients they don't like and discard them. If you've smothered everything in tomato sauce and your child doesn't like tomato sauce, the whole meal will be rejected.

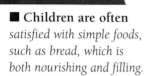

■ **Children are often** *satisfied with simple foods, such as bread, which is both nourishing and filling.*

ORGANIC FOODS

The use of chemicals, pesticides, and drugs in food production is a controversial issue – some people believe that their use can produce high levels of toxins, both in the environment and in the people who consume the food. Others believe that their use doesn't cause much harm at all. However, the general consensus now seems to be that these chemicals may be more harmful than was once thought, and that children are more likely to be affected than adults. An FDA directive has banned the use of certain pesticides in the production of baby food.

Organic foods are produced without the use of chemical fertilizers, pesticides, or drugs, and are becoming more and more popular with consumers. The downside to buying organic food is that it's often more expensive because organic farmers need more space to keep infestation and infection at bay, and they also have lower yields. If you haven't gone organic yet because of the high cost, at least consider buying cheese, milk, and meat from organic sources. Some chemicals stick to fats, so high-fat foods have higher concentrations of potentially harmful residues.

My, how you've grown!

THAT'S WHAT DOTING GRANDPARENTS *always say when they see their beloved grandchildren, even after a short absence. And the truth is, of course, that young children are growing all the time – although not always at a consistent rate.*

Perhaps you noticed big leaps in your child's growth over the first year or 18 months of her life, but after that it slowed down. Now, your child's growth will slow still further – she may gain only 5 or 6 lb (2.25–2.75 kg) in her third year, and even less in the following year.

There's no point in continual weighing and measuring at this stage, although if you're worried that your child looks a lot bigger or smaller than her peer group, consult your pediatrician.

It can be fun to have a height chart on your wall and to measure your child from time to time – maybe every birthday. If you don't have a chart, just measure your child against a wall and then use a tape measure to see what height she's reached. Some people like to reserve a part of wall as a permanent record of their children's growth over the years. What you will notice especially through this period is that your preschooler's proportions will alter dramatically. Until now, she's been a slightly pudgy toddler with a big head and a protruding stomach, but that's all changing now.

■ **Your little girl** *is no longer a baby – she's probably becoming tall, slim, and leggy.*

Play's the thing

PLAY IS SOMETIMES REFERRED TO *as a young child's "work," and in many ways that's exactly what it is. It isn't an add-on, a diversion, or a sideline, it's the very core of her development and learning. Nor is it merely for enjoyment or for fun (although, hopefully, it is both of these things too); play teaches your child a lot of what she needs to know about life.*

Rotate your child's toys to increase their novelty value. Keep some in a box out of sight, and when she's bored, swap them for the toys she's been playing with more recently.

Until the age of around two and a half, play is largely a solitary activity – it's as though there's so much to learn that your child isn't yet able to incorporate sociability into the equation. From around 30–36 months, however, other children will be incorporated into her play more and more.

Always be on hand to help settle fights when your child starts playing with another child. As time goes on, she'll learn to give and take, but for the moment, she needs help with this.

Playing with other children

The trouble is, of course, that this immediately brings compromises – sharing, taking turns, and doing things the way the other person wants them done. This is a lot for your little one to cope with and, almost inevitably, this results in arguments and fights. If you can, take time to play with your child and her friend for short periods. Explain as you go that Mia has to have a turn, and then Freddie can have his turn. Tell her that you're letting her have a turn and then you want a turn, but that you don't mind waiting for her to finish with the toy while you wait.

Fun games don't have to be very sophisticated. My preschooler loves nothing more than to play in the backyard on a warm day with a bowl full of lukewarm water; she just loves "washing up" her tea set.

Why play matters

Play expands the range of things your child can do – in particular, it allows her to refine her *fine motor skills*. Picking up toys, finding out how they work, and feeding bricks through shaped holes and building them one on top of the other are all ways your child learns to use her hands. Play also matters because it gives young children a "safe" forum to find out how to do things and how the world works. It's a kind of rehearsal for real life. It's interesting how often a child will act out adult roles and have conversations with teddies or imaginary characters. Often, their favorite toys are real things, such as an old set of keys or their mom's discarded handbag. They find these objects more intriguing than special children's versions.

> **DEFINITION**
>
> **Fine motor skills** *describe your child's ability to touch and grasp things with her hands, and to develop the use of her hands so that, in time, she will be able to carry out complex tasks such as writing. Gross motor skills involve the ability to move around, walk, and balance.*

If you haven't already started to do so, this is a good time to instil the idea that your child helps you pick up at the end of playtime – it will help deter her from dumping all her toys into a pile in the middle of the floor.

Different sorts of play

THERE'S A WHOLE RANGE of different kinds of play that appeal to children of this age, and your child needs to have opportunities to try all of them.

That doesn't mean that she has to spend the same amount of time painting as playing with the doll's house – let her make choices and, like everything else, there'll be some kinds of play that she enjoys and others she doesn't. Let her have a chance to sample as much as she can.

■ **Children love going** *to the woods, where there are trees and rocks to climb, things to collect, places to hide, and leaves to play in.*

Let your child's imagination grow

If you're one of those parents who insists on getting down on the floor to join in your children's games, pay attention: according to researchers at the American Psychological Society, too much of this can stifle your child's natural creativity. The trouble is that your involvement turns play into something structured, and your child's primary concern then becomes pleasing you, rather than following her own instincts.

To foster creativity and imagination, leave her alone and give her the opportunity to explore her own feelings.

Don't have just one big toy box — it's impossible to find anything. Sort toys and organize them by type.

Dressing-up and role-playing

If you have any old clothes or hats, your child can use these to stimulate ideas for who she wants to be. A dress-up box will really come into its own — if possible, choose outfits that are easy for your little one to put on and take off without help, so that she can play with them alone or with a friend. Many children enjoy props for their games, and often these are quite simple. Give your child a spoon and a pan, if she wants to be a cook, for example, or a toy stethoscope if she wants to be a doctor.

■ **Dressing-up** *is often a favorite childhood pursuit, because it allows children to live out their imaginary roles more fully — from being a ballerina to a doctor.*

BOYS WILL BE BOYS, GIRLS WILL BE GIRLS

That's what they say, anyway, as little boys settle down to play with a train set or race around the backyard like crazy, while little girls put new outfits on their dolls. The fact is that much of the way boys and girls play is about role models — from their earliest days, girls pick up how to play by watching how their mothers act, and little boys learn from watching their dads. However, there also seems to be inbuilt tendencies in each sex. For example, research shows that boys are better at activities controlled by the right side of the brain — that is, physical games — while girls are better at left side of the brain activities, such as writing and speaking.

Messy types of play

Your child needs opportunities to experiment with materials such as mud, paint, and wet sand without worrying about the mess she'll make or whether you'll get angry with her.

Be sure to give your child plenty of opportunities to paint and enjoy other sorts of messy play. It doesn't pay to be too tidy when you have a young child – neat, clutter-free living, and un-marked walls aren't easy to maintain with a preschooler in the house.

Why not rotate playdates with two or three friends and have a series of painting afternoons at each house? The mess is the same whether it's one child or five, and you'll all have more fun.

■ **Put your child** *in some old clothes and an apron and let her have fun expressing herself with paints.*

Toy people

Between the ages of two and a half and three, a lot of children start to play with toy people and action figures, acting out various scenarios. A set of small figures with an accompanying house, car, farm, and so on is the best toy investment I've ever made as a parent. Today, my children aged nine, six, and two all play happily with it.

Action figures and toy people are ideal to play with in the tub, too – my children have never particularly liked bath toys, but they've always chosen waterproof toys from their general collection to play with in the tub, where they pretend the toy is deep sea diving, water skiing, or learning to swim – or even simply taking a bath!

Try not to be rigid about where and how toys are played with – your child might like mixing cars from one game with people from another game, in order to create an original scenario of her own. It is best, at the end of the day, to put things back in the right boxes, but your child is actually being very creative when she mixes and matches, so don't be too controlling about how your child plays, even if it doesn't seem very ordered.

Trivia…

Children at a kindergarten in New Zealand have to apply for a "license" before they can play with a toy gun. The children have to answer questions and learn rules about "safe" gun play, such as never pointing your gun at anyone else. The child has to explain why he or she wants a gun, and what use he or she will put it to.

Television, videos, and computers

Love it or hate it, electronic media and communication are here to stay. They've become a big part of our lives, and there's little doubt that they will play an even bigger role in the lives of our children in the future. That doesn't mean, however, that all computer play, television programs, and videos are good news. Like all play, multimedia games and television viewing can be great for your child's development – providing that she gets the right amount, and that it's relevant to her age and stage.

Trivia...

Children are spending more time than ever playing computer games. In the year 2000–2001, there was a 40 percent rise in sales of computer games aimed specifically at children of preschool age.

Any television, video, or computer program will be a lot more helpful for your child if she shares it with you or another adult, so that she can talk about what she's seen and learned.

Playing outdoors

All children need the space to play outdoors sometimes. It's not just the chance to learn about hot and cold or sunshine and rain that's important – although clearly these things do matter. It's not even the chance to look at plants and discover how many colors flowers come in. The biggest advantage of outdoor play is the opportunity it gives your child to get further from you – safely, of course – to explore a little bit of the world on her own.

Make sure that your backyard is a safe play area for your child – make sure that garden tools are not accessible.

A playhouse can be a great asset and need not be prohibitively expensive if you buy one from a local garage sale or even make one yourself – from cardboard boxes.

■ **Children are curious** *about snow, whether they see the "real thing" or just a picture of it. They will be fascinated by how it changes the look of the world.*

Don't forget to read!

According to a recent study, bedtime stories are a thing of the past. The researchers found that, whereas 93 percent of parents remember having a bedtime story read to them, only 40 percent do the same for their children today. This story was widely reported and columnists everywhere lamented the fact that bedtime was no longer a time when children had a story read to them.

We all use reading in our daily lives, so whether you're a book-lover or not, let your child see you reading and she'll begin to understand how useful the printed word is. Remember, too, that all kinds of materials – magazines, catalogs, newspapers, and brochures – can introduce children to reading. You don't have to invest in specialized books.

INTERNET

www.toystogrowon.com

This web site has lots of ideas for children's toys, and may give you some inspiration for birthday presents.

Start introducing your child to letters using the first letter of her name. Pronounce letters carefully – my daughter Miranda calls herself Randa, so when I'm talking about the letter "M" I'm always very careful to say her name in full so that she makes the connection between the letter "M" and the "M" sound.

You don't have to teach your child to read before she goes to school, but it will help her enormously if you teach her what books are for and how they work.

■ **Whether your child is old enough to read** *or not, it's still important to share bedtime stories. It's a good chance for you both to enjoy spending quiet, quality time together too.*

A simple summary

✔ Your child is older now, but you may still encounter sleep problems. There are various ways to deal with these.

✔ Many 3-year-olds may still be taking a daytime nap. But, if you want your child to go to sleep at a reasonable hour at bedtime, naps after 3 P.M. are out and naps of longer than one hour before this aren't a good idea either.

✔ If your child's sleeplessness is really getting you down, talk to your pediatrician.

✔ If your child is an early riser and you don't want to be disturbed, make sure that she has things to occupy her when she wakes up.

✔ Fussy eaters are notorious at this age. Try to rise above it and don't invest a lot of effort in preparing complicated meals.

✔ Let your child make the connection between meal times and having fun.

✔ Don't fight over every mouthful. You'll only build up negative feelings about food, and this can be harmful in the long run.

✔ By 30 months, your child is able to play alone for short periods, but she also needs your input to keep her play rich and varied

✔ She's starting to play with friends, but she isn't very good at sharing yet; fights are inevitable.

✔ Play helps your child practice the things she's learning every day – her fine motor skills, her social skills, and her imaginary powers.

✔ Physical play, role play, quiet play, messy play – all are important for the development of your child.

✔ It's important to give your child the chance to explore outdoors, whatever the season.

✔ Reading is crucial in these early years – encourage your child to love books.

Chapter 21

Your Child's Expanding World

For the first couple years of your child's life, everything he encounters happens with either you or his caregiver by his side. By around 30 months, his world begins to change. He'll be going to preschool and getting ready for the world of "big" school. These opportunities will give him a greater taste of independence than he has ever known so far in his life.

In this chapter . . .

✓ Ready for preschool?

✓ The big day

✓ Learning how to behave

✓ Separation issues

✓ Playdates

✓ And so to "big" school

IS YOUR CHILD READY FOR THE WIDER WORLD OF PRESCHOOL?

Ready for preschool?

SO, YOU'VE CHOSEN THE PRESCHOOL *that you think will suit your child best, you've applied for a place well in advance, he's been accepted, and now the time is looming for him to start. But before he embarks on this new adventure, it's important to be sure that your child is truly ready to attend preschool.*

Deciding how ready your child is for preschool can be difficult. Try to imagine how well your child will cope outside his familiar environment. Ask yourself the following questions, and be realistic and honest with yourself:

- Is he confident about talking to people outside his trusted group of family and friends?
- Is he out of diapers during the day, and will he ask when he needs to go to the toilet?
- Does he play quite well on his own?
- Is he generally interested in other children and does he play happily with them – at least for some of the time?

As the big day draws nearer, you may decide that your child isn't ready to go to preschool for more than a few mornings a week. Many preschools offer flexible arrangements so don't hesitate to talk to staff about what will be best for your child.

■ **Think about** *how well your child interacts with other children and try to imagine him in a preschool environment.*

Preparing for the big day

Once all the arrangements for preschool have been made, all that's left for you to do is to prepare your child for his first day. What can you do to get ready? The obvious way, of course, is to talk to your child about what's in store. Tell him what children do in preschool and answer all his questions. If you can, buy or borrow a story book about preschool and share it with your child.

Introduce your child to slightly older children who have already been to or who are currently going to preschool.

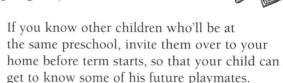

If you know other children who'll be at the same preschool, invite them over to your home before term starts, so that your child can get to know some of his future playmates.

■ **Talk to your child** *about preschool and discuss with him what some of the activities will be.*

The big day

WHAT MATTERS MOST is that your child finds preschool exciting and fun. This is his first introduction to the big world away from home and, if it can be a positive experience, will lay a good foundation for school and all the other institutions he'll be part of throughout his childhood.

Don't expect too much from his first day at preschool and don't leave him on his own for the whole session. Try to stay around for part of the time to help him through it.

Talk to the teachers about how to handle your child on his first day. Try to fit in with the way they like to do things – but if you feel strongly that they're asking too much of your child, explain what you're feeling and why. Any preschool worth its salt will recognize that you know your child better than anyone else. But don't forget that they're experts at dealing with cranky 2- to 3-year-olds who often kick up a fuss when their mommies or daddies are leaving – and then settle happily into play 5 minutes later.

Being there

On the first day, you'll probably be expected to stay for part of the session to play with your child and meet the other children and their parents. Take advantage of this opportunity – the more you know about what goes on at preschool or daycare, the more you'll be able to talk with your child about what's going on there, what he enjoys, and who he's been playing with every day.

If your child is confident enough, it's a good idea to leave him for 30 minutes or so of the first session, even if you just go into another room in the same building for a cup of coffee. Tell your child you're leaving, but explain that you'll be back very soon, and that you're just going to run a quick errand.

Getting settled

The first day is the beginning of settling in, and for some children it may be all that's required. Many children, however, take a little longer – sometimes weeks and even months – to settle into their preschool. The good news is that, however long it seems to take, your child will eventually settle in. Be guided by your own feelings about whether he's confident and happy enough to be left on his own. If you feel he's still a little young and shy, be prepared to stick around preschool or day care a little longer than other parents do. If the staff asks you to leave your child, explain that you'd like to remain on the premises, or ask them to call you if he doesn't settle in.

Once your child IS happy at his preschool, don't make the mistake of hanging around. Children tend not to settle very well if their parents are present – but will usually be fine within minutes of being left.

■ **Your child will soon get used** *to daycare or preschool and will enjoy spending time with children his own age. He'll come home with lots of things to tell you about what he has learned during the day.*

Learning how to behave

THIS ISN'T A NEW ISSUE – *you've probably been dealing with "misbehavior" since your child was 12 months old. Remember that children are still learning about the world, and "bad" behavior is just part of this process.*

■ **Children of preschool age** *find it hard to understand that they can't have everything their own way, and this can result in bossy behavior.*

Young children have lots of ideas of their own and can be determined to get their own way. The other day, my daughter had a friend over to play. After being bossed around for a good part of an hour, the other child decided that she'd had enough and wanted to go home. My daughter refused to accept this. She started hitting the friend and shouting "You've got to stay! I want you to stay!" The irony of the situation, the fact that the last thing she was going to achieve by her behavior was to encourage the friend to stay, was lost on her.

DEALING WITH FIGHTS OVER TOYS

"I had it first!" goes the cry, and you know you've got a fight on your hands. Whether it's between siblings or friends, it's never easy to know what to do – but here are a few ideas for how to nip it in the bud. If you know which child had the toy first, give it to that child and explain that he can have 2 minutes with it and then, when you say the word, he should hand it over to the other child. Point out that this will make it fair, because both children will get a turn. If the toy is a much-loved cuddly toy, return it to its owner and explain that it's something important – compare it to something special that belongs to the other child. If the fight continues, take the toy from both children and encourage them to play with something else.

Coping with difficult behavior

When your child gets into a fight with his friend, separate the children and try to explain to the aggressor why the tactics aren't actually going to work. Always comfort the injured party (usually, it's only their pride that's been hurt) and give most of your attention to him. Psychologists say we should be wary of giving attention to the child who is behaving badly, because a child may be encouraged to more naughtiness when he or she notices that this type of behavior draws an adult's attention.

Sharing isn't something preschoolers learn to do overnight. One of the most vital aspects of preschool education, both formal and home-based, is teaching a child that much of what's in the world has to be shared with others.

Enforcing time out

One of the best tactics for dealing with bad behavior is known as "time out." Basically, preschoolers want to be part of the action – they're not like older kids, who actually enjoy spending time in their bedrooms on their own. Your preschooler will always want to be where the action and the fun is, so what better way to drive home the message that certain behavior isn't acceptable than to banish him from the fun, even just for a minute or two?

Just as you may have done when your child was a toddler, you can still use the idea of a time-out chair where your child has to sit, away from the fun, to make clear that his behavior was not okay.

Don't use time-out as a threat. Mention it only when you're about to use it, and then pick your child up and take him there. Insist that he sit in the chair – even a minute will make the point.

Preschool fighting

Once your child starts at preschool or day care, you might find yourself worrying about the inevitable fights he'll get involved in when you're not around. It's understandable that you should be concerned, particularly if your little one is going through a stage when sharing seems particularly difficult.

Bear in mind that preschool staff have lots of experience with dealing with the tiffs that break out every few minutes at every session.

Asking for advice

If you're concerned about fights, why not talk to the staff about how they deal with squabbles and other bad behavior during play sessions? Tell them which tactics you use at home and compare notes. Talking to preschool or day care staff will not only reassure you that they know how to handle your child and the others in their care, but you might also gain some useful tips that you can use at home yourself. If you then use these tactics for coping with bad behavior at home, your child will be receiving the same clear messages from both his teachers and his parents.

Always remember to praise good behavior as well as making clear your disapproval of bad behavior. In fact, one effective tactic is to ignore bad behavior (unless it's potentially harmful to your child or others), but to lavish praise on good behavior instead.

Separation issues

ALL CHILDREN CAN BE *apprehensive in a new situation, but some children take longer to gain confidence than others. If your child refuses to let you out of his sight even several weeks into preschool or day care, try to analyze the problem. Is day care or preschool meeting his particular needs? How does he behave when you're not around? Is he really ready for a preschool?*

If the staff tell you that your child is happy enough when you're not around, you can at least console yourself with the thought that, however difficult the separation, your child will settle down soon after you leave.

■ **At preschool age,** *children are learning to be more independent, but it can be difficult when they've become used to the security of their parents' presence.*

If you find that you're consumed with guilt after leaving your child at day care bawling yet again, arrange to phone the staff half an hour later to find out how your child is doing, and to help put your mind at rest that he's okay.

Don't tell your child all about what you did while he was at preschool, or you'll make him wish he'd stayed with you. Ask him about what he did, who he played with, and so on.

Making the adjustment

If your child still isn't adjusting to day care or preschool after several weeks, and you've followed the staff's advice on how to help him settle in, think about whether it would be worth taking him out for the rest of the term.

You could then enroll him again next term, either at the same preschool, or at a different one. Don't just decide preschool isn't for him and leave it for months. Children have preferences, just as adults do, and it could be that the particular preschool wasn't right for your child, while another one will be fine.

Preschools often have a group of parents who spend some time helping out. The opportunity to participate on an occasional basis at your child's group is a welcome chance for you to find out more about how he's spending his time there, and means that you can talk to your child with more knowledge about what's gone on during the day in your absence.

■ **If your child** *is very shy in the company of other adults or children and has become even more clingy now that he's started preschool, it may be that he's just not ready for it yet.*

Playdates

GOING TO A FRIEND'S HOUSE *for a playdate is an exciting development in the life of any child. Some children start a social life at a very early age but, for many, invitations to play at others' homes don't begin until after they've started preschool.*

Going to a friend's house

It's usually a good idea to wait until your child is well settled into preschool before launching him into the world of playdates. Once he's happy, however, he'll love the chance to spend time in other people's houses, playing with his friends and their toys.

Children often feel a little worried when their mom or dad leaves them at a friend's house, unless they've spent time there before. If your child looks concerned, let him know that his friend's mother has your phone number and that if he needs you, you can be back within a few minutes. You don't want him to feel abandoned.

Don't be late in picking up your child from a friend's house – not only will the other parent have had enough by then, but your own child will pick up the vibe that it's time for him to be picked up, and he may become anxious.

Explain to your child how long he will be staying at his friend's house and tell him if he's staying for lunch or supper. Say you'll be back to pick him up after the meal so that he knows when to expect you.

■ **Your child's social life** *is beginning to expand. He will enjoy going to other children's houses to play.*

It's my party

Once your child is in preschool, he's probably ready to have a "real" birthday party. Until now, parties have probably been small affairs.

Parents of children under three in particular, and sometimes under four, almost always stay at a party. But once your child is three or four, most parents will leave their child in your care. My advice about children's parties is to try not to be too ambitious – keep it simple.

■ **Children love party foods.** *Favorite treats will include pizza, cookies, cake, and ice cream.*

Don't invite too many children – six or eight preschoolers are a good number – and don't arrange for it to go on for too long. A couple of hours is plenty.

Arranging parties

You might want to hire a clown, a magician, or some other form of entertainment – there's lots of it around – but my advice would be to wait until your children are older and will appreciate an act more. For younger kids, party games such as duck, duck goose, musical chairs, and some unstructured play time is all you'll need for a fun afternoon. Enlist the help of at least one other adult – or two, if you have a younger child to keep an eye on as well. Prepare the food in advance so that you have your hands free when the children arrive.

■ **For special occasions,** *and if it's summertime, set up a trampoline or hire a bouncey castle. These keep children happy for hours.*

You can put together boxed lunches with sandwiches and cookies. Once the children are sitting on the floor or on the grass in the backyard, you can hand out the boxes. This avoids the need to set up a table beforehand, which can be a waste of time when you have eight 4-year-olds running amok.

And so to "big" school

IT DOESN'T SEEM THAT LONG AGO that you were pushing him around in his stroller and now it's time to think about elementary school! It's one of the most important decisions you'll make as a parent, and certainly one of the most daunting. Which school will be best for your child and how do you actually get him in?

You often hear the phrase "parental choice" in reference to education, but that doesn't mean that you have an automatic right to select the school you want for your child. What "parental choice" actually means is that you have the right to express your preference – that's all. To find out what your preference is, you need to do your homework. Call your Local Board of Education and ask for a listing of all the schools that they have available – the listing may also give entrance criteria, or you may have to call individual schools to find out how they choose students. Use your local library or the Internet to look for general information about the schools you're considering.

Trivia...

Competition for the best schools can be steep. Some parents are resorting to employing private tutors for their 4-year-olds to help them pass class entrance tests. But teachers warn that this is too much pressure for many young children – there is a risk of "burning them out" by the age of six.

INTERNET

www.schoolmatch.com

This research and database service collects and processes information about public and private schools.

Comparing schools

Talk to other parents in your area about the schools they're looking at. Think of your child and his needs. What kind of atmosphere will he thrive in? Some children need a relaxed, social environment, while others do better in a more structured, academic setting. What's right for one child may be wrong for another. Look at a school's standards and find out about any extra-curricular activities it may offer. Visiting a school will give you an opportunity to see the place "as it is," and will give you an idea of how happy and motivated the children are.

Entry requirements

Finding the school you'd like your child to go to is the easy part, but try to keep an open mind instead of setting your heart on one particular school. Every school has a list of entry requirements, and the more closely your child matches the list, the more likely it is that he will get in.

The big day looms...

Most schools have open days or afternoons in the summer or early in the fall when children who are going to attend in September can come for an orientation session. If you haven't been told about one of these, be sure to ask. If there is an event scheduled, try and make every effort to go to it with your child – it really does help to give your child a preview of what the classroom looks like, and how much fun it will be.

■ **On the first day of school,** *reassure your child. Even if you're nervous yourself, don't let your child pick up on your mood.*

ARE YOU LOOKING FOR AN ALTERNATIVE?

Most parents choose a public or independent preparatory (private) school for their 4-year-olds, but these aren't the only choices. Other options include:

● **Home schooling:** You don't have to send your child to school at all. Educating children at home is perfectly legal, although your local school board may need to be notified

● **"Little" schools:** There are any number of small, independent schools around the country. Many of them have been opened as an alternative for parents who worry about big classes and the lack of individual attention in larger schools

● **Rudolph Steiner schools:** These delay formal teaching until children are six or seven in favor of a rounded, creative education early on

Settling in

The transition to elementary school is a huge one for a young child, even if he's already been attending preschool or day care. One of the big differences is size. Even a small school is a huge new world to a 4-year-old. In the first weeks of a new school, lunch time and play time are often especially traumatic for children. If this is the case with your child, talk to his teacher about it and see what can be done to make life easier. Some schools have a "buddy" system in which each incoming child is paired with a child from an upper grade to give practical and moral support, and this is often extremely helpful.

A simple summary

✔ Starting preschool will give your child his first taste of independent life away from you or his caregiver. Make sure that he's really ready for it.

✔ Talk to your child about preschool in the weeks leading up to his first day.

✔ Don't expect him to adjust immediately. You may need to stay with him for a while each day until he settles in.

✔ Talk to the staff about what you can do to help your child settle.

✔ The most important lesson your child will learn at preschool is the importance of cooperating and sharing with others.

✔ Find out how the staff at preschool deal with fights over toys, and try to follow the same policies at home.

✔ If your child is still very anxious and shy several weeks after starting preschool, think about whether it's right for him. Consider taking him out for a while and re-starting him later on.

✔ Once your child has adjusted to preschool, encourage him to have playdates with other children – at your home or theirs.

✔ Choosing an elementary school for your child can be daunting – and then once your child starts school, you'll need to offer him plenty of reassurance.

Further Resources

Recommended books

There is a bewildering array of books about baby and child care and parenthood on the market, and numerous methods put forward for how to bring up children. Where do you start? Here are just a few books that you could refer to:

The Baby and Child Question & Answer Book
Dr. Carol Cooper, Dorling Kindersley, 2000

Baby Play: 100 fun-filled activities to maximize your baby's potential
Dr. Wendy S. Masi and Dr. Roni Cohen Leiderman, Time Life Books, 2001

The Best Friends' Guide to Toddlers: A survival manual to the 'terrible twos' (and ones and threes) from the first step, the first potty and the first word ('no') to the last blanket
Vicki Iovine, Bloomsbury, 1999

Complete Baby and Childcare
Dr. Miriam Stoppard, Dorling Kindersley, 1995

Confident Children
Gael Lindenfield, Thorsons, 2000

Do Not Disturb: The benefits of relaxed parenting for you and your child
Deborah Jackson, Bloomsbury, 1993

First Time Parents: The essential guide for all new mothers and fathers
Dr. Miriam Stoppard, Dorling Kindersley, 1998

How To Behave So Your Children Will, Too!
Dr. Sal Severe, Vermillion, 2000

The Good Nanny Guide: The complete handbook on nannies, au pairs, mother's helps, childminders and day nurseries
Charlotte Breese and Hilaire Gomer, Vermillion, 2000

Immunization: Everything you need to know about vaccinations and immune-boosting therapies for your child
Harriet Griffey, Element, 2000

The National Childbirth Trust Book of Breastfeeding: Everything you need to know from the experts
Mary Smale, Vermillion, 1999

Nature's Masterpiece: A family survivalbook
Libby Purves, Hodder and Stoughton, 2000

The NCT Book of Crying Baby
Anna McGrail, Thorsons, 1998

The Parent Talk Guide to the Toddler Years
Steve Chalke, Hodder and Stoughton, 1999

Positive Parenting: Raising children with self-esteem
Elizabeth Hartley-Brewer, Vermillion, 1994

The Year After Childbirth
Sheila Kitzinger, Oxford University Press, 1994

Your Baby and Child
Penelope Leach, Penguin, 1997

Useful organizations

If you need information on specific issues, there are plenty of special organizations who can offer you advice and reassurance. Here are just a few:

Back to Sleep Campaign
31 Center Drive, MSC 2425
Bldg. 31, Room 2A32
Bethesda, MD 20892-2425
Tel: (301) 496-5133 or (800) 505-CRIB
www.nichd.nih.gov
Information on SIDS (Sudden Infant Death Syndrome).

Child Care Aware
2116 Campus Drive, S.E.
Rochester, MN 55904
Tel: (202) 393-5501
www.naccrra.org
Refers callers to local agencies that can provide lists of child care centers and family day care providers.

Consumer Product Safety Commission
Washington, DC 20207
Tel: (800) 638-2772
www.cpsc.gov
Establishes and monitors safety standards for children's products; provides information and lists of recalled items.

The Fatherhood Project
Bank Street College of Education
610 W. 112th Street
New York, NY 10025
Tel: (212) 465-2044
www.familiesandwork.org
Offers seminars, films, books, and training to support fathers in their parenting roles.

Health Canada
A.L. 0900C2
Ottawa, ON, K1A 0K9
Tel: (613) 957-2991
www.hc-sc.gc.ca
Provides information on a variety of healthcare issues and includes resources and web links.

Learning Disabilities Association of Canada
323 Chapel Street, Suite 200
Ottawa, ON, K1N 7Z2
Tel: (613) 238-5721
www.ldac-taac.ca
Offers information on learning disabilities and includes a directory of camps, schools, and assessment services.

National Organization of Mothers of Twins Clubs
Tel: 1-877-540-2200
www.nomotc.org
A valuable resource for parents of twins.

National Safe Kids Campaign
1301 Pennsylvania Avenue, NW
Washington, DC 20004
Tel: (202) 662-0600
www.safekids.org
Provides publications on child safety and childproofing.

9 to 5, National Association of Working Women
1430 West Peachtree St., Suite 610
Atlanta, Georgia 30309
Tel: (216) 566-9308 or (800) 522-0925
Information for women who are going back to work.

Parents Without Partners International, Inc.
1650 S. Dixie Highway
Boca Raton, Florida 33432
www.parentswithoutpartners.org
Information and support for single parents.

Safe Kids Canada
555 University Avenue
Toronto, ON, M5G 1X8
Tel: (416) 813-6715
www.safekidscanada.ca
Provides safety tips to keep kids safe.

Parenting on the Web

THE INTERNET IS A GREAT place to browse for information on baby and child care – ranging from tips on how to bath your baby to advice on how to deal with toddler tantrums. Here are some sites that you may find useful:

www.aap.org
The web site of the American Academy of Pediatrics provides parents with health-related information.

www.amshq.org
Information about the preschools that offer programs that follow the methods developed by Maria Montessori.

www.awsna.org
Find out about Waldorf/Rudolf Steiner schools.

www.babybag.com
Contains articles and links on a range of parenting topics.

www.babycenter.com
Packed with information on caring for newborns.

www.breastfeeding.com
Plenty of information about breastfeeding your baby.

www.breastfeeding-basics.com
More information about breastfeeding.

www.canadian-health-network.ca
Offers information on a variety of health issues.

www.cbcbooks.org
Find out about reading groups and events for children.

www.cdc.gov
Reliable information about immunizations.

www.cfc-efc.ca
The Child & Family Canada web site provides information on child care and family issues.

www.childsecure.com
Information on various aspects of child health, plus product information on various child-safety items.

www.contentedbaby.com
Information about implementing effective routines.

www.cps.ca
The web site of the Canadian Paediatric Society provides publications and resources on healthcare for children.

www.cpsc.gov
Information on product recalls on a range of consumer goods.

www.cwla.org
Information on all aspects of child welfare, including health and education.

www.dadscan.org
Provides articles on fatherhood.

www.dmoz.org
This site will help you locate child care agencies throughout the U.S.

www.drgreene.com
Useful information on every aspect of pediatric care..

www.familyplay.com
Activities to help keep children entertained.

www.gocitykids.com
Ideas about things to do and places to visit with your baby – it covers several major cities.

www.google.com
Visit this search engine and request "speech and language therapists" in your region.

www.huggies.com
Share tips and ideas with parents over the internet.

www.iapa.org
Information about the International Au Pair Association.

www.icomm.ca.daycare
A web site for day care providers.

www.immunize.cpha.ca
Offers information and advice on immunization and links to health organizations across Canada.

www.jpma.org
Detailed information about shopping for baby gear.

www.lalecheleague.org
Contains advice about breastfeeding.

www.medicinenet.com
Contains detailed information on diseases and drugs, plus a medical dictionary, and more.

www.momsonline.com
Useful information about pregnancy and babycare.

www.montessori.org
All about the Montessori approach to education.

www.nccanet.org
Operated by the National Child Care Association, this site assists parents in their search for child care.

www.nccic.org
The National Child Care Information Center web site.

www.nhsa.org
Information about subsidized early learning opportunities for preschool children.

www.obgyn.net
Browse here for advice about breastfeeding problems.

www.our-space.co.uk/sleep/htm
The web site of CRY-Sis, an organization providing advice to parents who are having problems with sleepless or excessively crying babies.

www.parentcenter.com
Ideas about how to entertain your toddler.

www.parenthoodweb.com
Features articles on parenting.

www.parentsplace.com/readroom/ACS
Contains advice about types of caregivers.

www.schoolmatch.com
Provides information on public and private schools.

www.sids-network.org
Contains information on Sudden Infant Death Syndrome (SIDS).

www.steps-charity.org.uk
Provides information about hip abnormalities in babies and children.

www.teamlollipop.co.uk
Details the many reusable diaper options open to you.

www.thelaboroflove.com
This site contains 500 birth stories.

www.toystogrowon.com
Lots of ideas for children's toys.

www.toy-testing.org
The Canadian Toy Testing Counil's site provides details on toy safety.

www.zerotothree.org
Advice about the health and welfare of toddlers.

A Simple Glossary

Alternative therapies Also known as complementary therapies, these include treatments such as osteopathy, homeopathy, and herbalism, which can be used to prevent or treat some types of medical conditions.

Antibiotics These are chemicals that are used to treat bacterial infections – either by killing bacteria, or by preventing them from multiplying so that the body's immune system can combat them more easily.

Apgar score An assessment that is carried out on a baby within the first few minutes of birth to rate his or her overall condition.

Asthma A respiratory condition in which the passageways in the lungs constrict, making breathing difficult.

Au pair A young woman, usually from a foreign country, aged 18 to 27, who lives as part of a family and helps around the home.

Babbling Your baby's first sounds – often, it's one sound that's being repeated, such as "baba" or "gaga".

Babysitter A caregiver who looks after your baby in your home.

Bear walking A variation on crawling – a baby gets onto his or her hands and feet and walks like a bear.

Blocked duct A milk duct within the breast that has become congested.

Breast pump A device for expressing milk (pumping milk out of the breasts) – the mother's milk can then be used for bottle-feeding.

Clicky hips Correctly called developmental dysplasia of the hip, it means that the hip joint is in the wrong place, or that it has a tendency to move too easily out of its socket.

Colic A bout of unexplained crying in a young baby, usually occurring in the early evening. Experts are undecided about what causes it.

Controlled crying A method of getting a baby to sleep at night. It involves resisting the impulse to go to your baby the moment he or she starts crying. Instead, the parent leaves the baby for a few minutes before going in to check on him or her.

Co-sleeping This is when a baby sleeps in his or her parents' bed.

Cracked nipples Painful nipples with tiny, bleeding cuts. The condition is usually caused by incorrect positioning during breastfeeding.

Cradle cap Common in young babies, this is a form of seborrhoea of the scalp, characterized by flaky skin.

Creeping A pre-crawling stage, whereby a baby moves around the floor by gradually inching forwards or backwards on his or her stomach.

Cruising A pre-walking stage in which a child moves around a room, holding on to furniture for support.

Day care center A child care center where babies and children are cared for while their parents are at work.

Diving instinct The phenomenon that enables young babies to hold their breath naturally when they are underwater.

Engorged breasts Breasts that are painfully full of milk. This is common during the early days of breastfeeding, when the mother's body is still adjusting to how much milk her baby needs.

Enuresis Bed-wetting or involuntary urination.

Expression The method of getting milk out of the breasts, either by hand or by using a breast pump.

Febrile seizures A convulsion in a baby or young child caused by a sudden rise in temperature due to an infection or illness.

Fine motor skills This refers to a child's ability to touch and grasp things and to carry out complex tasks with his or her hands, such as writing.

Fontanelles These are the soft spots on a baby's head that allow the skull to compress during the birth process. The fontanelles have usually closed up by the time a baby reaches 18 months of age.

Gross motor skills The ability to move around, walk, and balance.

Jaundice A condition caused by an excess of the chemical bilirubin in the body.

Latching on The correct positioning of the baby's mouth during breastfeeding.

Let-down reflex A hormone response that is triggered by a baby's sucking. It results in the flow of milk from the deeper reserves within the breast.

Mastitis An infection in the breast caused by a blocked duct.

Montessori schools Schools where children are allowed to develop and learn in a natural way.

Moro reflex A primitive reflex that babies are born with, whereby a baby will throw out his or her arms when startled, to alert his or her mother.

Mother's helper An untrained or inexperienced caregiver who provides help around the house.

Nanny A trained child care worker who will look after your child or children in your home.

Nanny agency A company that specializes in matching potential nannies with families.

Nursery school A first-stage educational establishment, catering for children from the age of two and a half or three to five.

Percentile chart A graph plotting your child's actual growth against his or her expected growth rate. This estimated rate is determined according to weight at birth.

Phobia An irrational fear of an object, situation, or animal – common in toddlers and young children.

Phototherapy A treatment for jaundice, using fluorescent-type lights to help break down excess bilirubin in a baby's body.

Pre-K A type of preschool.

Premature baby A baby born before the 37th week of pregnancy, usually weighing less than 5½ lb (2.5 kg).

Preschool Educational establishments for children between the ages of three and six.

Rescue breathing A life-saving system of getting air in and out of the lungs of a child or adult who has stopped breathing.

Reusable diaper A nappy that can be washed and used again, such as a terry nappy.

Sleep clinic A clinic that aims to uncover the cause of and suggest solutions to a child's sleeping problem.

Solids The name given to the first solid foods your baby moves on to after milk.

Special care unit A hospital unit that cares for newborn babies in need of special attention.

Speech therapy Assessment and treatment of communication and speech problems.

Steiner Waldorf kindergarten A type of preschool: the guiding philosophy is that children can suffer anxiety if they are pressurized into too much learning too soon.

Sudden infant death syndrome (SIDS) The unexpected death of a seemingly healthy infant, also known as crib death.

Supply and demand The system by which a mother produces enough milk to suit her baby's needs.

Teething The process by which a baby's first teeth, or "milk teeth," start to come through.

Toddler gyms Fun sessions for youngsters, aiming to encourage movement and mobility skills.

Topping and tailing A system of keeping your newborn baby clean by washing his face, neck, hands, and bottom – an alternative to bathing.

Umbilical stump The base of the umbilical cord, which temporarily remains attached to the baby's navel after the cord has been cut at birth.

Index

Acknowledgments

Publisher's Acknowledgments

Dorling Kindersley would like to thank Katy Wall for designing the jacket and
Melanie Simmonds for picture research.

Packager's Acknowledgments

Studio Cactus would like to thank Barry Robson for providing the dog illustrations,
Polly Boyd for proofreading, and Hilary Bird for compiling the index.

Picture Credits

t = top, b = bottom, c = center, r = right, l = left

Simon Brown: 2, 246
John Bulmer: 130, 131tl, 260
© Digital Vision: 8/9, 10/11, 14, 28, 30, 33, 44, 53, 56, 58, 59tr, 60, 64bl, 78, 81, 96, 99, 104, 134, 136br, 140, 164
Julie Fisher: 135
Damien Moore: 76, 84, 95, 114, 138cr, 151, 196tr, 197, 204, 210, 214, 218, 222, 244, 259, 272br
Photodisc: 25, 26, 37, 41, 42, 55, 63, 68, 71, 92, 97, 98, 101, 102, 106, 116, 128, 154, 157, 166, 170, 178, 185, 187, 188, 198, 203, 208, 212, 226, 234, 237, 254, 256, 262, 269, 270
Guy Ryecart: 75, 249

Jacket
Photographer: Dave King
Models: Hannah Brohier, Pui Ming Chow, Jacob Brubert

All other images © Dorling Kindersley
For further information see: www.dkimages.com

Note: The people illustrated in this book are models. Images are used for illustrative purposes
only and do not imply endorsement, use of, or a connection to any product, service, or subject.